WILD BILL HICKOK

WILD BILL HICKOK

Richard O'Connor

 LONGMEADOW PRESS

Published by Longmeadow Press, 201 High Ridge Road,
Stamford, CT 06904. All rights reserved. No part of this book
may be reproduced or utilized in any form or by an means,
electronic or mechanical, including photocopying, recording
or by any information storage and retrieval system, without
permission in writing from the Publisher. Longmeadow Press
and the colophon are registered trademarks.

This edition published by special arrangement with
William S. Konecky Associates, Inc. and McIntosh and
Otis, Inc.

Jacket design by Irving Freeman

ISBN: 0-681-20404-4

Printed in the United States of America

First Longmeadow Press Edition

0 9 8 7 6 5 4 3 2 1

CONTENTS

Introduction to a Gunfighter

Few people then or now have been able to agree on what kind of man James Butler Hickok was, a ruthless killer or a man dedicated to bringing law and order to the frontier, the deadliest gunfighter of them all or the creature of dime novelists and theatrical press agents, a homicidal psychopath or a harbinger of civilization. He may have been the deadliest gunfighter, though John Wesley Hardin and one or two others might have successfully disputed that, but he was not a homicidal maniac, nor was he a fervent disciple of law and order except as they pertained to his occasional employment as a peace officer. He was simply a man who went West and fell into a dangerous way of life, different from others essentially because of his amazing ability to fire a handgun in a hurry, usually under dire circumstances.

From the modern viewpoint, however, Hickok was a little too much of everything to be completely believable. The first publicist who came across him, Colonel George Ward Nichols of *Harper's*, said, "I thought John Wilkes Booth was the handsomest man I had ever known, but Wild Bill Hickok was handsomer . . . he had a finer, saner, better balanced, more magnetic face and head than Booth." It did not help the cause of realism that Hickok favored an elegance in dress, was courtly in manner, wore his Derringers tucked inside a flowered waistcoat among the ruffles of a spotless white shirt. He seems, in fact, fictional: a man who lived out his life as though anticipating his future glorification in a television serial.

It would be easier to believe in a gunfighter of the naturalistic school, a trifle verminous, ugly, illiterate, unkempt, unwashed, and uncomplicated. It is difficult enough for modern man, who is supposed to be sinking into the anonymous tide of conformity, standardization, and mass organization, to grasp that only a few generations ago men like Hickok, blazing individualists, walked this same prosaic earth. It is easy to forget that he was a product of a more exuberant America; that in his time it was still possible for a man to live without the bonds of a regular job, a Social Security number, several varieties of income tax, a permanent address, and visible means of support. Vagrancy, then, had a touch of class.

Even in his own time people did not find it easy to separate the man from the legend, and some found it simpler to assume that his fame was fraudulent and Hickok merely a blowhard who capitalized on everything the eastern penny-a-liners wrote about him. Shortly after his death the editor of a Cheyenne newspaper paid his respects by writing that the event was not generally lamented, that "If we could believe half of what has been written concerning his daring deeds, he must certainly have been one of the bravest and most unscrupulous characters of these lawless times. Contact with the man, however, dispelled all illusions, and of late years Wild Bill seems to have been a very tame and worthless bummer and loafer. He loved to drink the tenderfoot's liquor and regale him with wild stories of his hair-raising encounters with 'red fiends and white desperadoes.' In such moments he was the very personification of happiness." The editor was all too eager to believe that the Hickok he knew, "dispelling all illusions," was the whole man. Few things are more pleasurable than tipping idols off their pedestals.

Accuracy was certainly not one of the virtues of the majority of the people who knew Hickok or claimed to know him. Most who went West seemed to acquire a taste for exaggeration, hyperbole, and the stark colors of melodrama. Hickok, for instance, is mentioned prominently in what is now regarded as a semi-classic of the frontier, *My Reminiscences as a Cowboy*. Its author was Frank Harris, a picturesque and controversial figure of the Anglo-American literary world and the heartily disavowed biographer of George Bernard Shaw and Oscar Wilde.

In the preface to the 1930 edition of this work, Harris was quoted as saying, "I've never known Wild Bill as I've known Bernard Shaw, Oscar Wilde or a hundred of the most important men in art, literature and politics in Europe and America, but Wild Bill remains a hero to me still. Indeed I have only three heroes, Wild Bill, Shakespeare and Cervantes—all dead." Harris made this statement to H. M. Kallen, who wrote the preface to *Reminiscences*, at his villa in the South of France.

Certainly no more resounding tribute to Hickok has ever been paid than to link him with Shakespeare and Cervantes. It is doubtful, however, whether Harris had any more direct acquaintance with Hickok than he had with his other two heroes.

Harris wrote in his *Reminiscences* that when he knew Hickok the latter "had been City Marshal of one of the new towns springing up, Wichita or Dodge . . ." Hickok was never a peace officer in either of those two towns. Harris then related this incident:

". . . Within a week of his [Hickok's] election he had been called to a saloon where there was a row, and had settled it by shooting three of the most quarrelsome. Coming out of the saloon, Bill met a man who made an incautious gesture; quick as a flash he drew and shot a popular railway boss . . . A vigilance committee was formed and next morning two hundred armed men surrounded the marshal's house to drive him out of the country or kill him." Harris recounted that Hickok managed to disperse the mob and subsequently "he took a turn with us on the trail as a cowboy at $60 a month and grub."

No such incident ever occurred. Nor did Hickok ever work as a cow hand, being devoutly opposed to hard labor. One wonders just who Harris met in the guise of Wild Bill Hickok during his western travels.

Nothing has been more exaggerated about Hickok than the number of men he killed, nothing more mendacious than the repeated assertions that "Hickok got all his men by shooting them in the back or catching them unarmed." Equally false is the claim that he specialized in killing men incapable of putting up a good fight with a gun. Hickok took them as they came. All his opponents were armed and belligerent; often they had him outnumbered, and most of his shooting took place in towns a heartbeat away from erupting into the wildest lawlessness. Generally Hickok had only a fraction of a second in which to judge a man's intentions. He rarely gave the benefit of the doubt. Otherwise he would never have lived to the ripe old age of thirty-nine.

The only advantage Hickok took of his opponents was in being quicker and deadlier with the pistol. It was quite simple to avoid giving Hickok the bulge. All you had to do was mind your own business, keep your gun in your holster, and refrain from making a nuisance of yourself.

The number of Hickok's unsuccessful opponents has often been estimated at anywhere from seventy-five to a hundred, excluding Indians and Confederates. He is pictured as cutting them down in windrows as a lawman in Hays City and Abilene. He was supposed to have been the terror of Cheyenne, Deadwood, Laramie, and Medicine Lodge—all of which places, and many more, he visited without pulling a trigger. His total casualty list, so far as can be determined by fairly diligent research and a determined skepticism, was actually seventeen, again excluding Indians and Confederates. Enough, certainly, to give the ordinary citizen bad dreams. In all but three of his gun fights, however, he was wearing the badge of a city marshal, county sheriff, or deputy U.S. marshal. In the three exceptions the other men were the aggressors.

To show how even sober and conservative men were inclined to be misled by Hickok's publicity, Joseph G. McCoy, mayor of Abilene and a businessman not ordinarily given to miscalculation, reported that Hickok had killed forty-three men in gunfights before coming to Abilene. This was almost three times the correct figure. And at that, McCoy was more accurate than most.

Between his friends and his enemies, and Hickok himself, he became a mythical figure conjured up out of low-grade whiskey, endless saloon talk, and dime-novel pulp.

Yet it would seem that Hickok himself was not entirely deceived by the processes of either glorification or villification, equally unjustified by the facts of his existence.

Harry Young, the author of a lively memoir titled *Hard Knocks*, who knew Hickok long and well, told of listening to Hickok yarn away about himself in various barrooms. One of his favorite tales concerned the time when he was scouting for Custer in southwestern Kansas. Hickok was far in advance of the column. Subsequently he found himself in a dead-end canyon with a narrow passageway leading into it. "I remarked to myself what a great protection from Indians this would be if one were hard-pressed—the entrance being so narrow that one could secrete himself on the inside and kill

13

any number of them, since they could enter only one at a time. I was armed with a six-shooter and a large knife. The thought had hardly passed through my head, when in looking at the entrance I saw an Indian approaching. Knowing he was hostile, I shot him. Another came; I also shot him.

"They kept coming one by one until I had discharged the six shots that my gun contained. In those days we used the powder and ball six-shooters with caps on the nipples. Not having any extra ammunition with me, I was unable to reload. More Indians kept coming. I then drew my knife from my belt and backed up against the wall at the farther end, while in the meantime the open space became crowded with Indians."

At this point in his story Hickok would wait until someone prodded him to tell what happened next.

"What could I do?" he asked. "There were many of them, well armed, and I had only my knife."

"Well, then," someone would demand, "what *did* you do?"

"By God, they killed me, boys," Hickok would reply, laughing uproariously.

That Hickok could ridicule his own awesome reputation would indicate at least one saving grace in his character, and not the least of them.

WILD BILL HICKOK

CHAPTER 1

An Occurrence at Rock Creek

In the summer of 1861 James Butler Hickok, later known as Wild Bill, was something less than the "knight chivalric of the plains" so glowingly described by his subsequent admirers. A half-dozen years hence he would be the glamour boy of the western plainsmen with a shoulder-length mane of wavy hair, a brace of ivory-handled revolvers, a costume that included silk-lined capes and waistcoats in flowered brocade, and a faithful nimbus of hero-worshipers who dogged his long-striding footsteps. But now, in this first summer of the Civil War, Hickok was merely a frontier roustabout, dressed in hickory shirt and jeans, cutting hay for a few dollars a month and board. He was twenty-four years old and employed at the Rock Creek Station as a stock tender.

Several months before coming to this Nebraska stage stop he had engaged in a Davy Crockett-like scrimmage with a grizzly bear in Raton Pass. He had come out of that encounter severely mauled, with a torn scalp, a badly clawed left arm, and lacerations all over his body. To recuperate from these wounds he had been sent by his employers to the station in southeastern Nebraska.

The Rock Creek Station was a busy place, located on the Oregon Trail near what is now the town of Beatrice. There were wagon trains bound for the Pacific Northwest passing through, a heavy traffic in freight wagons, the Overland Stage's bustling passenger service, and the hard-riding relays of the Pony Express. All stopped at the Rock Creek Station, operated by Russell, Majors & Waddell, owners of the Overland Stage and Pony Express lines, for water, feed, fresh horses, wagon repairs. It was a sort of prairie caravansary, with a ranch house on either side of Rock Creek, stables, barn, and corral, at which travelers could pause for a certain amount of rough comfort. A toll bridge over the creek brought in a handsome revenue. Over the rolling horizon to the west, across the Little Blue River a few miles away, there was only the vast wilderness of the short-grass plains, a few trails, the wide, shallow prairie rivers . . . emptiness . . . Indian Country.

So Rock Creek Station was an outpost, and people who man outposts are seldom noted for gentility, refinement, or their moral standards. They were pioneers, the first wave, and toughness was the prime requisite. They would have roared with laughter, or possibly indignation, at what their descendants have made of them—sunbonneted and saintly women, strong silent men, in a cinematic setting of house-raisings, quilting bees, and square dances. Actually they were a noisy and robust lot, not a great deal more civilized than the "barbarians" they had pre-empted.

The leading citizen of the vicinity was David C. McCanles, a swarthy, bull-shouldered, and aggressive man, whose income from various enterprises was said to average a thousand dollars a month. This made him the local tycoon, a man growingly accustomed to having his own way. It was young Hickok's misfortune that he somehow aroused McCanles' enmity, and it was McCanles' misfortune that he underestimated the weedy young stock tender. Their showdown one blazing July afternoon was to become as celebrated, and even more exaggerated, in western legend as the Earp brothers' fusillade in the O. K. Corral many years later.

McCanles' credentials were not of the best. He had absconded as sheriff of his native Watauga County, North Carolina, early in 1859 with the intention of joining the Pikes Peak gold rush. To ease the rigors of the journey he took with him one Sarah Shull, who was twenty-six years old, dark-haired, blue-eyed, and attractive. Mrs. McCanles and the children, of course, were left behind. The thirty-one-year-old McCanles and his traveling companion journeyed by horseback, railroad, and steamboat to Leavenworth, Kansas, and then set out on the trek to Colorado. Along the Oregon Trail they met the backwash from the Pikes Peak country, returning stampeders who reported that all the best claims had been staked. Sarah and Dave halted at the point where the Oregon Trail crossed Rock Creek and settled down to build the station. McCanles quickly became the dominant figure in the neighborhood, which was largely settled by Southerners. The nearest town site, at the intersection of the Oregon Trail and the Big Blue River, was named Palmetto, testifying to a nostalgia for the Carolinas.

The stage station prospered, but apparently unwedded bliss with Sarah had its limits. Undoubtedly, too, McCanles had the Southerner's strong feeling for his clan. He sent for his wife, his children, his brother J. L. McCanles, and his family. Sarah was understandably displeased but not so outraged that she took her departure. She stayed on at Rock Creek, ambiguous though her position may have been. The McCanles clan established itself at the east ranch house, Sarah across the creek in the west ranch house, which made a nice stroll in the moonlight for the virile McCanles. The situation was accepted calmly, if not with rejoicing, by Mrs. McCanles. Of this arrangement Charles Dawson, who later owned the Rock Creek ranch on which these events occurred, wrote somewhat cryptically (in *Pioneer Tales of the Oregon Trail*, privately published, 1912), "The motive that impelled her [Sarah Shull] to reside at Rock Creek Station was concealed in the hearts of the few. At least her charms (as Dame Gossip says) were reserved to this circle, and that fact caused domestic troubles."

It may have been Mrs. McCanles' growing restiveness at having her comely rival established only a stone's throw away that impelled her husband to sell the Rock Creek Station to Russell, Majors & Waddell early in 1861. The McCanleses were then transplanted to a ranch on the Little Blue several miles away. Dave McCanles, however, continued to take a lively proprietorial interest in Sarah.

In May of 1861 the Rock Creek Station was taken over by Horace Wellman as agent for the stage line. The east ranch house and its outbuildings, as well as the toll bridge, were included in the transaction. Sarah Shull, however, continued to live in the west ranch house.

Wellman and his common-law wife were assisted in operating the station by Hickok, the stock tender, and J. W. (Doc) Brink, the stable hand. This little group soon found itself in bad odor with Dave McCanles.

McCanles was irked by the fact that Russell, Majors & Waddell was dilatory in paying him for hay furnished by his ranch on the Little Blue as well as installments due on the property itself. Violent and unreasonable, McCanles blamed the Wellmans for the slow payment of these debts and made numerous and harassing visits to the station to demand that they do something about it.

And Dave McCanles took a strong personal dislike to their stock tender. Hickok was an inoffensive loner, who did his work and lived in a dugout not far from the stables and asked only to be left alone. He wanted nothing to do with the loud, swaggering Carolinian and tried to avoid him. McCanles accordingly took delight in tormenting him. He called Hickok "Duck Bill," apparently in reference to a rather protruding upper lip which Hickok later concealed under stallion-tail mustachios. When there were bystanders around, McCanles delighted in pouncing on Hickok, despite his disabled left arm, and throwing him to the ground. It was said, too, that there was another cause for bad feeling between the two men—Sarah Shull—and that Hickok had taken to straying across the creek to the west ranch house. Charles Dawson, without citing any supporting evidence, stated that McCanles warned Hickok "on the penalty of violence or death not to cross the creek where she lived."

McCanles, with all the southern mountaineer's love of a feud, directed his energies at making life miserable for the people at Rock Creek Station.

Under this senseless but continual harassment, Wellman left the station early in July for the division offices of Russell, Majors & Waddell at Brownsville, on the Missouri River, to beg that McCanles be paid off as soon as possible. Knowing this, but still unpacified, McCanles paid daily visits to the station to shout threats and denunciations at Mrs. Wellman. Hickok, who was the stationmaster in Wellman's absence, shared in the abuse. He took it so meekly, in fact, that McCanles undoubtedly was convinced that "Duck Bill" was incapable of defending himself.

On the evening of July 11, Wellman returned to Rock Creek, his mission a failure. The division offices of his company had proven unwilling or unable to provide an immediate payment on the money owed McCanles. The latter's probable reaction to this news was predictable enough to the men at the station. Undoubtedly he would try to repossess it by force as he had been threatening. They also feared he would have plenty of help from Southerners in the neighborhood, many of whom were preparing to leave the territory to join the Confederate Army. Wellman and Hickok presumably decided that night not to give up the station without a battle.

Next morning McCanles learned that Wellman had returned from Brownsville empty-handed and roared that he would "clean up on the people at the station."

That day, July 12, 1861, a more important date in his life than he could have imagined when he rolled out of bed that morning, was a nerve-racking one for Hickok. The jittery Wellmans summoned him to the ranch house and asked him to stand by, along with Doc Brink, the stable hand. Also in the house was Sarah Kelsey, the station girl of all work. The defense force, it seemed to Hickok, was inconsiderable. Hickok himself was armed with a revolver, Doc Brink with a shotgun, Wellman with only a hoe. They all looked to Hickok as the man to handle McCanles, although his only recommendation was that victory over the grizzly bear. At this stage Hickok had never been involved in a gun fight; he was not exactly a stranger to violence and trouble, but he had no reason to believe he was capable, particularly with his barely healed wounds, of coping with a hell-roarer like McCanles and whomever he might muster.

In the forenoon McCanles appeared in the station yard and shouted a demand that Wellman surrender the station. Wellman refused. McCanles rode off threatening to take it by force later in the day. More hours of waiting in the oppressive heat of the ranch house. The tension was growing unbearable.

Late in the afternoon McCanles reappeared at the station, this time with three companions. They included his twelve-year-old son Monroe, his cousin James Woods, and James Gordon, an employee on the McCanles ranch. McCanles anticipated little or no trouble in "cleaning up" on the people at the station, for he ordered his son and the two young men with him to wait at the barn while he went up to the ranch house alone.

Mrs. Wellman answered his thunderous summons, coming to the kitchen door and somewhat unnecessarily asking what he wanted.

"I want to settle with your husband," McCanles said.

"He won't come out," Mrs. Wellman replied.

"Send him out or I'll come in and drag him out!"

While Wellman cowered inside, Hickok was persuaded to go out and try to parley with McCanles.

"What the hell have you got to do with this?" McCanles demanded. "All right, if you want to take a hand in this, come out and we'll settle it like men."

Hickok knew he was incapable of meeting McCanles on anything like equal terms in an eye-gouging, groin-kneeing, ear-chewing, all-out, frontier-style combat. He could see no reason why he should allow McCanles to commit mayhem on him as a means of relieving his annoyance with the Overland Stage. He had also reached the end of his patience with being bullied, degraded, and humiliated by McCanles.

Hickok stayed in the doorway, refusing the invitation.

"All right then, send Wellman out or I'll come in after him," McCanles said.

Hickok went back in the house. The anxious people inside, peering out, saw McCanles move around the house from the kitchen door on the west side to the front door on the south side. From the front McCanles had a clear view of the interior, except for a portion of the front room which was partitioned off by a calico curtain concealing two beds.

His gun drawn, Hickok waited behind the calico curtain.

McCanles apparently spotted his movement behind the curtain and called out to him to "come out and fight fair."

The rancher then stepped across the threshold.

Hickok fired from behind the curtain. Either his hand was surprisingly steady or his luck was with him in that moment. The bullet struck McCanles in the heart and he fell mortally wounded on the doorstep.

were buried in tandem on what is known as Soldier Hill. By sunset all three were interred without the benefit of any religious rites . . . or mourners.

Three days later Hickok, Wellman, and Brink were arrested by the sheriff of Gage County and taken before Justice of the Peace T. M. Coulter. Their plea was self-defense, with the further contention that they were defending government property—that is, the wagons, stages, and horses used in carrying the United States mail. Justice Coulter accepted this plea without further ado and turned all three men loose without the necessity of standing trial.

Just what happened at that briskly conducted hearing is still not entirely clear. For years the only documentary proof that such a hearing was even held was a line in the Appearance Docket of the Clerk of the District Court of Gage County, which read:

"The Territory of Nebraska vs. William B. Hickok [sic], J. W. Brink and Horrace [sic] Wellman."

In 1926, however, members of the Nebraska Historical Society unearthed a box of moldering old documents in the basement of the courthouse at Beatrice. Several of the papers concerned the preliminary hearing in the McCanles case. They indicated that young Monroe McCanles was summoned as a witness but for some unexplained reason was not permitted to testify, although he was the only witness to his father's death aside from the people at the station. Both he and his mother, in fact, were excluded from Justice Coulter's courtroom while the hearing was being held. The only witnesses heard were the accused men and Mrs. Wellman. Even allowing for certain crudities in the administration of territorial justice, this would seem to have been a suspiciously hasty and prejudicial procedure. Presumably the citizenry of Beatrice tolerated it because the McCanleses were Southerners and there was much bitterness against the settlers around Palmetto, in particular, because many were preparing to join the Confederate Army.

Most historians, in fact, have claimed that the real reason for the gunfire at Rock Creek Station was that McCanles was the leader of a band of southern patriots and that he and his henchmen appeared at the station that day to steal the horses and turn them over to the Confederate cavalry. This theory collapses rapidly under the weight of the more reliable evidence.

In the first place, the McCanles clan was pro-Union. Their native Watauga County, in western North Carolina, was a stronghold of Unionist sentiment. The McCanleses were of the Whig-Republican persuasion, living in one of these southern backwaters where the people owned no slaves and wanted no part of the slaveowners' grandiose visions of a new agrarian republic below the Mason-Dixon line. The surviving McCanleses, in fact, remained loyal to the Union throughout the Civil War, although many of their neighbors went South to join the "erring sisters."

In any event, the horse-stealing theory was ridiculous on other grounds. It would hardly have been worth a murderous raid to steal the horse herd at the station that day—it included only six horses and two ponies—and then drive them all the way through Union territory, through Kansas and Missouri, to the Confederate cavalry's remount stables.

The one person who might have cleared up a number of mysteries concerning the shooting, Sarah Shull, vanished from the scene the next morning. She was placed on a westbound stage—by whom it was never ascertained—and managed to conceal her identity for some sixty-five years, during which she lived in Utah, Colorado, Florida, and Tennessee. At the age of ninety-three she was located by a Hickok biographer, Frank J. Wilstach (*The Plainsman*, 1926), who incidentally held to the theory that McCanles intended to steal the station's horse herd and operate along the Oregon

Trail with a band of anti-Union guerrillas. Wilstach did not state where he found the aged Sarah, but "inducing her to talk was much like opening an oyster with a blade of grass." Her relationship with McCanles was not discussed. About the only significant statement made by Sarah was that "on the morning of the tragedy I heard McCanles say that he was going to clean up on the people at the station." Asked if she believed that Hickok shot in self-defense, she replied, "Certainly—yes." Although she must have been a witness to the whole affair at Rock Creek Station, there was nothing else she would add, by Wilstach's account, to the story of that bloodletting except the incomprehensible statement that Mc-Canles went there to "steal horses for the Confederate cavalry." It would seem that all the facts will never be known.

The one sure fact was that Hickok, under rather squalid circumstances, killed one man and wounded two others who were dispatched by his friends. Out of this seedling of truth grew the legend of the "massacre at Rock Creek Station," which was the foundation of the picturesque fable that represents Hickok's life to most people. Even relatively sober-sided historians have referred to it as "the greatest one-man gunfight in history."

Hickok's life was extraordinary enough without the embellishments of either his admirers or detractors. He had more than his share of both, and both were equally imaginative, eloquent, and industrious. The present intention is not to debunk Wild Bill Hickok, any more than it is to glorify him, but simply to arrive at an approximation of the truth. In this connection it might be instructive to study what the legend makers did with the occurrence at Rock Creek Station.

The first romancer who happened on the story was George Ward Nichols, whose account appeared in *Harper's New Monthly Magazine* of February 1867. Mr. Nichols cited "an officer of the regular army, who, an hour after the affair, saw Bill and the ten dead men—some killed with bullets, others hacked and slashed to death with a knife." The victims of this slaughter, according to Nichols, were Dave McCanles and nine members of his "party of ruffians." Nichols related that the ten marauders broke into the station and were confronted by Hickok with a rifle, six-shooter, and Bowie knife. When the dust settled, all ten were lying on the floor dead or mortally wounded.

Nichols claimed to have heard part of the story from Hickok's own lips, a claim which Hickok later repudiated. The writer said he was "conscious of its extreme improbability" but "as I looked upon this magnificent example of human strength and daring, he appeared to me to realize the powers of Samson and Hercules combined, and I should not have been likely to place any limit on his achievements." In his account McCanles is referred to as "M'Kandlas" and Wellman as "Waltman."

Nichols quoted Hickok as saying one of his assailants struck him with a rifle butt and, "Then I got ugly and I remember that I got hold of a knife, and then it was all cloudy-like and I was wild and I struck savage blows, following the devils up from one side to the other of the room and into the corners striking and slashing until I knew that every one was dead."

It was, as Nichols said, a "terrible tale."

Fourteen years later—but no closer to the truth—J. W. Buel, who knew Hickok as a reporter for the Kansas City *Journal*, published a sketch of Wild Bill in *Heroes of the Plains* (1881) in which the death toll at Rock Creek still stood at ten. He identified the army officer, apparently the same one quoted anonymously by Nichols, as Captain E. W. Kingsbury, of Kansas City, then U.S. chief storekeeper for the western district of Missouri. Captain Kingsbury, Buel said, was one of six passengers who arrived at Rock Creek on the westbound stage an hour after the shootings. This account was

somewhat enhanced by Captain Kingsbury's description of
Hickok still on his feet after having suffered a frontal skull
fracture, three "terrible" gashes on his chest, four bullets in
his body, his scalp almost detached and hanging over his
eyes, and various lesser knife wounds. Buel said he also interviewed a Dr. Joshua Thorne, who told of patching Hickok
up after the battle.

According to Buel, the McCanles "gang" had "killed more
than a score of innocent men and women for the purpose of
robbery, and yet their power was such that no civil officer
dared undertake their arrest." Buel's account continued:

"Early in the morning of the day in question, Jim [sic]
McCandlas [sic] rode by Rock Creek station in company
with four of his men. McCandlas was leading an old man,
known as Parson Shapley, by a lariat which was around the
old man's neck. Coming up to Bill the party stopped, and
McCandlas entered into a conversation, in which he tried to
persuade Bill to enter the Confederate service and to turn
over all the horses at the station to him. Bill, a stranger to
the sensation of fear, told McCandlas to go to hell; that if
he did any fighting it would be on the side of the Union.
McCandlas then told Bill that if he didn't have the horses
ready for delivery by the time of his return . . . 'there would
be a small murder at the Rock Creek station, and the stage
company would have to get another man.'"

When McCanles and his henchmen returned, according
to Buel, Hickok engaged them hand-to-hand in a small log
hut which would hardly have provided elbow room for eleven
desperate men wielding rifles, knives, and revolvers. Hickok
had barricaded himself in the hut at the approach of the
McCanles gang with a "Mississippi Yager rifle, two revolvers,
and a Bowie knife." The ruffians outside used a log to batter
down the door, and the bloody skirmish was on.

Even gaudier, as was to be expected, was the account
published by Beadle's Dime Library on January 11, 1882,

under the title *Wild Bill, The Pistol Deadshot*. Its author was a man who styled himself Colonel Prentiss Ingraham, who was almost as prolific and equally as careless with the facts as the redoubtable Ned Buntline.

Both the ubiquitous Captain Kingsbury and the garrulous Dr. Thorne showed up in this account. With the passage of time Hickok's wounds became more numerous in the good doctor's memory. Recalling his surgical masterpiece, Dr. Thorne said he "removed eleven bullets from the person of Wild Bill, nearly all of which were planted within him at the Rock Creek fight." Hickok remained conscious during this operation, waving off whatever analgesics and anesthetics were available, Dr. Thorne said, and "gave expression only to sympathetic words for the ferocious enemies he had slain in that memorable encounter."

Down through the years, as the Hickok legend proliferated, the story of the Rock Creek killings (they could hardly be dignified as a gunfight) suffered little downgrading in the telling. A few details were changed, but it was still an epic battle. Emerson Hough in his near-classic *The Story of the Outlaw* (1905) stated that "there were six dead men on the floor of the dugout" when the shooting ended. Mr. Hough trimmed the death toll by four and shifted the scene of the shooting from the east ranch house to Hickok's dugout, which was so small that the dead men would have had to be accommodating enough to stack themselves like cordwood before expiring. A more sanguinary tale written seven years later, possibly without the devoted help of Dr. Thorne, said that "Hickok was wounded by three bullets, 11 buckshot and was cut in 13 places." This was the first time a shotgun was listed in the armory of weapons employed by the "McCanles gang." As late as 1926, Fred E. Sutton, a former Kansas marshal, wrote in *The Saturday Evening Post* that Hickok did indeed snuff out ten lives in the Rock Creek battle. There was a downward revision of the death toll, finally, in the two latter-day biographies of Hickok, Wilstach's *The Plainsman* (1926) and William E. Connelley's *Wild Bill and His Era* (1933), both of which credited him with only the deaths of McCanles, Woods, and Gordon.

From the scant evidence available it appears that Hickok shot and killed McCanles rather than take a beating. McCanles was something of a brute and a bully, but he had never killed a man and probably had no intention of killing anyone at the station. He had made the sorry mistake of overestimating the amount of bullying people will take.

Hickok apparently shot Woods and Gordon in a panic, believing they were coming to McCanles' assistance. The indications are that they were not even armed; otherwise they would have defended themselves against Brink with his shotgun and Wellman with his murderous hoe.

A sordid frontier brawl, gleefully exaggerated by the tall-tale tellers of the border, made Hickok one of the most famous men in America in the decade following the Civil War. His tragedy, perhaps, was that he had to spend the rest of his life trying to live up to his legend.

CHAPTER 2

The Small World of Troy Grove

Near the state highway that skirts the town of Troy Grove in La Salle County in northern Illinois a rough-hewn monument stands, somewhat surprisingly looming out of the picnicking grounds of the state park. It was dedicated on August 29, 1930, in the presence of twelve hundred persons, more than half a century after its subject died suddenly of a bullet in the brain on the sawdust of a South Dakota saloon. This fact was ignored in the speeches which preceded the ceremonial undraping of the monument, in which the subject was eulogized as "dead square . . . dead honest . . . and a dead shot." A bronze plaque imbedded in the chunk of granite asserted, "He contributed largely in making the West a safe place for women and children. His sterling courage was always at the service of right and justice."

No mention was made of the fact that this local hero ran away from home as a youth, believing that he was fleeing a possible murder charge. Nor that he returned to Troy Grove only once in later life. Like most heroes, he required wider horizons, and the population of Troy Grove never managed to rise above the three-hundred mark.

This was the home town of Wild Bill Hickok. He was born there under the less flamboyant name of James Butler Hickok on May 27, 1837, and spent eighteen years of his life, almost half of it, among its groves and river bottoms and prairie vistas.

He was descended from a long line of God-fearing, patriotic New Englanders, the first of whom barely missed taking passage on the Mayflower. The first Hickoks established themselves in Connecticut Colony, then spread out through New England, particularly Vermont. They fought with Ethan Allen's Boys during the American Revolution. His grandfather, Otis Hickok, was one of the heroes of the Battle of Plattsburg during the War of 1812.

His father, William Alonzo Hickok, was born at North Hero, Vermont, and was of less military, though no less militant, turn of mind. William Alonzo, having given early indications of piety, was consigned to the ministry by his family. Apparently his intellect did not quite match his spiritual fervor. He was forced to concentrate so intensively on his studies that he suffered a breakdown. It was diagnosed as an attack of brain fever, which could mean almost anything in those days. For some time he suffered from amnesia and his recovery was slow. When his memory finally cleared and his health was partly restored, his family decided that William Alonzo was better suited to the plow than the pulpit. At the age of twenty-six he married Polly Butler, nine years younger, the daughter of a neighboring farmer. They came West in 1834, finally settled at Troy Grove in 1836, the year before James Butler Hickok was born. The latter had three older brothers—Oliver, Lorenzo, and Horace—and eventually two younger sisters, Celinda and Lydia.

The Hickok family first lived in a frame house built out on the prairie, half a mile from Little Vermillion Creek, where William Alonzo broke the sod and tried farming. His health still wasn't quite up to it, so he opened the first store in the hamlet of Troy Grove. The general store occupied a ground-floor room in the village tavern, known as the Green Mountain House.

Jim Hickok's boyhood apparently was fairly typical of the time and place. He led a semi-savage life, roaming the creek bottoms and racing over the prairie, modified only by the demands of a country schoolmaster and the lectures of his sternly religious father, who was a deacon in the local church. It would appear that the schoolmaster, with his whistling hickory rod, exerted a stronger influence on young Jim than his father. From the way he spoke and the letters he wrote in later life, he seemed to have acquired an education better than most such graduates of prairie schools. The religious teachings of his father, however, failed to take hold. They didn't seem to fit the brutal facts of life on the frontier. And Illinois, during his boyhood, was still part of the frontier; Black Hawk's war, with young Abraham Lincoln as a young captain of Illinois militia, had been fought shortly before Jim Hickok's birth.

Firearms fascinated the boy from the day he was strong enough to heft the heavy, cumbersome weapons of the period. His first gun was an old flintlock pistol, which he acquired through barter and used on hunting expeditions along the creek bottoms. Jim's fondness for guns—it rapidly became an obsession—and his proclivities as a hunter did not please his family, although the birds and other small game he shot went into the family pot. The elder Hickoks wanted something better for their sons than the rough, hazardous life of the frontiersman. Jim, however, a true contemporary of Mark Twain, had his eyes, heart, and mind fixed on the Great Plains and adventure in the West. Most red-blooded boys did. Nothing was less appealing than his parents' hope that he would become a small-town lawyer, doctor, minister, or businessman. Young Abe may have studied the Bible, Milton, and Shakespeare by firelight, but young Jim had *The Trapper's Guide*

34

and *The Life of Kit Carson* squirreled away in his attic room and pored over them when he should have been delving into the mysteries of long division and the subordinate clause.

When he was twelve years old, he managed to acquire a good rifle and a Colt's revolving pistol by trading furs for them. He soon became the best marksman in that part of the country. A few years later he beat all the crack shots in northern Illinois shooting at targets with a percussion revolver. Illinois, in fact, was the cradle of the West's top guns. Wyatt Earp and Bat Masterson, among others, were born in that state. Hickok would meet them later—as friends, fortunately for all concerned.

His elder brothers did not share, at least not to an equal degree, Jim's fateful interest in firearms. Oliver, the eldest, was fascinated by horses and became a driver and trainer of trotting horses, among them St. Julian, the greatest trotter of his day. Lorenzo went out West for a time but returned to become a surveyor. Horace, the only son to satisfy his parents' longings for a professional career, served for many years as a justice of the peace. All his brothers survived Jim by many years, thanks mostly to their more peaceable inclinations. In later years Horace said that Jim, during his boyhood, showed few signs of aggressiveness. "He never started a quarrel, was always good-tempered."

The Hickok brothers shared at least one enthusiasm with their father, a strong belief in Abolition, which William Alonzo brought with him from his native Vermont long before *Uncle Tom's Cabin* made Abolition a popular and respectable cause in the North. Curiously and ironically enough, it was this idealistic zeal for freeing the slaves, transmitted by his father, which was partly responsible for Jim's career as a man of violence. His anti-Southern bias, his enthusiasm for Free Soil and other Abolitionist causes first encouraged Jim to lift his sights from small game to other human beings. And most of his opponents, from one end of the border to the other, aside from Indians, were Southerners. Sectional and political strife became part of Jim's life from early boyhood. The bitter nourishment provided by this atmosphere—though it was far from his father's intention—helped to turn Jim's footsteps toward that slow, ominous stalk known as the "gunman's walk."

Pious and law-abiding though he was in other matters, William Alonzo Hickok did not hesitate to flout the laws concerning fugitive slaves. It was then the law of the land that a runaway slave must be returned to his owner, even in a northern state. William Hickok, however, established a way station of the Underground Railroad at the Green Mountain House, along which runaway slaves were hurried to freedom and safety in Canada. From Troy Grove the fugitives were conveyed to the next station at Panton's Mills.

It was a strange midnight traffic, full of risk and charged with melodrama, and must have left a more indelible mark on his youngest son than on the three older ones. Late at night the fugitives would be brought to the Hickok store and hidden through the following day under a trap door. The following night they would be conveyed to Panton's Mills.

Often the professional slave catchers, human bloodhounds employed by the plantation owners, were in hot pursuit. They were bounty hunters, paid so much per head on the recaptured slaves, and with this incentive went about their work with a ferocious enthusiasm.

Since the slave catchers did not hesitate to fire on wagons suspected of transporting fugitive slaves, the traffic was a dangerous one for the Underground agents and their charges alike. The elder Hickok had a team of fast Kentucky horses especially for use on the Underground.

Jim often went along on the midnight gallops to Panton's Mills, huddling in the wagon box with the terrified Negroes while their pursuers' bullets whistled around the rocketing conveyance.

All that came to an end when the elder Hickok died in 1852. Jim was fifteen years old at his father's death and had to help support the family. He hunted wolves for bounty, did odd jobs around Troy Grove, and drove wagon teams for the local merchants.

Jim Hickok might have settled down to the humdrum life of the Illinois village if the Illinois and Michigan Canal hadn't been extended through the district at that time and if a brawl hadn't sent him on his way westward, believing he was a fugitive from justice. He went to work driving a mule team for the canal builders. His fellow workers were a rough, brawling, and tumultuous lot. None was tougher and meaner than another teamster named Charles Hudson.

Something about Jim Hickok in his youth seemed to attract the attention of bullies. Perhaps he had grown accustomed to solitude as a hunter. He was quiet, indrawn, minded his own business, and was anything but gregarious. People who knew him as a youth said he was "hard to get acquainted with." Undoubtedly some of his fellow teamsters —Hudson in particular—misinterpreted his solitary nature as standoffishness or snobbery, especially since Hickok was soft-spoken and better educated than his companions.

One afternoon in the summer of 1855, when Hickok was eighteen, he took more than the usual amount of abuse from Hudson while they were on the towpath alongside the canal. Suddenly Hickok flew at Hudson with fists flailing. Hudson was so surprised that he soon found himself taking a terrific beating from the younger and smaller Hickok. He grappled with the boy, and together they toppled into the canal. The struggle continued in the water, with the opponents earnestly doing their best to drown each other.

Fellow teamsters finally broke up the fight by dragging Hickok out of the canal. Hudson was still floundering somewhere in its depths. Someone shouted that "Charlie Hudson's dead." Rescuers began diving into the canal to find him.

Panic overwhelmed young Hickok. Listening to the shouts of his fellow teamsters and the frantic sounds of the rescue attempt, Hickok was convinced that he had committed murder. Charlie Hudson's lifeless body must be lying at the bottom of the canal.

Jim Hickok lit out across country. If he was a murderer, he had no intention of standing trial. A moment or two after the panic-stricken youth took off, Hudson was hauled out of the water, weak and battered, but still alive.

Hickok kept going, expecting any minute to hear the sounds of pursuit behind him. He didn't stop until he reached the Mississippi four days later. At a steamboat landing he loaded slab wood on a stern-wheeler and thus worked his passage to St. Louis. Jim Hickok, at eighteen, was on his own and headed West.

CHAPTER 3

The Blood-dimmed Tide

After hanging around the levees at St. Louis for several days, young Jim Hickok, still believing himself to be a fugitive from the gallows, worked his way upriver on a paddle-wheeler to Leavenworth, Kansas.

It was a fateful choice, dictated at least in part by the Abolitionist sympathies he had acquired from his earliest years. The Territory of Kansas was then a battleground between bloody-minded fanatics and idealists from both North and South. Undoubtedly the youthful Hickok's experiences with the night riders of "bleeding Kansas" were the determining factor in what he became, the deadliest of the gunfighters. At eighteen, certainly, Hickok had few inclinations toward the career of a professional killer. He was a gentle enough and generally amiable boy, a dutiful son and affectionate brother. His wild assault on teamster Hudson came about only after he had been bullied and tormented beyond endurance. There was no evidence of the born killer, the instinctive aggressor, about him. Had he ventured anywhere but Kansas, he might have lived out his days as peacefully as his brothers.

When the steamboat tied up at Leavenworth that summer day in 1855, the border town was in turmoil. The authorities had decided that no passengers would be permitted to disembark, since the town already was bulging with troublemakers from both factions, pro-slavery and Abolitionist. Hickok, however, jumped over the side and mingled with the roustabouts unloading freight from the steamboat's hold, then took the first opportunity to slip away from the dock.

He worked for a farmer homesteading on the prairie a few miles west of Leavenworth to acquire a small stake and size up the situation. A few months later he journeyed farther west to what is now Monticello Township in Johnson County. There again he hired himself out as a farm laborer, meanwhile looking around for a piece of land he could work for himself.

Kansas in those pristine days had a virginal beauty that attracted less poetic souls than Hickok's. It was a great rolling grassland, a fertile steppe, through which coursed the calm prairie rivers. There were frequent patches of timber, walnut, hickory, oak, elm, willow, buttonwood, and cottonwood. The clear cool water of many creeks cut through limestone hills. In season the prairie flowered magnificently with blue lupine, primroses, wild strawberry, elderberry, and plum blossoms threw banners of color and fragrance against grassy slopes and blue horizons. The land was thick with edible game, quail, prairie chicken, wild turkey. It was living virgin soil, green-cloaked for centuries, plentifully veined with water, unspoiled and uncultivated. It could have been paradise.

Instead it became the first battleground of North and South, the proving ground of the Civil War, where sectional rivalry, hatred, and prejudice had their violent collision. Here was loosed the "blood-dimmed tide" of which Yeats wrote, in which "the best lack all conviction while the worst are filled with a passionate intensity."

Goaded on by ambitious demagogues and financed by

southern slaveholders and northern manufacturers, the Border Ruffians from Missouri and the Free-Soil partisans fought it out in an undeclared war, the dirtiest kind of war, ambushes, massacres, bushwhackings, neighborly murders, town-burnings, and lynchings.

The mischief began in Washington the year before young Hickok arrived in the Territory of Kansas. Until 1854, by terms of the Missouri Compromise, a makeshift but serviceable bulwark against civil war, Kansas and Nebraska were designated non-slavery territories. In 1854, however, the supple and devious Senator Stephen Douglas of Illinois and his supporters eased through the Kansas-Nebraska Act, repealing the Missouri Compromise and allowing the citizens of those territories to decide for themselves whether they would permit or forbid slavery.

Both sides were determined to tip the balance in their own favor by rushing in thousands of settlers, a migration which was just beginning when Hickok jumped ship at Leavenworth.

Northerners had the edge from the outset, thanks to the endeavors of the New England Emigrant Aid Society and the contributions of Amos Lawrence and other wealthy New Englanders. These settlers of the Free-Soil persuasion were not only given all kinds of assistance in establishing homesteads for themselves but were provided with shipments of the new and highly efficient Sharps rifles, jocularly called "Beecher's bibles" in honor of that eminent Christian, the Rev. Henry Ward Beecher, who believed there was nothing like a judicious amount of gunfire to further a holy cause.

This well-armed migration was viewed with justifiable alarm by the slaveholders of Missouri and the plantation aristocrats of the Deep South. There were fifty thousand slaves, representing a thirty-million-dollar investment, in Missouri's border counties. Former U. S. Senator David R. Atchison, leader of the pro-slavery forces in Missouri, grimly informed his sympathizers, "To have a free state as our western neighbor would spell disaster." He and his followers established pro-slavery strongholds in Leavenworth, Kickapoo, and Atchison, Kansas, but for the most part Missourians preferred raiding across the border and illegal expeditions into Kansas to vote in the territorial elections to settling there. They preferred working their river-bottom lands to the backbreaking job of breaking sod on the Kansas prairie. Susceptible as they were to oratorical appeals, they resisted such calls to armed migration as were sounded by Senator Atchison's *Platte Argus:* "Stake out your claims and woe be to the Abolitionists who shall intrude upon it or come within range of your long rifles, or within pointblank shot of your revolvers." The pro-slavery Missourians made up in violence what they lacked in numbers, answering such trumpetings as those of Dr. John Stringfellow, editor of Atchison's *Squatter Sovereign* and one of Atchison's more vituperative propagandists, who howled at a crowd in St. Joseph, Missouri, "Vote at the point of Bowie knife and revolver . . . I tell you to mark every scoundrel among you that is the least tainted with free-soilism, or Abolitionism, and exterminate him." After listening to the fulminations of their leaders at pro-slavery rallies, they were all too eager to join the "Blue Lodges" and "Friendly Societies," which were simply bands of bushwhackers organized to raid across the border. Their passions were further inflamed by sessions at the crossroads general stores, where barrels of "Old Monongahela" were on tap, a distillation which had the "strength of forty jackasses, guaranteed to kill forty rods around the corner." Between the backwoods oratory and the "Old Monongahela," the Missourians, rejoicing in the title of "Border Ruffians," joined battle with the Free-State partisans across the Missouri with a remorseless enthusiasm. It occurred to very few of them that they were dupes in a struggle which could only benefit those who incited and manipulated them from their distant manor houses.

Nor was the state of political morality—no matter how elevated and ministerial its tone—much better on the other side. In the Free-Soil camp, too, there was that strain of hoodlumism, of which Bruce Catton (*The Hallowed Ground*) has written, "Like an ape behind a mask, it can display itself suddenly with terrifying effect. It is slack-jawed, with leering eyes and loose wet lips, with heavy feet and ponderous cunning hands; now and then, when something tickles it, it guffaws, and when it is made angry it snarls; and it can be aroused much more easily than it can be quieted . . . Judge Lynch is one of its creations; and when it comes lumbering forth it can make the whole country step in time to its own frantic irregular pulse-beat." In retaliation for the Missourians' rowdy invasions, the Free-Staters were quick to fall on isolated settlers suspected of pro-slavery sentiments, burn down their houses, and drive them out of the country without the semblance of a hearing. And in the summer of 1856, when the Free-State militiamen, grandly styling themselves the "Army of the North," attacked various southern settlements, they equaled, if they did not exceed, the Missourians in brutality.

Young Hickok, of course, could not long escape being embroiled in the war for Kansas. He joined the Free-State Militia, later known as the "Red Legs," a conglomeration of several hundred men who marched about, rather ineffectually, in an attempt to counter the invasions from Missouri. Their commander was one of the more picturesque figures in the history of the Middle Border, James H. Lane, a former congressman and lawyer from Indiana. He had commanded an Indiana infantry regiment in the Mexican War and had an undeniable talent for leadership, military and political.

Rough-hewn Jim Lane formed a strong contrast to his opposite number in the pro-slavery camp, Senator Atchison.

At the sound of the shot Woods, Gordon, and young Monroe McCanles ran toward the house from the barn, evidently believing that Dave McCanles had begun "cleaning up" on the people at the station. This was a serious error in judgment. Woods ran to the kitchen door, where Hickok fired twice and wounded him. A moment later Gordon appeared at the front door. Hickok, racing from room to room, winged Gordon with one shot.

Both Woods and Gordon attempted to flee for their lives. As far as Hickok was concerned, they would have been allowed to escape. He had shot and killed one man—the cause of all the trouble—and wounded two others, who may or may not have been coming at him with homicidal intent. That was enough shooting for one day. But the other people at the station, terrified until now, had their blood up. A grisly sort of chase ensued. Wellman, with his grubbing hoe, and Doc Brink, with his shotgun, took out after the two wounded men.

Dave McCanles had just breathed his last in the arms of his twelve-year-old son.

Mrs. Wellman, untouched by this scene, pointed at young Monroe and screamed at Hickok, "Kill him, kill him!"

But Hickok shook his head and slipped his gun into its holster.

The two wounded men fared less well. Wellman caught up with Woods in a clump of weeds at the east end of the station and chopped the life out of him with his hoe.

Gordon, less seriously wounded, was running for his life along the creek bottom with Brink and his shotgun in pursuit. Brink caught up with him and fired a blast of pellets into his body. Gordon slumped and died at the base of a tree.

Hasty burials were arranged by the people at the station without consulting the McCanles family. Gordon was buried in a blanket under the tree where he fell. An outsize coffin was hammered together for McCanles and Woods, and they

The latter was described as a "florid, sociable man-mountain, fond of horses, hunting, fishing and liquor." He liked to introduce himself in his booming voice as "born in Frogtown, Kentucky, where I was the biggest frog in the puddle." Lane, in contrast to this jovial hulk, was primarily an ambition-driven agitator, lean, burning-eyed, haggard, with an unkempt beard and a "demoralized wardrobe."

Lane was a hero in search of a cause. A Democrat, he had supported Douglas and Atchison in their campaign to shove the Kansas-Nebraska Act through Congress. He came to Kansas in the spring of 1855, saying he would "just as soon buy a nigger as a mule." Scenting opportunities for a heroic role in the Free-State cause, he quickly and radically changed his viewpoint. Soon he was the loudest and most effective of the Free-Soil demagogues, "a perfect specimen of the *chamoleon politico*," as Alice Nichols wrote in her excellent *Bleeding Kansas*. Among the Kansas settlers he made an instantly winning impression. He worked hard to unite all the anti-slavery factions. Standing before a crowd of Free-Staters at one of their gatherings—which were as emotional if not as alcoholic as those across the Missouri border—he would gnaw off a chaw of tobacco, take a deep breath, and launch into a stream of invective and exhortation that would keep his audience spellbound for hours under the glaring sun of a town square. Much as it promised, his career following the border war fizzled out and ended in suicide. Just after the Civil War broke out, he appeared in Washington with a tatterdemalion "Frontier Guard" which bivouacked in the East Room of the White House during the tense days of April 1861. President Lincoln was fascinated with his energy and self-confidence, appointed him a brigadier general of Volunteers. Lane commanded the Kansas Brigade which jayhawked the property of Confederate and Union sympathizers alike in freebooting campaigns through western Missouri. He was returned to Congress after the war but shot himself to death in July of

1866 after being charged with irregularities in connection with Indian Bureau contracts.

Hickok, though only a gangling youth approaching his nineteenth birthday, attached himself to Jim Lane as his bodyguard. There is a splendid little story concerning this accomplishment. According to one of Hickok's earlier biographers, he was personally enrolled in the Free-State commando by the commandant himself. Lane, according to this account, was holding a shooting contest for his marksmen. All his crack shots took their turn at the targets and missed. Hickok, not yet a member of Lane's force, brashly stepped up and announced he could puncture every target in view. Amid much scoffing he proceeded to do so, and Lane exclaimed, "By heaven, the best shot in three hundred!" Thereupon, it was stated, Lane himself "enrolled Hickok in the Red Legs." Unfortunately this never happened; the mounted legion calling themselves "Red Legs" were not organized until several years later. Actually Hickok's enlistment was a more prosaic affair. He and a neighboring farmer named John Owen signed up without any sensational display of marksmanship. Hickok gravitated to Jim Lane's side as his unofficial bodyguard through the sheer magnetism of hero-worship; he hung around Lane so much that the latter, secretly flattered, no doubt, finally accepted his services. Lane subsequently praised him as "one of the most effective men of my command." Just what those services were, to earn such a compliment, was not recorded. One catches only occasional glimpses of the young Hickok in the confusion of the guerrilla campaigning.

Once when Lane was treating the folks at Grasshopper Falls to a sample of his firebrand oratory, denouncing the Border Ruffians as the spawn of Beelzebub, Hickok stationed himself in front of the wagon box from which Lane was delivering his harangue. He spotted a Missourian in the crowd who surreptitiously began to reach for his gun. Hickok

45

covered the Missourian with his revolver until the latter slunk away, with Lane continuing his speech unaware of the fact that he had barely escaped assassination.

Hostility between pro- and anti-slavery forces reached the flash point in the spring of 1856. A territorial grand jury indicted a number of the leading citizens of Lawrence, charging them with treason and assorted other crimes. Lawrence was the fortress of abolition in Kansas, named for the Massachusetts manufacturer who was foremost in financing the movement. All the citizens indicted by the pro-slavery grand jury were Free-Staters, of course. A United States marshal was ordered to arrest the Free-State leaders. When he whistled for a posse, a thousand armed Missourians sprang to his side. This was the opportunity the Border Ruffians had been waiting for; it gave them an excuse to march into Lawrence, the focal point of their hatreds, and clean out the Yankee hellhole. The huge posse hauled along five cannon and was hopeful of resistance.

Lawrence stood out on the prairie like the mockup of a white-steepled, colonial-styled New England town. Behind the stage effects, however, there was a grim purpose. The buildings were stoutly constructed to resist a siege; the inhabitants were armed with "Beecher's bibles," and every house was a small fort. The strong point of this Abolitionist hedgehog was the thick-walled Free State Hotel, with its windows designed to serve as embrasures for riflemen.

On May 21, 1856, the outsize posse of Missourians marched into Lawrence behind the U.S. marshal.

The citizens of Lawrence offered no resistance, allowed the marshal to serve his warrants. The marshal then announced that his task was completed and the posse could disband.

Waving their long rifles and their half-empty jugs of forty-rod, the Missourians decided en masse against disbandment. There was more work for the posse than merely serving a few warrants. Senator Atchison, who just happened to be along, bellowed at the mob: "Be brave, be orderly, and if any man or woman stand in your way, blow them to hell with a chunk of cold lead."

Then began the sack of Lawrence. The cannon opened up on the Free State Hotel but made little impression on its stout masonry. The Missourians set fire to it, likewise the home of the man who had set himself up as "governor of Free-State Kansas." Then they swarmed all over the town, burning, looting, shooting up the place. Two citizens were killed by Atchison's "chunks of cold lead." The offices of the two Free-State newspapers, *Herald of Freedom* and *Kansas Free State*, were wrecked and their presses and type cases dumped into the river. Wobbly-legged and empty-jugged, the Border Ruffians finally withdrew from Lawrence and camped a few miles outside the pillaged town.

Free-State militiamen began converging on Lawrence from all directions, too late to catch up with the Missourians, who broke up into small bands and drifted back across the border.

Among the Free-State militiamen who arrived at Lawrence too late to wreak vengeance on the Border Ruffians was a lank, hot-eyed fanatic named John Brown, who came to Kansas to "meddle directly with the peculiar institution of slavery" and lived in a feverish dream of drowning the South in its own blood. This psychopath and his seven followers, four of them his own sons, all of them settlers at Osawatomie, were wild with frustration at having arrived too late to join battle with the Missourians. "Something must be done to show these barbarians that we too have rights," Brown told his followers. It was agreed that they would take their artillery broadswords and descend on the pro-slavery settlement along Pottawatomie Creek. Three nights after the sack of Lawrence they dragged five men from their beds and hacked them to death with their broadswords. Then they washed their swords in the creek and went home.

After that it was a bloody summer along the Kansas-Mis-

souri border, a holiday for terrorists. Each side could pretend
to righteousness. The Missourians pointed to the massacre of
Pottawatomie Creek, the Free-Staters to the atrocities of
Lawrence.

Jim Lane and his commando, now styling itself the "Army
of the North," took the field. Hickok, of course, abandoned
farm work and hurried to his hero's side. Tremendous clashes
were predicted between the Free-State forces and Atchison's "Grand Army." Northern and southern newspapers
foresaw rivers of blood coursing over the Great Plains when
both sides collided.

But it was a comic-opera war, unfunny though it was to
most of the participants. Lane's and Atchison's "armies"
threatened to have at it late in August 1856 on Bull Creek,
fifteen miles north of Osawatomie. The "Battle of Osawatomie" was widely heralded before the two forces came
within shouting distance of each other. Both sides, however,
were so skittery, having swallowed each other's vehement
propaganda, that they had no heart for a pitched battle. Out-
riders of both forces collided, exchanged a few shots, and
withdrew in mutual alarm. Border Ruffians and Free-Staters
eyed each other across the creek, each imagining the other
was nine feet tall and almost as nasty as the orators claimed.
Senator-General Atchison thundered to his followers that
they would march on Lawrence and "destroy that Boston
Abolition town." Lane was in a mood to wipe out half of
Missouri.

When the yelling subsided, each generalissimo came to the
conclusion that it would be indiscreet to fight it out on Bull
Creek. A Federal cavalry commander, Colonel Philip St.
George Cooke, rode up with a squadron from Fort Leavenworth and saved face all around. He told both sides to with-
draw, which was exactly what they did, with secret rejoicing.
The Missouri-Kansas War continued to be an affair of barn-
burnings, lynchings, and ambushes.

Hickok and his comrades, coaxed along by Jim Lane, made a number of such marches and fought a dozen similar skirmishes. It was probably an exciting life, with Lane proclaiming his grandiose visions around the campfires and encouraging his men to think of themselves as the vanguard of a liberating army. Hickok naturally got a great deal of boyish pleasure out of guarding Lane from assassins. And, of course, he got his first taste of the pleasures of violence. He'd had shots fired at him, and he'd fired back, probably with no ill effects to anyone. He became accustomed to the idea of gun-play. He was indoctrinated with the theory, contrary to the teachings of his deacon-father, that it is permissible to ignore the commandment "Thou shalt not kill" on occasion, that there is such a thing as justifiable homicide. All this was a very necessary part of the education of the future gunfighter: it enabled him to pull the trigger.

Eventually the border quieted down, the Missourians wearied of raiding and being raided, and there were only occasional outbreaks of jayhawking and boozy night riding. Hickok went back to peaceful occupations around Monticello. He filed a claim for a quarter section, 160 acres, out on the prairie and built himself a dugout there. But he lived most of the time at Monticello Tavern, for which he contracted to cut prairie hay as provender. Later he also took on the job of caring for the stage horses and taking charge of the stable. According to the family of John M. Reed, the proprietor of the tavern, Hickok was a cheerful worker, a nice fellow to have around. He was popular with the townspeople and respected by them. Before he was old enough to vote, he was elected constable of Monticello Township. It was a quiet place, and there is no record that he ever had to draw his gun in the performance of his duties.

Hickok was particularly friendly with John Owen, the farmer with whom he had enlisted in the Free-State Army. Owen had married a Shawnee woman named Patinuxa and was formally "adopted" by her tribesmen. In-laws, among the Indians, were treated with great generosity and respect.

Hickok fell in love with Owen's daughter, Mary Jane, who was said to have inherited her mother's beauty and intelligence. Old settlers of Johnson County, interviewed by the late William E. Connelley when he was secretary of the Kansas State Historical Society, said the girl was a good cook, an excellent housekeeper, and well respected in the neighborhood, "half-breed" though she may have been.

In the letters Hickok wrote home at the time—he was now aware of the fact that Charlie Hudson had suffered no more from the towpath fight than a good soaking—he told of working hard and living a clean life: "Mother mentioned something about drinking and gambling in her letter. Well, now, I will tell you what is a fact. I have not drank a pint of liquor in a year, and I have not played for a cent in twice that time." He wrote of his ambition to acquire part of the Delaware tribal lands which were going on sale. "There is one section over there that I would like to have for us four brothers. There are about one hundred acres of timber on the section and the rest beautiful prairie that can't be beat in the country."

He mentioned Mary Jane Owen frequently and fondly in his letters home: "I went to see my girl yesterday and ate blackberries that she picked Saturday. You ought to be there to eat some of her biscuits. She is the only one I ever saw that could beat Mother making biscuits, and I ought to know, for I can eat a few, you know . . ." "Mary cut off a lock of my hair yesterday and said for me to send it to my mother or sisters. If she had not thought a great deal of you all she would not have cut it off, for she thinks a great deal of it. At least she is always combing and curling it, that is, when I am there . . ." "I received a letter from Celinda Friday. Mary got it and read it for she reads every letter that I get and said she would answer it and tell Celinda all about that girl she spoke of and tell her her name . . ."

Hickok must have been serious about Mary Jane to make such an effort to present her in a favorable light to his family. The legend makers, in fact, had it that Hickok married Mary Jane and lived as a "squaw man" for a time among the Shawnees. This was a fabrication. The records of Johnson County show no such marriage was performed, and Mary Jane Owen, with at least one foot in the white world and her full share of respectability, would not have consented to one of those informal and temporary arrangements which were common enough on the frontier at the time. Nor would Hickok have entered into such an arrangement with the daughter of his best friend. Apparently Hickok and Mary Jane drifted apart when he became a stage driver; Mary Jane, at any rate, subsequently married a doctor named Harris.

Hickok took to the highroad between Independence, Missouri, and Santa Fe, New Mexico—following the old Santa Fe Trail—in his twenty-first year, driving first a freight wagon, then a stage carrying mail and passengers. It was hard, dangerous work, paying about twenty dollars a month and board. In those pre-railroad days, wagon freighting was big business. A train carrying a hundred tons of freight, at eight dollars per hundred pounds, between Missouri and the terminus at Santa Fe earned sixteen thousand dollars for the transportation company . . . little of which filtered down to the hired help.

Driving wagons or stages across the prairies was simple enough, provided a man had wrists capable of handling a fistful of reins and a team of wild horses or recalcitrant mules, but the later stages of the journey took nerves as well as muscles of steel. The Santa Fe Trail wound into the hills in the upper reaches of the Arkansas River, turned up the Purgatoire ("River of Lost Souls"), and then climbed into the Raton Mountains. Often the road led over shelves curving around breath-taking gorges or made breakneck descents

51

that required a strong hand on the brakes. Beautiful, deadly scenery.

Hickok was a popular figure among the hard-living stage drivers and freighters of the Santa Fe Trail. In this period, it seems, he was first called Bill—not yet Wild Bill. Many earnest attempts have been made to learn how Jim Hickok became Bill Hickok. The most plausible explanation seems to be that his brother Lorenzo—who had been a famous wagon master on government trains—was known as Billy Barnes in the West. According to the Hickok family, that was his childhood nickname and it carried over into his frontier years. The Bill passed from Lorenzo to his younger brother, apparently, as a family trademark. So henceforth in this account he will be referred to as Bill Hickok. He was known as James Butler Hickok only to his family and his home town.

Hickok, when he graduated to the passenger runs, cut a dashing figure. When the stage neared Santa Fe, he liked to give the horses their head on the last stretch of road to "jolt the cricks out of the passengers' backs." He claimed to have great faith in the therapeutic value of such a shaking up. Hickok's stage, it was said, entered Santa Fe "lurching the passengers from side to side, dishing up dyspeptics, phlegmatics, and rollicking dispositions indiscriminately, and bowling into the town finally the center of a dust bank and the object of excited interest to everyone in the ancient Mexican city." Hickok already grasped the value of showmanship, a subject he had studied close up as one of Jim Lane's most trusted followers.

During one of his stays in Santa Fe, Hickok met Kit Carson, the hero of his boyhood and the No. 1 celebrity of the frontier. Although Kit was almost thirty years older than Hickok, they became friends and frequent companions during the latter's stopovers in Santa Fe. Carson was a small, sandy-haired man, gentle of manner, soft-spoken, and extremely modest. There were no lessons in swashbuckling to be learned from him, although he was reputed to be Jim Bridger's equal as a practitioner of the frontier trades, trapping, buffalo hunting, and Indian fighting. The Kentucky-born Carson had served on John C. Frémont's three expeditions in 1842, 1843, and 1845. Around the time Hickok met him, Carson was working a farm near Taos, having married Maria Josefa Jaramillo, sister-in-law of Charles Bent of Bent's Fort. He had recently driven sixty-five hundred sheep to Sacramento, California, and sold them for a good profit. There was no more highly respected character in the West. During the Civil War he was given a brigadier's star, despite the fact he could barely write his own name, and General William T. Sherman said of him, "His integrity is simply perfect."

How the two men became friends, being so widely separated in years and accomplishments, is something of a mystery, except that Hickok had a habit of tagging along after great men and ingratiating himself with them. He was determined to learn from them, and even men more spoiled by fame than Kit Carson can be flattered by that.

Carson took him on the rounds of Santa Fe night life, which was colorful, noisy, and frequently violent. The center of cosmopolitan drinking and bickering was the bar of the United States Hotel, crowded with hunters and trappers wearing fringed buckskin and armed with Hawkins rifles and Bowie knives, Santa Fe merchants and traders, Mexican entrepreneurs, freighters, teamsters, and passing strangers whose business was their own. They bargained, quarreled, sang, and joked in a variety of tongues, French, Spanish, German, and English. A river of whiskey and a cascade of beer poured down their throats, most of them being lonely men down from the mountains beyond Taos.

The most popular gambling house was an L-shaped, flat-roofed adobe house down in the Mexican quarter. It had an earthen floor slippery with tobacco juice and was crudely appointed, but a lot of money changed hands in that smoky, dimly lighted room. Monte was the favored game, and the "banks" at which patrons were accommodated were stacked high with Spanish doubloons, Mexican gold and silver. The notorious Señora Dona Gertrudis Barcelo was in charge of the play at the monte banks, the only female professional gambler in the Territory of New Mexico, "the bejeweled, painted and powdered, hard, black-eyed queen of Santa Fe, whom for a long time it was a fashionable thing for American traders and trappers, as well as Mexican caballeros, to lose their money to."

Señora Barcelo is said to have looked over Hickok, when he entered with Carson, with an expert eye. She was taken with his looks and told a dealer in Spanish, "Let the handsome young American win."

Hickok won a couple of hundred dollars and would have gladly continued the game, except that Carson, who understood Spanish and did not want his protégé to take too much advantage of the señora's weakness for handsome young fellows, told him, "You'd better stop while you're ahead, Bill," adding with mock piety, "Cards are the devil's prayer book, you know."

Carson also took Hickok to a Mexican dance hall near the plaza, one of the sights of the town, where the youth of Santa Fe danced the fandango and fought with knives whenever honor could be satisfied no other way.

Soon after the two men entered, a violent argument broke out between a couple of young Mexicans over which would have the honor of the first dance with a local beauty. The señorita settled the matter and made her choice. The unsuccessful aspirant, eyes glittering with rage, left the dance hall.

"Well, I guess that little argument is settled," Hickok said.

"Just wait and see," suggested Carson.

A few minutes later the youth who had been dancing with the girl was summoned outside. His rival promptly stabbed him in the heart. There was a flurry of excitement in the dance hall over this event, but the dancing was resumed after a moment's pause.

Carson had seen some gory sights as an old Indian fighter, but a battle in a Mexican dance hall was too much for him. "Let's get out of here before the usual riot begins," he said.

Hickok often recalled his guided tour of Santa Fe's night world, his first fascinated glimpse of the drinking, gambling, and womanizing circuit which was to engross him for the rest of his life. The clink of glasses, the rattle of chips and coins, the rowdy beat of a dance-hall piano formed the most pleasing of melodies for him. A free-and-easy life among the high-rollers and wine buyers seemed ideal to him—certainly not the first farm boy or deacon's son to be enchanted in that fashion.

But a young man had to work for a living, no matter what his inclinations. In the fall of 1860, Hickok was engaged by Russell, Majors & Waddell as wagon master of freight trains moving through Raton Pass. It was a rather sanctimonious outfit, considering the rough nature of its enterprises and the venturesomeness required of its employees. Hickok, like all others signed on by the company, had to sign the following pledge:

"I do hereby swear, before the Great and Living God, that during my engagement, and while I am an employe of Russell, Majors & Waddell, I will, under no circumstances, use profane language; that I will drink no intoxicating liquors; that I will not quarrel or fight with any other employe of the firm, and that in every respect I will conduct myself honestly, be faithful to my duties, and so direct all my acts as to win the confidence of my employers. So help me God."

It is doubtful whether any company—despite this pledge— had a more profane, hard-drinking, and quarrelsome lot of employees. One of its most notable field executives, for instance, was the notorious Jack Slade, the wild man of the

Nebraska steppe, who was division agent at Platte Crossing near Fort Kearney. Slade was credited with killing twenty-six men in the course of his career, and his reputation as a gunman persuaded horse thieves and bandits to stay well away from his territory. Vigilantes disposed of Mr. Slade some years later at Virginia City, Montana.

One of the more difficult phases of Hickok's work as wagon master was guiding the trains through the rock-strewn and tortuous corridors of Raton Pass. Riding up and down the length of the train, he had to space the wagons a safe distance apart and escort each one separately over dangerous stretches of the trail.

One day, while riding back to pick up another wagon, he entered a patch of stunted pines. A large female grizzly bear lumbered out of the clump of pines where her two cubs were hidden, determined to protect them from the intruder. Hickok's horse reared in panic, threw him out of the saddle, and bolted down the trail. Unmounted and shaken by his fall, with no help in shouting distance, Hickok had to face the enraged grizzly with only the weapons attached to his person.

He emptied his revolver at the approaching bear, but she soaked up bullets with a mere grunt of disapproval and kept coming on.

Hickok managed to draw his Bowie knife just as she closed in with murderous swats of her huge paws. In the ensuing struggle he had his scalp, arms, legs, and torso ripped repeatedly by her claws. Blood was streaming from his wounds. Just before she could move in and hug him to death, he managed to drive his heavy blade into her belly and disembowel her.

When the next wagon came up the trail, the driver found Hickok lying unconscious under the dead bear.

The young wagon master was hurried back to Santa Fe,

more dead than alive, and given medical care. Later he was
sent to Kansas City for further repairs. Early in 1861 he began
slowly to mend, and Russell, Majors & Waddell sent him to
their Rock Creek station on the Oregon Trail. And there, still
convalescent, he attracted the hostile eye of Dave McCanles.

CHAPTER 4

Spy, Scout, and Sharpshooter

In August of 1861, after being turned loose by the Nebraska court in the killing of Dave McCanles and his two companions, Hickok departed from Rock Creek and headed for even less peaceful scenes, the battlefields of the Civil War in the Southwest. Hickok did not actually enlist in the Union Army. Like many Westerners and frontiersmen, he had no use for formal soldiering, for taking orders, saluting officers, living under military discipline. He wanted to be a one-man army.

He succeeded in extraordinary measure, from all accounts, and risked his neck oftener than would have been required of a soldier in the ranks. George Ward Nichols, a colonel on General William T. Sherman's staff during the war, whose *Harper's Magazine* articles made Hickok nationally famous, recalled, "Whenever I had met an officer or soldier who had served in the Southwest I heard of Wild Bill and his exploits, until these stories became so frequent and of such an extraordinary character as to quite outstrip personal knowledge of adventure by camp and field; and the hero of these strange tales took shape in my mind as did Jack the

Giant Killer or Sinbad the Sailor in childhood's days. As then, I now had the most implicit faith in the existence of the individual; but how one man could accomplish such prodigies of strength and feats of daring was a continued wonder." Colonel Nichols said, however, that tales of Hickok's wartime exploits were "confirmed in all important points by many witnesses."

Hickok began his service with, but not in, the Union Army at Fort Leavenworth. He found that his fame—and the wild exaggerations of Captain Kingsbury and Dr. Thorne—had preceded him and that people shrank back at the approach of the man who was supposed to have killed ten men in less than an hour. Hickok, possibly because of this partly undeserved notoriety, was appointed brigade wagon master in Major General John C. Frémont's Army of the Southwest.

His first assignment was to take a supply train from Fort Leavenworth to Sedalia, Missouri, through country infested with guerrillas. Apparently the rascals had never heard of Hickok or his supposed massacre at Rock Creek. Three days out of Leavenworth, Hickok and his twelve-man guard were attacked by a partisan band. The train was captured. Later that day Hickok rode into Independence, where there was a Union garrison, and told of escaping from the ambush. He claimed to have shot and killed four of his pursuers, although how he could have determined this while fleeing for his life was not made clear.

During his brief stay in Independence he acquired the sobriquet of "Wild Bill." A bartender with whom he was friendly shot a man who was causing a disturbance in his saloon. The wounded man's friends, fifteen or twenty teamsters and other tough characters who had been terrorizing the town, chased the bartender into a nearby house and ordered him to come out and submit to punishment. Hickok appeared on the scene slapping leather. Ordering the mob to disperse, he added the threat, "If you don't, there'll be more dead men around here than the town can bury." Obviously it would have been possible for up to a score of armed men to dispose of Hickok with little damage to themselves, but they had all heard of how Hickok had wiped out the McCanles "gang" singlehanded. They slunk away. The value of a reputation was thus impressed on Hickok.

A large crowd had gathered in the town square to watch the outcome of this lynching bee. Among them was a woman who called out as Hickok strolled nonchalantly away:

"Good for you, Wild Bill!"

Henceforth, except in letters home, he would always be known as Wild Bill Hickok.

He began to dress the part now, going in for fancy buckskins and colorful neckerchiefs while on field service and patronizing the better Kansas City tailors and haberdashers for his town costume, long-tailed dark coats, embroidered vests, fine linen shirts, and fifty-dollar boots fashioned from French calf. He wore his hair, generally described as a "golden brown," shoulder length. This hair style, of course, was not a sign of effeminacy or dandyism. It was a challenge to one and all: "Lift my scalp if you dare." The long upper lip which had caused Dave McCanles to call him "Duck Bill" was concealed by two large curving mustaches with the fine sweep of a bull's horns. He was a magnificent figure of a man—even his enemies conceded that while insinuating there was something a trifle stagey about his appearance. He was about six feet two inches tall and carried himself with an easy grace, was broad-shouldered and slim-hipped, and walked like a king. His eyes were a light blue-gray—the true killer's color, according to frontier physiognomists. His nose was aquiline and his jaw firm. He was soft-spoken, courteous, and unaggressive, until the moment came for a shoot-out. While most of his colleagues were scraggly and villainous, not to say verminous, Hickok was well-barbered and bathed with a startling regularity. He was, in brief, a fastidious man in a very unfastidious time and place; no casting director could pick a better type for the role of "knight chivalric of the plains."

Soon after the wagon-train incident, he was enrolled as a scout attached to the headquarters of the Army of the Southwest and was involved in that peculiar, shadowy war which was fought as a sort of side show to the larger and bloodier campaigns to the east. An extension of the pre-war hostilities between the Border Ruffians and the Free-State Army, it was fought over southern and western Missouri, a state sorely divided between the Unionists of the cities and the Secessionists in the countryside, parts of Kansas, Arkansas, and the Indian Territory (later Oklahoma). There were only two major battles—at Wilson's Creek and Pea Ridge—but countless skirmishes, ambushes, night raids, murder in retail and wholesale lots . . . the bitterest and dirtiest kind of fighting. In the border states families were divided and brothers marched off in different directions, a tragedy best epitomized by the marker erected over the graves of two brothers who fought in the opposing armies: "God knows which was right." Neighbors bushwhacked neighbors, and "dead men ornamented trees by the roadside, and were found lying in the fields and in byways."

In the battle of Wilson's Creek, in southwestern Missouri, Hickok was employed as a scout and sharpshooter. He rode ahead of the Union Army commanded by the redheaded New England-born Abolitionist Brigadier General Nathaniel Lyon as it maneuvered ten miles outside of Springfield toward the twelve thousand men under Generals Sterling Price and Ben McCulloch. On the other side of the creek with Price and McCulloch were the Missouri aristocrat Jo Shelby, who liked to quote Sir Walter Scott and write his reports in blank verse, and his reckless, ruffianly riders, Charles Quantrill, the Younger brothers, the James brothers, and other bravos.

As the two forces approached the point of collision, it was Hickok's job to locate a masked battery, which was waiting

61

to fire on the Union advance. The battery opened fire the moment he caught a glimpse of the gunners moving behind their camouflage of brush and branches. Hickok said later, "It was the first time I was ever under artillery fire, and I was so frightened that I couldn't move for a minute or so, and when I did go back the boys asked me if I had seen a ghost."

A short time later Hickok heard General Lyon haranguing his troops: ". . . Don't get scared—it's no part of a soldier's duty to get scared."

It turned out, however, that the Union troops had every reason to get scared. Lyon foolishly divided his forces in the presence of a strong and aggressive enemy, trying a flank attack around the Confederate left. The flanking maneuver went awry, and the balance of Lyon's brigades ran into a long line of Confederate riflemen banked four deep. The opposing infantry blazed away at each other with muzzle-loaders at a range of fifty yards. Lyon was killed. With more than twelve hundred lost on each side, the casualty rate was twice as high as First Bull Run. Unable to budge the Confederate line, and with a fourth of their men lying dead or wounded in the fields bordering Wilson's Creek, the Union commanders ordered a retreat to the railhead at Rolla.

Hickok and a number of other scouts, acting as sharpshooters to discourage the bolder spirits among the enemy, helped to cover the retreat.

The command of the Army of the Southwest subsequently passed into the more capable hands of Major General Samuel R. Curtis, a West Pointer who had created a highly effective espionage system during the Mexican War and had an excellent appreciation for men like Hickok who could think and act independently and ferret out the enemy's intentions by roving behind his lines. General Curtis was a large, ponderous man with a bulging forehead and the bluff manner of an English squire. He asked Hickok, who, being an independent contractor in the business of war, could not be commanded to such duty, to attach himself to army headquarters as a spy and scout. Hickok was on the verge of joining his old chief, Jim Lane, now forming his Kansas Brigade with the fetching slogan, "Everything disloyal, from a Shanghai rooster to a Durham cow, must be cleaned out."

Joining Lane's military plunderbund must have been a tempting thought, but Hickok accepted General Curtis' offer and stayed with him for several years through a series of adventures often more picaresque than military. Much of his intelligence work consisted of living behind the Confederate lines, gathering information on enemy troop movements, and forwarding it to army headquarters. Hickok and his colleagues, half scouts and half spies, sometimes disguised themselves as Ozark hillbillies and traveled the back-country roads. They hid in the woods by day, particularly when Confederate patrols were active, and slipped out at night to attend those thumpingly patriotic rallies called "Secesh Balls."

In the interval between the lost battle of Wilson's Creek and a renewal of the effort to drive the Confederates out of southwestern Missouri, the Union command was particularly anxious to learn every disposition made by "Pap" Price and his subordinates. Hickok roved all through the Ozark country and finally settled down at Yellville, Arkansas, a center of Confederate activity. A thousand enemy troops were garrisoned there to protect one of the few large arsenals in the Trans-Mississippi theater. The Confederacy had a large saltpeter works in the vicinity; lead was mined nearby, and the arsenal produced much of the ammunition used by the Confederate forces in the Southwest. During the forthcoming campaign General Curtis, acting on Hickok's information, sent a raiding column into Yellville to destroy the arsenal, storehouses, and powder works.

Later, on his return from that foray behind the lines, Hickok was detailed to act as a courier, carrying dispatches from headquarters to two battalions of mounted riflemen under

Major Charles Zagonyi, who was operating in the vicinity of Springfield and doing his best to make things miserable for "Pap" Price's Confederates as long as they chose to hold the place. Zagonyi, a dashing Hungarian, had about three hundred men in his command, with which he decided to attack Springfield, although that city was occupied by more than fifteen hundred Confederates.

The enemy was holding positions west of the city and apparently had been alerted to the possibility of an attack. Zagonyi's battalions were just debouching from a woods, preparatory to deploying for the charge, when Hickok came up with dispatches. Wild Bill was so exhilarated at the chance to participate in a cavalry charge—there were very few in the Civil War, despite the evidence of old lithographs and woodcuts—that he forgot to deliver his messages to Major Zagonyi.

The Hungarian and his horsemen had to pass down a long lane under an intensive cross fire, yelling, "The Union forever!" as they rode the gauntlet.

Emerging from the lane, the Union battalions formed line of battle and swept down on the main Confederate positions. The secessionists broke and fled through the town, despite their considerable advantage in numbers.

Zagonyi's men occupied Springfield for a few hours and raised the Stars and Stripes over the courthouse. For this dubious reward the Federals suffered a casualty list of sixteen dead and twenty-six wounded. At nightfall, with the enemy gathering from all directions to retake Springfield, Zagonyi was forced to order a withdrawal. Hickok suddenly remembered then that he had dispatches to deliver to the major, several hours late. But Major Zagonyi was still too flushed with elation over his spectacular charge and bootless victory to take note of the lapse.

Toward the end of 1861 General Curtis increased the pressure on the Confederates occupying southwestern Missouri. The Lincoln administration was extremely concerned about the border states, and clearing the Confederates from Missouri was being given a top priority. Pap Price and his divisions reluctantly yielded up Springfield and withdrew toward their bases across the Arkansas line. In advance of a campaign planned for several months hence, General Curtis, from his headquarters at Rolla, sent his scouts through the enemy line in various disguises. Some were dressed as Confederate soldiers, some as peddlers and vagrants, others as Ozark hillmen.

Hickok was sent on such a mission in a group including John R. Kelso, John W. Allen, John C. McKoin, Zeke Stone, and a man named Adkins. Most of them were natives of the Ozarks or the Cherokee Nation and knew the country like the inside of their pockets. All were dressed in Confederate uniforms, with Hickok decked out in a captain's braid and epaulets. They were to pose as a group of soldiers on detached service, make their way through Confederate territory, and gather all the information they could. The Union Army would be moving out in a few weeks, and General Curtis, a cautious planner, wanted to know just what he would encounter in an invasion of northwestern Arkansas.

"Captain" Hickok and his fellow spies left Springfield on the night of February 14, 1862, and by midmorning the following day they were well inside the Confederate lines.

They fell in with a Confederate foraging party of twelve men and ten wagons, six of which were loaded with corn, oats, hay, and other supplies requisitioned from farmers in the valley of Flat Creek.

Informality being a keynote of the Confederate service, the foragers were delighted to have the company of Captain Hickok and his men. Sometimes the Ozark farmers, growing restive under the demands of the Confederate commissary, were inclined to resist foragers. This also was a land filled with the spirit of vendetta, and one never knew when someone was going to spring an ambush. The Confederate captain—

a real one—who commanded the foraging detail was only too glad to have temporary reinforcements.

The party came on a creek-bottom farm owned by a widow whose husband had been slain by guerrillas for his Unionist sentiments. Against the widow's protests, her stacks of grain and the contents of bulging corncribs were confiscated. Then she was ordered to prepare dinner for exactly twenty-two men, which she did with the help of her five daughters.

After dinner, while the genuine Confederates were out raiding the beehives, Hickok argued with the Confederate captain that this widow and her daughters should not be deprived of the corn and grain they needed to see them through the winter. Rather eloquently Hickok inquired, "Must our glorious Confederacy be founded on the robbery of defenseless women? Can we endure only by preying on the helpless?"

A vote was taken, and the majority signified they were in favor of not confiscating her provender. Southern chivalry had prevailed, or perhaps the widow's daughters were as toothsome as the dinner they prepared. The soldiers solemnly unloaded the widow's grain and corn from their wagons, and the foraging party proceeded down Flat Creek.

Darkness had fallen by the time the detail, with Hickok and his detachment still riding along, reached the Wire Road. This thoroughfare was the old mail route from Rolla, Missouri, to Van Buren, Arkansas, along which a telegraph wire had been stretched. At the moment it was the main artery of the Confederate withdrawal. Campfires extended for miles along the road; wagon trains were moving south, and regiments were marching in the same direction.

Hickok and his fellow spies separated from the foraging detail on the Wire Road and mingled with the retreating regiments. It was their job to find out just where the Confederates intended to halt and form a line of resistance. They went from campfire to campfire, listening to the talk. Apparently the Confederates were concentrating in the vicinity of Elkhorn Tavern on the Wire Road to the south. Adkins was sent back to Union headquarters with this information.

Hickok and the others rode south with the slowly retreating southern army. Next day they turned off on the road to Bentonville to explore the enemy's right wing and study the countryside into which the Union forces would be advancing in a week or two. Fortunately security arrangements in the Confederate Army were haphazard; no one challenged their identity or their purpose in roving around an area of active operations. For that matter, similar groups of Confederate scouts were nosing around the Union Army to the north and enjoying an equal freedom to observe troop movements. Spying in the Civil War, with both sides speaking the same language and knowing each other so intimately, was a relatively simple matter. Furthermore, the battle lines were so extended in all theaters of the war that they could be penetrated with ease. And what the spies couldn't find out the newspapers on both sides printed with only the flimsiest regard for military security and censorship almost nonexistent. A shrewd general, in fact, had little need for an intelligence service, provided he had a steady supply of newspapers published in enemy territory.

Hickok and his little band of fake Confederates ran into trouble on the Bentonville road, through bad luck rather than any sudden efficiency of the Confederate spy catchers. They came across a group of about fifteen Confederates riding in the opposite direction. As the two parties approached each other, one of the Confederates—possibly a former Border Ruffian—recognized Hickok. He gave a yell, and the Confederates opened fire on the Federal scouts. There was a brisk little fire fight, in which several of the Confederates fell, then Hickok and his companions fled into the brush at top speed. A long pursuit followed, winding into the scrubby hills bordering the Bentonville road. The pursuers gradually became discouraged, several of them having been shot out of the saddle by the scouts. The Union men finally succeeded in shaking off the pursuit and paused to take stock of their situation. Hickok's horse had come up lame; McKoin's horse was wounded, and Allen was wounded in the left forearm. They needed food, medical assistance, fodder, and remounts—and there was no place to apply except the Confederate Army, which had been quite accommodating thus far.

Hickok and his comrades boldly rode into the nearest Confederate camp, loudly complaining that they had been ambushed by some low, sneaking Yankee guerrillas. Their sympathetic hosts not only supplied them with fresh horses and everything else they needed but turned over their own sleeping quarters to the visitors.

For the next several days Hickok and his friends continued to sample southern hospitality and soak up military information. They rode to Bentonville and conducted a leisurely survey of Benton and Washington counties and one night camped near Elkhorn Tavern on ground that would soon be fought over. They studied the back-country roads, the mountain trails, river crossings, and forest paths, so that they would be able to find their way through the choppy Ozark countryside in the confusion of battle or at night. All these findings were kept in their heads for personal transmittal to the Union commanders.

On March 4 they began to turn northward to return to their own lines. From all the signs a battle was imminent: the Confederate Army was concentrating, digging in along the ridges, moving up trains of artillery and supply wagons to Elkhorn Tavern. Preoccupied as they were with preparations for the coming battle, the Southerners' hospitality never failed. Hickok and his companions, still posing as a troop on detached service, rode along with various cavalry regiments and listened to the talk around the campfires.

When they saw Louisiana and Texas infantry regiments marching to the front with Pap Price's Missourians—and heard that Major General Earl Van Dorn, an old-army regular of high repute, had taken command of the combined Confederate forces—they knew it was time to be clearing out. This would soon be a combat area. They swung east to get clear of the military traffic and pounded up the roads to reach Union Army headquarters with their information. One of the most ticklish moments in the expedition came when they approached the first Union pickets in their Confederate uniforms; it took a lot of fast talking to persuade the Union cavalrymen not to cut loose.

They reached Cross Hollows, General Curtis' advance headquarters, just before the battle erupted on March 7.

Just as they rode up to report to General Curtis, a bandy-legged, narrow-eyed little quartermaster captain mounted and trotted away. His name was Phil Sheridan, future lieutenant general. Hickok and Sheridan were not yet acquainted, but some years distant from that pre-battle morning in Cross Hollow their paths would cross again with explosive results.

Partly on the basis of his scouts' information General Curtis decided to concentrate his forces between Sugar Creek and Pea Ridge, just across the Arkansas line. The opposing battle lines swayed together and murderously collided. The Battle of Pea Ridge (called Elkhorn Tavern on the Confederate side) was on. It broke up into a dozen bloody fragments in the rough terrain. There were sharp little clashes in hidden valleys, cannon booming across ravines, cavalry clashing in the meadows and at crossroads, bitter skirmishes in creek bottoms.

Pea Ridge was the kind of battle that can get out of control, but somehow General Curtis kept the reins of command in hand, and by the evening of March 7 the Confederates were being driven back all along the line. Curtis retained control, in large measure, because he had been thoroughly briefed by his scouts, had a pretty good idea of the country in which he was fighting and considerable information on the enemy's dispositions. He also had the service of his scouts, including Hickok, who acted as couriers once the battle was joined. Since they knew the country, no messages went astray, no reports were delayed.

The corps of couriers was kept on the run for two days, dashing back and forth along the dirt roads behind the battle line, riding hell for leather across fields swept by rifle and artillery fire, jumping rail fences, jerking their horses to a halt before various regimental headquarters.

In this frantic exercise Hickok used up four horses, three of them dropping from exhaustion, the fourth shot out from under him.

On March 8 the Confederates began a hasty withdrawal. Van Dorn split away from the action to march his divisions toward Shiloh and another terrific set-to. The remnants of Pap Price's army pulled back on the roads leading to Little Rock, with Curtis cautiously pursuing.

With that stroke the battle for Missouri was won. The Rebs would come back, raiding, looting, barn-burning, but never to stay. General Halleck, the western commander in chief at St. Louis, exulted a trifle prematurely that there would be "no more insurrections and bridge-burnings and hoisting of Rebel flags." Missouri, however, was secured to the Union. In the congratulatory atmosphere of General Curtis' headquarters Hickok and his fellow scouts came in for their share of the praise, and apparently they deserved every word of it.

(The legend makers were not satisfied with this creditable performance of Hickok's, however, and one of the gaudier fragments of the Hickok myth was that he served as a sharpshooter at the Battle of Pea Ridge, posting himself in an advanced position behind a log. He was said to have killed exactly thirty-five Confederates, although who counted the corpses for him was not stated. While popping away in Cross Timbers Hollow, according to one of his early biographers [Buel, *Heroes of the Plains*], he drew a bead on the Confederate General McCulloch and killed him. McCulloch actually was killed north of Leetown, more than two miles away from the scene of Hickok's imaginary feat of marksmanship, and *Official Records* credited his death to a private in the 36th Illinois Infantry.)

Hickok spent the rest of the war attached to General Curtis' headquarters. There were no more battles in the Southwest of a size or ferocity to compete for the headlines with those across the Mississippi. Many of the troops used to clear Missouri were sent to the armies of the Cumberland, Tennessee, and Potomac, and relatively small forces were retained under Curtis' command to fend off the Confederates and their Indian allies. The fighting on the border continued to have the character of the mountain feud, a large-scale vendetta between good strong haters on both sides. It was a private, regional war, beyond the end of the line from both Washington and Richmond. And though it was a smaller war than the one the Easterners fought, it fomented more enduring hatred, possibly because of the character of the contestants. Every man who fought in it, due to its rustic and curiously personal nature, made a number of lifelong enemies for himself. His neighbors, who may have fought on the other side, knew exactly what he did . . . and never forgot it.

Hickok, too, would never be allowed to forget what he did as a Union scout and spy. The flamboyant nature of his exploits—and the manner in which they were exaggerated by the ubiquitous tellers of tall tales—made him a prime target for revenge. It would be an honor to kill a man like that; his celebrity would rub off on his slayer.

Hickok added to his fame during the intermittent campaigning which followed Pea Ridge. Under Curtis' orders he was constantly roaming behind the Confederate lines in

Arkansas and even southward to Texas and Louisiana. Once, legend says, he was audacious enough to wangle a post on Pap Price's staff. This may seem improbable, but considering the ease with which spies on both sides penetrated the various headquarters during the war, even in the more security-conscious East, with its swarm of Pinkertons and other supposedly secret agents, it was not impossible.

On one of these undercover missions he was almost bushwhacked by three guerrillas who were intent on robbing anyone who came down the pike. One of the men, mounted on a magnificent black mare, gave him a terrific chase, which ended only when Hickok managed to put a bullet through him. Hickok confiscated the mare and named her Black Nell. She became almost as famous as her master. Justly so, if certain stories can be believed. According to Colonel Nichols, the *Harper's* correspondent, Black Nell was an extraordinarily intelligent and obedient creature. He claimed to have watched while Hickok showed off her company manners. At a whistled command she climbed the steps to a saloon, walked in, clambered up on a pool table, and lay down. Another whistle from Hickok and she climbed off the table and trotted back to her stable. One thing is certain about that tale: it was based on a mighty stout pool table.

Hickok and John W. Allen, who was married to an Indian wife in the Cherokee Nation, spent most of the winter of 1863–64 roving the rear areas of the Confederacy's Trans-Mississippi army commanded by Lieutenant General E. Kirby-Smith. The previous summer was a bad one for Unionists on the border, largely because of the depredations of Quantrill and other guerrillas. Quantrill had swooped down on Lawrence, Kansas, and burned out that Abolitionist stronghold, causing the death of 150 persons. The Union commanders were determined to push the Confederates farther south, away from Union territory. They were preparing to cut deep into the southern tier of the Confederate States in the spring of 1864. Major General Nathaniel Banks was to march through the Red River valley with forty-thousand men and teach the Louisianans and Texans the meaning of war, while Major General Frederick Steele slashed deep into Arkansas.

It was Hickok's and Allen's assignment to find out all they could about Confederate troop movements, dispositions, and morale in advance of Banks' and Steele's twin offensives. In civilian clothes they made their way to Dallas, Texas, then to Texarkana, where they posed as contractors buying cattle for delivery to the Confederate Army. Then they crossed into Arkansas and proceeded to Camden, a Confederate head-quarters and the objective of General Steele's coming cam-paign. They changed costumes again, this time fobbing them-selves off in ragged farm clothes as a pair of country boys eager to join the southern army. The Confederate recruiters accepted them immediately.

Hickok and Allen served in the Confederate forces until mid-April, when General Steele advanced into Arkansas and reached the vicinity of Prairie d'Ane, where a brisk little cavalry battle was fought. It was time to change sides. The two Union spies made a break for the Federal lines but were spotted by a couple of Confederate officers who were deter-mined to prevent any such defections. In the pursuit between the lines Allen was killed but Hickok made it safely to the Union positions. Legend says that a great shout went up from the Federal troops—"Here comes Wild Bill, the Union scout!" —but just how thousands of soldiers would simultaneously recognize Hickok in a ragged Confederate uniform was not explained.

Steele's corps took Camden as scheduled, but Banks bogged down in his Red River campaign, so Steele was forced to with-draw and it all came to nought.

Late that summer Pap Price was emboldened to gather up all available forces, launch his last thunderbolt at the North, and throw a real scare into the Unionists of Kansas. It was

73

a grim autumn for the Confederacy, with Grant fighting his way through the Wilderness toward Richmond and Sherman cutting across Georgia to the sea. This might be the last chance to make the Yankees howl.

On September 7, Price began his drive northward while most of the regular troops in General Curtis' Department of Kansas were down in the Indian Territory fighting Stand Watie and the Confederates' Indian allies. His intention was to march straight up the middle of Missouri, execute a left-face at Jefferson City, head for Kansas City, destroy it, and then raise hell with Kansas. Union General Alfred Pleasonton, with three cavalry brigades, began dogging his heels while General Curtis proclaimed martial law along the border and called out the Kansas militia. Price, as he sliced up the middle of Missouri and made his left-angled turn toward Kansas City, hauled along a wagon train a dozen miles long, laden with everything his bummers could root out of the war-impoverished countryside, farm implements, furniture, bedding, pots and pans, baling wire and buggy whips, children's clothing—the most pathetic sort of loot.

Hickok was appointed chief of scouts attached to Curtis' headquarters. He and his colleagues were in the saddle day and night, riding around the Confederate advance and charting its course for the Union command. Since most of the cavalry was with Pleasonton in the Confederate rear, the job of reconnaissance was left entirely to the scouts.

Price crossed the Little Blue, then the Big Blue, and pulled up at Westport, Missouri, on October 22 in battle formation. Kansas City was within striking distance. But Price now had Pleasonton closing in on his rear and Curtis' Kansas regiments facing him in two fair-sized divisions.

There was heavy fighting around Byram's Ford and Hickman's Mills, but Price was caught in a nutcracker between Curtis and Pleasonton, and the Battle of Westport ended with the Confederates in a precipitous retreat. The Union forces pursued them across the Arkansas River, and about all the Confederates salvaged from their campaign was their wagon train of loot.

That ended the formal warfare on the border.

Hickok, however, had at least one desperate battle of his own before Appomattox rang down the curtain on the Civil War. He accompanied General Curtis to Fort Leavenworth, where the latter set up his headquarters for closer observation of the guerrillas and the outlaws who were running wild while the regular troops and militia were occupied with fending off Price's invasion. This was in January of 1865. The following month came reports that the Indians—particularly the Choctaws, the Cherokees, the Creeks, and Osages—were planning to stage an uprising in Kansas. Their chiefs were boasting that an all-out massacre of the white settlers would take place.

At this point began the sanguinary drama involving Hickok and a Sioux chief named Conquering Bear, whose band had been more or less loyalist and served with Jim Lane's Kansas Brigade. The story of his deadly grapple with Conquering Bear was told by Hickok to his early biographers (Buel and Nichols).

Conquering Bear came to General Curtis with a report that five hundred Choctaws, who had been fighting down in the Indian Nations as allies of the Confederacy, were camped on the Kaw River ten miles west of Lawrence.

Curtis asked Hickok whether he believed Conquering Bear's report, not to mention his professions of friendship for the whites, could be trusted.

"I don't know much about Conquering Bear," Hickok said, "but I always get suspicious when an Indian claims he loves the white man."

He suggested that General Curtis send him, along with Conquering Bear, to investigate the report on the spot.

"It seems to me you ought to take a couple hundred men with you, if there's anything to Conquering Bear's story."

"I don't want anyone but Conquering Bear with me, General," Hickok replied. "And it's him or me if that Indian's lying or trying to lead us into a trap."

General Curtis finally agreed.

Hickok and Conquering Bear set out for Lawrence, the latter assuring the scout that Sioux enmity for the Choctaw made him as eager as any white to disperse the tribesmen on the Kaw.

On arriving at Lawrence, the pair went first to Conquering Bear's village a few miles outside the town, then shortly after dark ventured out on the prairie to scout the Choctaw camp. When they were about halfway between the two camps, Conquering Bear suddenly gave a startling whoop and ducked into the brush. Hickok found himself encircled by a band of Choctaws, all determined to cut him down with their knives and axes.

Hickok shot his way out of that melee and galloped back to the safety of Lawrence.

Then he rode on to report to General Curtis at Fort Leavenworth, brooding darkly all the way. What was Conquering Bear's motive for leading him into the ambush? Were the Sioux meditating an alliance with the Choctaw for the purpose of starting a border war while the Union armies were busy in the East? Or had some personal enemy put the Sioux chief up to it? In any case, Hickok was in a cold rage that demanded satisfaction.

He asked for a week's furlough from duty at headquarters, which General Curtis granted. Then he went back to Lawrence. Patiently enough for a man of his temperament, he eased his way into the confidence of one of Conquering Bear's young tribesmen who liked to hang around the streets of Lawrence, plying him with whiskey, presents, and sweet talk. In a few days he persuaded the young Sioux to arrange a

76

meeting with Conquering Bear, without telling the latter who wanted to see him. The rendezvous was to be a clearing about three miles east of town.

Late in the afternoon Conquering Bear kept the appointment and, according to Hickok, was frightened out of his wits when he saw who was waiting for him. Both agreed to fight it out with Bowie knives in a circle ten feet in diameter. They advanced on each other, heavy blades swinging in murderous arcs. Grappling and slashing, they fought for some time without either gaining the advantage. Then Hickok managed to inflict a long gash on the Indian's chest. In desperation Conquering Bear struck for Hickok's heart, missed, but ripped open Hickok's arm from wrist to elbow.

The Indian grew weaker from his exertions and loss of blood. Hickok parried one of his blows, leaped for Conquering Bear's throat, and slashed his jugular vein.

A moment later the Indian fell face forward and died thrashing in the dust.

That was Hickok's last action in the Civil War, the Sioux and Choctaw subsequently dispersing without going on the warpath. Hickok's fighting career, for all his wartime adventures, was just beginning.

CHAPTER 5

Enter Dave Tutt, Exit Dave Tutt

After the Confederate surrender and his formal discharge as chief of scouts to General Curtis, Hickok, like the fighting men of all wars, had to face his personal readjustment problem. His family wanted him to return to Troy Grove and settle down to a gainful and respectable life, but Hickok didn't fancy a return to the narrow horizons and humdrum concerns of his Illinois birthplace. He could have gone back to driving stages for the Overland Express, but that was hard work. Gainful employment would never again have the slightest appeal to Wild Bill Hickok.

He wanted ease, excitement, public attention. He fancied a sleep-till-noon life. The atmosphere of the gambling saloons suited him fine. Nothing pleased him more than strolling into a well-appointed barroom just as the place was coming to life and spending the rest of the night there until the swamper began sweeping up the sawdust, cleaning out the spittoons, and turning down the lamps.

He liked to drift from town to town, going where the action was, where the smell of money and excitement was in the air.

He loved the buzz of comment that arose when he made an appearance, immaculate in black broadcloth and white linen, carrying himself with the pride of a man who has never been downed. What were they saying? Here comes Wild Bill, the Union scout. Here comes Hickok, the killer. Here comes Wild Bill Hickok, the man who wiped out the Mc-Canles gang . . . Well, it didn't matter what they were saying, just so long as they took notice. He was a celebrity wherever he went on the frontier. How could he go back to Troy Grove now? How could he go back to driving a stage for $30 a month? The world expected more than that of Wild Bill Hickok.

Immediately after the war ended he went to Springfield, Missouri, which was probably the liveliest—and the deadliest—town on the border. He had spent much of the war in that neighborhood, and it was well supplied with both friends and enemies. And Appomattox had not ended the killing, though it now assumed a less formal and legalized character, in the Ozark country. The feuding and night riding, in fact, became more ferocious than ever. During the war southern sympathizers had the upper hand in southwest Missouri, driving many of the Unionists out of the country. Now the Unionists were back and thirsty for revenge. With encouragement from the Federal authorities they organized the "Regulators," a sort of Unionist Ku Klux Klan, to make things especially hot for Confederate veterans returning to their homesteads. Four thousand ex-secessionists were slaughtered in southwest Missouri during the year following Appomattox. "A swift bullet and a short rope for returned Rebels" was the prescription of the Regulators. In this moral and political climate violence was as palpable as the fog which rose from the creek bottoms in this summer of 1861.

The Regulators naturally sought to enlist Hickok, but he sensibly replied:

79

"I buried the hatchet when the war ended, and I won't fight again unless put upon."

It was a promise he soon found himself unable to keep.

Hickok had always been fascinated by gambling, and now he turned to it as a profession. Poker was his principal vice, along with an affinity for violence. And there was always a high-stake game going in Springfield that post-war summer. Returning soldiers had their pockets full of discharge pay; anyone with anything to sell commanded a seller's market, and there were plenty of greenbacks wadded in the pokes of the citizenry, those who hadn't picked the wrong side.

Springfield then had a population of three thousand, not counting the considerable number of transients. It was filled with an Ozarkian lethargy by day. Colonel Nichols, recently of General Sherman's staff but now a *Harper's* correspondent, described the scene:

"On a warm summer day I sat watching from the shadow of a broad awning the coming and going of the strange, half-civilized people, who, from all the country round, made this a place for barter and trade. Men and women dressed in queer costumes; men with coats and trousers made of skins, but so thickly covered with dirt and grease as to have defied the identity of the animal when walking in the flesh. Others wore homespun gear, which oftentimes appeared to have seen lengthy service. Many of these people were mounted on horses or mules, while others urged forward the unwilling cattle, attached to creaking, heavily laden wagons, their drivers snapping their long whips with a report like that of a pistol shot.

"In front of the shops, which lined both sides of the main business street, and about the public square, were groups of men lolling against posts, lying upon the wooden sidewalks, or sitting in chairs. These men were temporary or permanent denizens of the city, and were lazily occupied in doing nothing. The most marked characteristic of the inhabitants seemed to be an indisposition to move, and their highest ambition to let their hair and beards grow.

"Here and there upon the street the appearance of the army blue beckoned the presence of a returned Union soldier, and the jaunty, confident air with which they carried themselves was all the more striking in its contrast with the indolence which appeared to belong to the place. The only indication of action was the inevitable revolver, which everybody, excepting perhaps the women, wore about their persons. When people moved about in this lazy city, they did so slowly and without method. No one seemed in haste. A huge hog wallowed in luxurious ease in a nice bed of mud on the other side of the way, giving vent to gentle grunts of satisfaction. On the platform at my feet lay a large wolf-dog, literally asleep with one eye open. He, too, seemed contented to let the world wag idly on . . ."

The drowsy colonel was aroused a short time later, he reported, by the thunder of Black Nell's hoofs. Wild Bill Hickok rode up and was introduced to Colonel Nichols.

A rather girlish enthusiasm—or perhaps it was only the vibrant literary style of the day—seemed to have seized Colonel Nichols when he set down his first impression of Hickok. He wrote, "Wild Bill stood six feet and an inch in his bright yellow moccasins. A deerskin shirt, or frock it might have been called, hung jauntily over his shoulders, revealing a chest whose breadth and depth were remarkable. These lungs had breathed for some twenty [sic] years the free air of the Rocky Mountains. His small round waist was girthed by a belt which held two of Colt's navy revolvers. His legs sloped gradually from the compact thigh to the feet, which were small and turned inward as he walked.

"There was a singular grace and dignity of carriage about that figure which would have attracted your attention, meet it where you would. The head which crowned it was now

covered by a large sombrero, underneath which there shone
out a quiet, manly face, so gentle in its expression as he
greets you as utterly to belie the history of its owner, yet it
is a face not to be trifled with. The lips, thin and sensitive,
the jaw not too square, the cheek bones slightly prominent,
a mass of fine brown hair falls below the neck to the shoulders.
The eyes, now that you are in friendly intercourse, are as
gentle as a woman's . . . In vain did I examine the scout's
face for some evidence of murderous propensity. It was a
gentle face, singular only in the sharp angle of the eye, and
without any physiognomical reason for the opinion, I have
thought his wonderful accuracy of aim was indicated by this
peculiarity."

A somewhat different picture of Hickok at the time, more
darkly shadowed than Colonel Nichol's portrait of the lithe
outdoorsman, was provided by "Buffalo Bill," or Colonel
William F. Cody, to give him his full title. Cody, nine years
younger than the twenty-eight-year-old Hickok, had met him
before Springfield and was a friend of his. According to
Cody (*An Autobiography of Buffalo Bill*), Hickok could
usually be seen that summer hunched over the poker table
rather than vaulting out of the saddle after a canter into
the countryside.

Cody wrote of watching Hickok playing in a high-stake
game in which undercurrents of larceny were visible even to
young Cody's inexperienced eye: "Sitting by the table, I
noticed that he seemed sleepy and inattentive. So I kept a
close watch on the other fellows. Presently I observed that
one of his opponents was occasionally dropping a card in
his hat, which he held in his lap, until a number of cards had
been laid away for future use in the game. The pot had gone
around several times and was steadily raised by some of the
players, Bill staying right along, though he still seemed to be
drowsy.

"The bets kept rising. At last the man with the hatful of

cards picked a hand out of his reserves, put the hat on his head and raised Bill two hundred dollars. Bill came back with a raise of two hundred, and as the other covered it he quietly shoved a pistol into his face and observed, 'I'm calling the hand that's in your hat.'"

Hickok, according to Cody, then swept up the money in the pot with his left hand while holding the gun on the rest of the players.

"Any objections, gentlemen?" Hickok inquired.

The other players shook their heads, and Hickok and Cody strolled out of the place.

"Bill," said Cody, "I was noticing that fellow's play right along, but I thought you hadn't. I was going to get into the game myself if he beat you out of that money."

"Billy, I don't want you ever to learn it," Hickok said, "but that is one of my favorite poker tricks. It always wins against crooked players."

Even more sinisterly shadowed than his gambling activities were Hickok's relations with two other members of Springfield's transient population. They were Dave Tutt and Susanna Moore. They had been friends of his—Susanna perhaps more than a friend—but now they had fallen out. The exact relationship of the three has never been determined and probably never will be, since it is fogged with rumor, romance, and a final drift of gun smoke.

Tutt was a gunman-gambler from Arkansas, born near Yellville, where Hickok did much of his undercover work during the war. He came of a family renowned as good haters. In the long pre-war feud of the Tutt and Everett clans, forty-five men were killed along Crooked Creek in Marion County. Tutt served in the Confederate Army until early in 1862, when Curtis turned the tide at Pea Ridge. He then deserted and joined the Union Army as a scout and served with Hickok. There was a strong possibility, in fact, that Hickok had persuaded him to change sides. Until early

83

She came to Springfield shortly after Hickok and Dave Tutt arrived there, hoping to revive the wartime romance.

When she found that Hickok had cooled toward her, she fastened her attentions on his friend, probably in hope of annoying Hickok or recapturing his interest.

By mid-July Hickok and Tutt were no longer friends.

Not only Susanna had stirred up trouble between them, "bad blood" that was soon to result in gunfire. "The fact is," wrote Colonel Nichols in his *Harper's* report, "there was an undercurrent of a woman in that fight." Aside from whatever differences they had over Susanna and whatever ill feeling she managed to stir up between them, both men were determined to be the kingpin gambler of Springfield. They were out to break each other.

Tutt began associating with Hickok's enemies around Springfield and doing everything he could to taunt and harass his ex-friend. An expert *pistolero* himself, Tutt was not afraid of Hickok's reputation as a gun slinger.

One of their principal jousting grounds, over the poker table, was the Lyon House, formerly the Old Southern Hotel, on South Street just off the huge public square. The bar of the Lyon House was the scene of most of the high-limit games in town.

Hickok apparently did his best to head off a showdown with Tutt and finally refused to play at the same table with his former friend.

Tutt then took to standing behind one of Hickok's opponents in a game, encouraging him, coaching him on how to beat Hickok. This alone would have been provocation for slapping leather with most gamblers, but Hickok was determined to avoid a fight.

On the night of July 20 at the Lyon House, Tutt not only advised one of Hickok's opponents at the table but lent him money to keep him in the game. He was infuriated when

Hickok cleaned him out and started to rise from the table with two hundred dollars in winnings.

Tutt, halting him before he could leave the table, reminded Hickok of another matter that increased the sense of grievance between the two men. At their last set-to, before Hickok announced he would not play in any game with Tutt, Hickok had been cleaned out and still owed Tutt a disputed sum of money. Tutt said it was thirty-five dollars. Hickok claimed it was twenty-five dollars. In any case, Tutt wanted his money now.

Dave reached over and grabbed Hickok's Waltham watch, to which Hickok later claimed he had a strong sentimental attachment. It had been lying on the table in front of Hickok.

"I'll just keep this watch until you pay up," Tutt said.

The enraged Hickok, trying to control himself, told his creditor, "I don't want to make a row in this house, but you'd better put that watch back on the table."

Tutt laughed, tucked the watch in his pocket, and walked away.

Hickok called after him, "As a special favor to me, Dave, don't wear that watch in public. I wouldn't want people to know it had changed hands, even temporarily."

"I'll be wearing it tomorrow morning right out on the public square," Tutt replied.

"Don't come across the square with that watch on you," Hickok said deliberately. "If you do I'll shoot you."

He had the rest of the night to brood over the situation; thus when he stepped out of the Lyon House shortly before nine o'clock that morning, July 21, 1865, he had a Colt's Dragoon swinging easily in the holster on his right flank. His touchy pride was too inflamed—not only by Tutt's seizure of the watch but the fact that Susanna Moore had so nimbly transferred her affections from him to Dave Tutt, whom he regarded as an unworthy successor—to permit reflection on the fact that he was ready to kill a man over such a trifle. Hickok was an intelligent man, better educated than most of his associates, brought up in a religious home, sternly grounded in moral principles. But he had now spent ten years on the frontier, a decade of border fighting and civil war. Death itself was a trivial matter, less consequential than an affront to a man's pride. Perhaps, too, Hickok realized that sooner or later, whatever the issue, he would have to shoot it out with Dave Tutt. And as always in such matters, it might as well be sooner.

Half the town was waiting to watch a man die—Wild Bill Hickok or Dave Tutt—it didn't much matter which to most of the spectators. Word had spread around the small city that they would shoot it out the next time they met. All around the four sides of the square the people waited in the shadow of the courthouse, that dwelling place of a justice which had abdicated its responsibilities to the six-shooter and the lynch rope, for Hickok and Tutt to settle their dispute. The sheriff of Greene County and numerous other servants of that discredited justice were among the spectators loitering at the hitching racks and under the awnings of the stores and the arches of the courthouse. They made no effort to interfere; such a gesture would have cost them the votes of every good citizen gathered to share in the excitement.

From the entrance of the Lyon House, Hickok surveyed the scene: the dusty streets entering the three-acre public square, the massive, elm-shaded courthouse, the hogs lying in their wallows, the ox teams moving slowly along the north side of the square, and all the people hanging around, avid for the sight of blood. The sun was bright, and the heat of midmorning was already oppressive.

Across the square, standing in the door of the livery stable at the northwest corner, was Dave Tutt. He watched Hickok come out of the Lyon House and slowly began walking south-ward on the west side of the square.

Hickok caught sight of Tutt and started walking up South Street to the southeast corner of the square, a few hundred feet away.

He asked a bystander whether he had seen Tutt that morn-ing and whether Tutt was wearing Hickok's watch. The man said he had seen Tutt but didn't know if he was wearing the watch.

"If he's wearing it there'll be merry hell," Hickok said.

Tutt had begun to cut across the square to confront Hickok. Everybody scattered to take cover.

Hickok and Tutt slowly approached each other, each con-fident of his superior skill.

When they were about seventy-five yards apart Hickok called out, "Don't come any closer, Dave." It was Tutt's last chance to avoid a showdown.

Tutt replied by drawing quickly and firing. Hickok fired so quickly afterward, using his left arm as a rest to steady his aim, according to some witnesses, that both shots sounded like one. For a moment both men froze in their tracks and spectators couldn't see which one, if either, had been shot. At a range of seventy-five yards it wouldn't have been at all surprising if both had missed.

Then Tutt, stiff as a board, fell on his face. He had been shot clean through the heart.

Hickok wheeled to confront a number of Tutt's friends who had been gathering menacingly at his rear and de-manded, "Are you satisfied, gentlemen? Put up your guns or there'll be more dead men here."

Satisfied there was no more shooting to do, Hickok walked over to the sheriff, handed over his revolver, and surrendered himself. The Circuit Court of Greene County was then in session, and he did not have to wait long for a trial. There was talk of arranging a lynching among Tutt's friends, who said Hickok had so many highly placed, Unionist friends in Greene County that he could be acquitted on almost any charge.

Hickok, at any rate, was represented by the ablest and most respectable legal counsel in those parts when the case came to trial. His attorney was the Hon. John S. Phelps, former congressman and wartime governor of Arkansas, whose farm near Springfield had been devastated with unusual thoroughness by the Confederates. Hickok had served as a scout with the regiment commanded by his son, Colonel John E. Phelps, during Price's last campaign.

The jury voted for an acquittal after Tutt's gun, with one empty chamber, was placed in evidence and it was testified that Tutt appeared to be the aggressor.

The town generally approved the verdict, and Hickok, continuing his career as a gambler, stayed on in Springfield for several months after the trial.

Nothing better described the times than the fact that dangling a watch held as security for a poker debt was widely regarded as a justifiable provocation for resorting to firearms.

CHAPTER 6

Man About Kansas City

Eventually Wild Bill Hickok wearied of being the top celebrity of Springfield, following the Tutt shooting, and decided to leave the Ozark country and the many wartime enmities he had incurred there. It was about time to live among friends for a change. Besides, the easy money, which had been flowing through the saloons and gambling rooms during the post-war turmoil, was beginning to dry up. Late in January or early in February he was invited to return to the government payroll and readily accepted.

The senior officers at Fort Riley in Kansas Territory had appealed to their superiors for the appointment of a deputy United States marshal to help them cope with lawlessness on and around the post. Victory seemed to have demoralized the Union Army. A number of officers were short in their accounts and faced the usual remedy of being cashiered and possibly sent to military prison. In the ranks, government funds being inaccessible, desertion was the principal crime. Worse yet, the deserters rode off on government horses and mules.

Hickok was appointed to halt these forays against government property and discourage horse thieves lurking around the remount stables and corrals of the big cavalry post on the recommendation of Captain Owens, the provost marshal, and General Eaton, chief quartermaster of the department, who knew something of his efficiency. Their confidence in Hickok was vindicated almost immediately. A few weeks after his appointment he pursued a pair of deserters to the upper waters of the Little Arkansas and brought them back along with nine mules they had stolen.

When his duties as lawman permitted, Hickok also acted as a scout and guide for various troop movements along the border. He escorted a column under General William T. Sherman, now head of the Indian-fighting army, from Fort Leavenworth to Fort McPherson in the spring of 1866. On a subsequent expedition into Nebraska, Hickok visited a familiar but not necessarily pleasant scene of his youth, Rock Creek Station, where McCanles and his two friends had been dispatched to their deaths five years ago. Frank Helvey, then in charge of the stage stop, said Hickok encamped with General Sherman and his troops nearby on the Little Sandy. "Before they got fairly settled, General Sherman with Wild Bill accompanying him rode up to the station and warned us not to let the soldiers have any whiskey," Helvey later recounted. Hickok did not linger at the memory-haunted station but rode back to the bivouac immediately with General Sherman.

For all his rumored profligacy, Hickok, among gentle people, conducted himself with a modesty and a courtesy that reflected his upbringing in Troy Grove. All through the reminiscences of the people who knew him in peaceful circumstances runs an account—paralleling but certainly not contradicting the stories of his resort to violence, his fondness for saloon life, and his association with women who, in that fine old phrase, were "no better than they should be"—

of his love of children and his gentle manner in decent company. Hickok always adapted his demeanor to the circumstances in which he found himself. Thus it was difficult for many respectable people to believe that the Hickok they knew could be the Wild Bill of the gunfights and bushwhackings.

One of Hickok's missions in the autumn of 1866 was to escort Dr. William Finlaw, the army surgeon, from Fort McPherson to his regular post at Fort Riley. Along the way he took Dr. Finlaw's little daughter with him to hunt bullfrogs in the sloughs of the Blue River. A rather meager escort of ten soldiers was detailed to accompany Dr. Finlaw and his family, traveling in an ambulance wagon, through restive Indian country. Hickok, concerned for their safety, was in the saddle long before sunrise and long after sundown, scouting the country through which they passed with extreme thoroughness. And at night he rolled himself up in his blankets and slept under the ambulance to keep the closest possible watch on the surgeon and his family.

Dr. Finlaw found him sleeping there in the middle of the night and remonstrated with Hickok for not finding a more comfortable place to bed down. He said Hickok replied:

"Think of the Indians getting the baby! Your children are in my care, and I would not let anything happen to them for the world."

While serving as U.S. marshal at Fort Riley, Hickok made the acquaintance of Henry M. Stanley, who had come West as the correspondent of the New York *Herald*. He was the Stanley who, somewhat later, found Livingstone in Africa. He was somewhat less successful, judging by the account in his autobiography, in trying to locate the real Hickok behind the jungle-like growth of legend surrounding him. Yet it was not for lack of trying; Stanley and Hickok became boon companions, drinking companions at any rate. In the diary of George Snyder, sutler at Fort Riley, was found the signif-

icant entry, "Henry M. Stanley and Wild Bill my guests until 3 A.M."

Stanley wrote that he once asked Hickok, "How many white
men have you killed to your certain knowledge?"

He quoted Hickok as replying "after a little deliberation":
"I suppose I have killed considerably over a hundred."

"What made you kill all those men? Did you kill them
without cause or provocation?"

"No, by heaven, I never killed one man without good
cause."

Stanley said Hickok told him he was twenty-eight years
old when he first killed a man (actually he was twenty-four,
and the victim was McCanles). According to Stanley, who
was the kind of reporter who sometimes flinched at letting
the facts stand in the way of a good story, Hickok then
spun a horrendous tale of knifing and shooting a swath
through a pack of ruffians in a Leavenworth hotel.

"I ordered a room, and as I had some money about me, I
thought I would retire to it. I had lain some thirty minutes
on the bed when I heard men at my door. I pulled out my
revolver and Bowie knife, and held them ready, but half
concealed, and pretended to be asleep. The door was opened,
and five men entered the room. They whispered together,
and one said, 'Let us kill the son of a ——, I'll bet he has got
money.' Gentlemen, that was a time—an awful time. I kept
perfectly still until just as the knife touched my breast; I
sprung aside and buried mine in his heart, and then used
my revolvers on the others right and left. One was killed,
and another was wounded; and then, gentlemen, I dashed
through the room and rushed to the fort, where I procured a
lot of soldiers, and returning to the hotel, captured the whole
gang of them, fifteen in all. We searched the cellar and
found eleven bodies buried in it—the remains of those who
had been murdered by those villains."

According to this account, the massacre in the Leaven-

worth hotel took place in 1865, Hickok's twenty-eight year.
He was General Curtis' chief of scouts during the early
months of that year, with headquarters at Fort Leavenworth.
No record can be found, covering that period, of any such
bloody event requiring the intervention of the military. Later
in 1865 he was far away, gambling in Springfield, Missouri,
and gunning down Dave Tutt.

The brand of whiskey dispensed by the sutler at Fort
Riley must have been extraordinarily potent.

In between various missions for the army and the U. S.
Government, Hickok spent considerable time in Kansas City,
the Paris of the prairies, in 1866 and 1867. To the frontiersman it was the center of civilization, a metropolitan playground where he could find the best in food, liquor, and
entertainment, the prettiest and frequently the most accommodating women, the heartiest companionship, the fanciest
clothes—everything his lonely soul hankered for after many
months of sweating out a living on the plains or in a dreary
prairie settlement.

On his first trip to Kansas City the rumor flew around
town that he was determined on a showdown with Jim Crow
Chiles, the titular head of the rudimentary underworld and
proprietor of a prospering gambling house called The Headquarters. The basis for this rumor seemed to be the fact that
Chiles had been a leading desperado on the Confederate
side before and during the late hostilities. He rode with
Quantrill's raiders, served under Price and Shelby in the
Missouri campaigns, and was supposed to be Kansas City's
toughest citizen, a large, belligerent character who went for
his gun at the slightest provocation.

A large crowd appeared on the bluffs of the Missouri over-
looking the mouth of the Kaw just before the steamboat on
which Hickok was traveling came around the bend and tied
up at the foot of Delaware Street.

As he disembarked, someone yelled at Hickok, "Going over to The Headquarters, Wild Bill?"

Hickok nodded in the affirmative. The crowd, crowing with delight at the prospect of bloodshed, eagerly trailed after him.

Hickok strolled up to Main Street and entered The Headquarters. The crowd gathered to gape from the doorway, unmindful of statistics which indicated more innocent bystanders than belligerents often were slaughtered in a gunslinging contest.

To their amazement, Chiles came forward to greet Hickok with Mine-Host chuckles and backslapping.

"How are you, Bill?" Chiles inquired. "I haven't seen you since you gave us a heap of trouble down in Arkansas, spying for the Yankee army. Glad to see you, Bill."

Hickok shook hands warmly and said, "How about staking me to a stack of chips, Jim? They cleaned me out in Leavenworth on the way down-river."

"Sure, Bill, your credit's good here any time."

The crowd, grumbling in disappointment, quickly dispersed.

A short time later Jim Crow Chiles was killed by Marshal Jim Peacock of Independence when he refused to stop carousing and bothering the churchgoing folks on the street one drunken Sunday morning.

The Kansas City to which Hickok repaired as often as his fortunes would permit was a fast-growing boom town in the decade following the Civil War. Its population was approaching the thirty-thousand mark; it was a rising power in commerce and industry; it was the hub of rail and waterway transportation. Cattle barons from Texas, gold and silver kings from Colorado, ranchers from beyond the Pecos whose spreads were so vast only an eagle could survey them, the men who controlled the freight and stage lines to the farther West, the men who were building the railroads, the stockyards, and the meat-packing industries, all met, mingled, and connived in K.C., Mo. They transacted their business in the city's mahogany-lined saloons, its plushier gambling houses, and among the Parisian splendors of its more elegant parlor houses. In these places commerce acquired an intriguing scent of bourbon, cigar smoke, and even a hint of patchouli. Tycoons talking million-dollar transactions in beef, metal, and land rubbed elbows with gunfighters, gamblers, buffalo hunters, traders from Taos, dead-eyed drifters from nowhere.

It was Wild Bill Hickok's kind of town—none ever suited him better. A man could relax here as long as his money lasted. By common agreement, among the professionals at least, Kansas City was off limits to gunplay, a sort of neutral zone where grudges were held in abeyance and settled in more seemly places at more appropriate times. There was a murder or two a day during the height of the summer social season, but they generally involved drunks, brawlers, and disappointed small-fry gamblers who were outside Hickok's circle of frontier celebrities.

Gambling, Hickok's favorite vice, was wide open and almost as respectable as selling groceries. "Games of chance, cards, keno, faro, roulette, dice, cock-mains, dog-fighting and kindred means for hazarding money flourished day and night," wrote an early historian, and Kansas City was "the parent block off which was chipped all the gambling towns along the Kansas Pacific railroad."

Luxurious, up-a-flight gambling houses lined the west side of Main Street between Fourth Street and Missouri Avenue, while the sleazier, less reputable, and less honest operated on Fifth Street between Walnut and Main. All sorts of sex traps were waiting for the plainsman at the lower end of Main Street and along the levee—parlor houses in charge of madames whose manner was so chillingly refined that many a visiting roughneck thought he'd been directed to the wrong place, brass-check brothels with a rapid turnover, houses of assignation, cribs, panel joints with wallet-snatching creepers in the woodwork—all part of a well-organized and profitable whoring industry.

The principal hangout of the plainsmen in Kansas City, however, was Market Square, where the buffalo hunters, scouts, guides, stage drivers and teamsters, gunfighters (lawmen and outlaws alike), and professional gamblers congregated. Here they all came to exchange information on the movement of the buffalo herds, which towns along the frontier were booming, how the Indians were behaving in various localities. Here they came to find out what had happened to long-separated friends or relatives. From morning to midnight they sat under the awnings, in the saloons and hotel lobbies, on the hitching racks and store benches, gossiping, exchanging trade secrets, spinning yarns, listening in on the grapevine of the Great Plains which brought news faster than any electric telegraph.

Here Hickok would greet such contemporaries as Wyatt Earp, marshal of Wichita; the dapper young Bat Masterson, sheriff of Ford County, Kansas, in which Dodge City was the county seat; Luke Short, the little gunman-gambler who could quote Shakespeare by the hour; Doc Holliday, the rachitic and homicidal dentist from Georgia; Clay Allison, the gun-slinging terror of the Cimarron; Mysterious Dave Mather, Smoky Hill Thompson, Joshua Webb, Jim Marshall, and Billy Brooks. Also the wild and woolly buffalo hunters, Prairie Dog Dave, Blue Pete, Dirty-Face Charlie, The Off-Wheeler and his pal The Near-Wheeler, Eat 'Em Up Jake, Shoot 'Em Up Mike, the Hoodoo Kid, Light-Fingered Jack, Shotgun Collins, Black Kelly, The Stuttering Kid, Bull Whack Joe, Conch Jones, Hurricane Bill, and Shoot-His-Eye-Out-Jack, all of whom dispensed with surnames, and Jack Martin, Billy Dixon, Billy Tyler, Kirk Jordan, Billy Ogg, Bermuda Carlisle, Tom O'Keefe, Jim Hanrahan, and Old Man Keeler. Also the celebrated scout, Jack Gallagher.

In the afternoons Tom Speers, the much-respected chief of police, held court at a bench in front of the police station. Only the elite of the frontier was permitted to gather around Speers' bench, which was almost as exclusive as King Arthur's Round Table.

"Wild Bill and Gallagher were respected around Tom Speers' bench," Wyatt Earp recalled (in Stuart Lake's *Wyatt Earp, Frontier Marshal*). "They were accepted as authorities on buffalo-killing, and their opinions settled many a Market Square argument over man-killing as well. They knew Indians inside-out, and both had participated in or witnessed gunfights between white men that were talked of all over the West. Gallagher certainly knew more of buffalo-hunting and Indian battles, but Bill Hickok was regarded as the deadliest pistol-shot alive, as well as a man of great courage."

Earp said there were "few gunfights in Kansas City . . . none between men of reputation that I recall; and, unless participants in a killing were well known, no one gave much attention to what they did. The prominent characters were not trouble-hunters, as a rule; and their relations with Tom Speers placed them under obligation to save him the embarrassment which might follow if topnotchers went to shooting." And, besides, "topnotchers" had an understandable reluctance to try their skill on each other; it was an unseemly risk.

Tom Speers' bench, with Speers, Gallagher, and Hickok the leading lights, served as a sort of forum for gunfighters in which the arts of survival were discussed with deadly seriousness. Earp credited "the lessons learned in Market Square" for a large share of his own survival as marshal of Witchita, Dodge City, and Tombstone.

Aside from the seminar on gunfighting, Hickok was a leading figure in the social life of Market Square. Even the shaggiest and most verminous of buffalo hunters spruced up when they hit the square, and the frontiersman who spent most of his days in greasy buckskins blew a good part of his roll—aside from a rousing good spree when he first came to town—on a silk hat, brocaded vest, calfskin boots, velvet-collared frock coat, and fine linen. Hickok, with his flair for wearing the most spectacular tailoring, was easily the most resplendent; he had the manner, the bearing, as well as the haberdashery.

He spent his days renewing old friendships around the square, went to the theaters and variety halls in the evening, and from midnight to dawn bucked the tiger at faro, monte, and poker. He drank sparingly, since these pursuits would only be dulled by an overdose of whiskey.

Hickok had another enthusiasm, baseball, unlikely as it may seem for a man of his calling. The game was just developing into an American institution and was taken as seriously by its devotees as politics or Indian affairs. A riot was quite as likely to develop in Kansas City over an umpire's bad call as it was some time later on a frantic Sunday afternoon in the old home of the Brooklyn Dodgers.

Wild Bill was a regular attendant Saturday afternoons at the games played by the Kansas City Antelopes on a diamond near Fourteenth and Oak streets. There were few amenities for the fans: no grandstand, no scoreboard, no shelter against the sun. When a close play occurred or the umpire was rash enough to decide against the home team in a crucial matter, everyone swarmed out on the field to participate in the argument, sometimes with fists, bottles, and whatever came to hand.

The Antelopes beat down all challengers on their home grounds but on one occasion ventured to Atchison to play the Pomeroys, who roundly defeated them. Next time the Antelopes and the Pomeroys played in Kansas City and the game ended in a riot, with the umpire fleeing for his life.

The headline over the Kansas City *Times* account of this Donnybrook read:

THE TOWN IS
DISGRACED

With apologies all around, it was agreed to replay the game the following Saturday. This time, it was also agreed, the game must be supervised by someone respected—and feared—by players and spectators alike. What more eminent and authoritative umpire than Wild Bill Hickok could be found?

A delegation was sent to Hickok, who was located in Jake Fourcade's gambling rooms at Fourth and Main playing poker with one of the city fathers.

Hickok accepted the honor. When the Antelopes and the Pomeroys met that Saturday afternoon, Hickok was behind the plate with full armament. Riotous as the previous game had been, this one was played without a dissenting murmur from the crowd or even the mildest dispute from the players. An umpire with a pair of six-shooters presided over one of the most decorous games ever played in baseball history. The Antelopes won by a basketball-sized score, 48 to 28.

The Antelope partisans were so pleased with Hickok's umpiring that he was asked how he "might like to be repaid," after he was proclaimed the "distinguished guest of Kansas City for the day"—an honor unique in all the somber annals of umpiring.

"I'll tell you what I'd like," Hickok said after a moment's thought. "Send down to Frank Short's livery stable for an open carriage with his matched pair of white horses."

Hickok drove back to Market Square in the handsomest possible style, cheered along the way by a grateful citizenry.

The pleasures of Kansas City never entirely distracted him from his professional concerns, his determination to wield the handgun with greater expertness and efficiency than anyone else. Hardly a day passed that he did not practice drawing and shooting, perfecting his timing. He never tired of exhibiting his marksmanship apparently, and his ammunition bills must have been enormous.

In the opinion of experts who saw him perform at targets of all kinds, including human ones, Hickok was a virtuoso with any type of handgun. The grace and precision with which he drew and fired a revolver must have had something of the classic endowment of the ballet about them. Mythical as were many phases of his life, there was nothing imaginary about his skill at handling his weapons. The late Tom Lewis, a magazine writer who knew many figures of the Old West, asked Wyatt Earp, Bat Masterson, Billy Tilghman, and Charlie Siringo (who hated Kansas lawmen) which was the deadliest shot of them all. All four, Lewis said, replied without hesitation, "Wild Bill Hickok." Earp told his biographer, "There was no man in the Kansas City group who was Wild Bill's equal with a six-gun . . . Legend and the imaginations of certain people have exaggerated the number of men he killed in gunfights and have misrepresented the manner in which he did his killing . . . they could not very well overdo his skill with pistols." Generals Custer and Sheridan, who were not easily impressed by civilian heroics, considered Hickok the most expert gunman they ever saw on the frontier. Buffalo Bill, whose exploits were exaggerated by the most brazen press agentry but who was not quite the fraud latter-day revisionists have made him out, told a newspaper interviewer (Chicago *Inter-Ocean*, October 15, 1911):

"Wild Bill was one of the best revolver shots ever produced in the West. He certainly was the best shot in a fight. It is one thing to shoot accurately at a target and another to be able to shoot accurately at a man who is shooting at you . . . He was devoid of nerves; his mind was clear, his hand steady and his marksmanship certain in the most desperate situation. He never became excited. A cool man is often a phlegmatic man, but Wild Bill was the reverse. He was not only perfectly cool but he was always alert and nimble of wit, and in action as quick as lightning."

Some of Hickok's feats of gun-handling, certified by reliable and fairly sober witnesses, were:

Having a tomato can thrown in the air and riddling it with twelve bullets before it fell back to the ground.

Driving a cork through the neck of a whiskey bottle at about twenty paces.

Splitting a bullet on the edge of a dime at the same distance.

For all-around shooting Hickok, unlike most of his gunfighting contemporaries, favored the double-action Colt .44 with the catch filed down for hair-trigger quickness in squeezing out every bullet in its chambers. Most gunfighters used the single-action army Colt .45, filed down and reassembled so that it was fired by thumbing back the hammer. When he patrolled the streets of a lawless town, Hickok was often a walking arsenal. In addition to a pair of .44s strapped to his thighs he would carry a brace of .41 Derringers in his side pockets, a Bowie knife in his belt, a shotgun or repeating rifle crooked in his arm, which made a total of five guns and one knife. On the dressier or less dangerous occasions he often disdained the use of a holster and tucked one gun in the waistband of his trousers. In the practice of gunfighting—which has been debated elsewhere with greater authority, particularly in Eugene Cunningham's *Triggernometry*—many of the professionals held that it was better to fire only once or twice and make sure of hitting your opponent than squeezing off a greater number of shots. Hickok, however, believed in fire power. When he cut loose at a man or men with his double-action revolvers, it sounded, from all accounts, like a Gatling gun spraying the landscape. Perhaps he believed there was a certain psychological effect achieved in such a fusillade; it was often necessary for Hickok not only to dispose of one opponent but to dissuade the man's friends from joining in the argument.

There was no doubt about Hickok's ability to shoot accurately as well as rapidly. Earp told of watching Hickok demonstrate his marksmanship for Tom Speers one afternoon in Kansas City:

"Diagonally across Market Square, possibly one hundred yards away, was a saloon, and on the side-wall toward the police station a sign that carried a capital letter O. The sign ran off at an angle from Hickok's line of sight, yet, before anyone guessed what his target was, Wild Bill had fired five shots from the gun in his right hand, shifted weapons, and fired five more shots. Then he told Tom to send someone over to look at the O. All ten of Bill's slugs were found inside the ring of the letter.

"That was shooting. I am not belittling Wild Bill when I bear witness that while he was shooting at the O, he held his gun as almost every man skilled in such matters preferred to hold one when in action, with a half-bent elbow that brought the gun slightly in front of his body at about, or slightly above, the level of the waist.

"It may surprise some to know that a man of Hickok's skill could make a six-gun effective up to four hundred yards . . . Luck figured largely in such shooting, and a man had to know his gun to score, but I have known them to kill at that range."

Perhaps the most objective report on Hickok's marksmanship was written by the late Robert A. Kane, a big-game hunter, authority on handguns and editor of *Outdoor Life*, who witnessed a shooting exhibition by Hickok when the latter was on tour with a theatrical company. Kane and several other sportsmen called on Hickok at his hotel in Milwaukee. "Mr. Hickok treated us with great courtesy, showed us his weapons, and offered to do a little shooting for us if it could be arranged for outside the city limits. Accordingly the early hours of the afternoon found us on our way to the outskirts of the city. Mr. Hickok's weapons were a pair of beautifully silver-plated S.A. .44 Colt revolvers. Both had pearl handles and were tastefully engraved. He also had a pair of Remington revolvers of the same caliber. The more showy pair of Colts were used in his stage performance. On reaching a place suitable for our purpose, Mr. Hickok proceeded to entertain us with some of the best pistol work which it has ever been my good fortune to witness.

"Standing on a railroad track, in a deep cut, his pistols cracking with the regularity and cadence of an old house clock, he struck and dislodged the bleaching pebbles sticking in the face of the bank, at a distance of about 15 yards.

"Standing about 30 feet from the shooter, one of the party tossed a quart can in the air to the height of about 30 feet. This was perforated three times before it reached the ground, twice with the right and once with the left hand.

"Standing midway between the fences of a country road, which is four rods wide, Mr. Hickok's instinct of location was so accurate that he placed a bullet in each of the fence posts on opposite sides. Both shots were fired simultaneously.

"Located midway between two telegraph poles he placed a bullet in one of them, then wheeled and with the same weapon planted another in the second. Telegraph poles in this country run about 30 to the mile, or 170 feet distant from each other.

"Two common bricks were placed on the top board of a fence, about two feet apart and about 15 yards from the shooter. These were broken with two shots fired from the pistol in either hand, the reports so nearly together that they seemed but one.

"His last feat was to me the most remarkable of all: A quart can was thrown by Mr. Hickok himself, which dropped about 10 or 12 yards distant. Quickly whipping out his weapons, he fired alternately with right and left. Advancing a step with each shot, his bullets striking the earth just under the can kept it in continuous motion until his pistols were empty."

(It may be noted that Hickok's more enthusiastic admirers claimed he could put a dozen bullets into a tomato can tossed into the air while the more dispassionate Mr. Kane counted only three holes. Quite possibly, however, Hickok's skill had deteriorated somewhat between his days as an active frontiersman and his subsequent interlude as an actor.)

Several years later, writing on the same subject for his magazine, Kane recalled he was "deeply impressed with his [Hickok's] almost exasperating deliberation," and continued:

"No matter how elusive the target, even when shooting at objects tossed in the air, he never seemed hurried. This trait was, of course, natural, and in part due to his superb physique and superior mentality, which, combined with and supplemented by his methods of practice and free, wild life in the open, developed in him that perfect coordination of hand and eye which was essential to perfect mastery of the one-hand gun."

That exhibition, Kane said, left him "prepared to believe any story of his skill or prowess that does not conflict with the laws of gravitation and physics."

CHAPTER 7

A Private Shooting Gallery

For almost four years, from 1866 to 1869, Hickok was in the government service as a deputy marshal, scout, guide, and dispatch rider. The pay was low, the work hard and dangerous. Wild Bill Hickok was almost a household name in the East after the publication of Colonel Nichols' panegyric in *Harper's*, Henry M. Stanley's accounts in the New York *Herald*, and various other newspaper stories detailing his exploits, but the desperadoes of the border apparently were not acquainted with his press clippings. They insisted on matching their skill as gunmen against his, with uniformly disastrous results.

Hickok ranged all through western Kansas and Nebraska, tracking down army deserters, horse thieves, and other outlaws with a low regard for the sanctity of government property. The Solomon River valley was a favorite hangout of the marauders, and Hickok often roved there at considerable danger to himself. In January of 1867, with the assistance of a squad of cavalry from Fort Riley, he rounded up more than two hundred horses and mules which had been stolen from government stables and corrals and brought them back to the cavalry post. The thieves, however, had escaped. Next time he ventured into the Solomon valley without a squad of soldiers to attract attention to himself and was more successful. A brief item in the Topeka *Leader* stated that Hickok and "Buffalo Bill" Cody, whom it identified as "a government detective," had "brought eleven prisoners and lodged them in our calaboose on Monday last—a band of robbers having their headquarters on the Solomon, charged with stealing Government property and desertion." Hickok was also successful in halting the depredations of a group of men who were cutting timber on government lands and selling it to contractors working on the Kansas Pacific Railroad. The Topeka *Leader* reported Hickok brought in twenty-nine prisoners after a raid on their hangout along Paradise Creek. Presumably he also had a little help in that roundup.

Somehow, wherever he went, trouble followed him, even when he wasn't running down lawbreakers. Somehow, without knowing who he was, there was always someone who felt called upon to test his courage. There were thousands of men who lived in the West, worked, and went their way without ever raising their fists, let alone drawing a gun. Hickok, it appeared, couldn't walk down a street without arousing homicidal thoughts. His proud carriage, his acquiline features, and his somewhat challenging manner may have had something to do with it. To some knavish, ill-favored lout in a border saloon he must have seemed like a man well worth killing—out of sheer envy, if nothing else.

His career was full of stupid, meaningless encounters in which one or more men gave up their lives, thrashing about the sawdust and spittoons of a barroom floor, simply because of a few ill-chosen words. Hickok's temper, like his guns, was on a hair trigger. His revolvers came flashing out at the first sign of belligerence. He was always perfectly courteous to anyone without a chip on his shoulder, but a strong sense of survival made him quick to comply with the adage, "Shoot first and ask questions afterward."

"As to killing," he once told a newspaperman, "I never think much about it. I don't believe in ghosts, and I don't keep the lights burning all night to keep them away. That's because I'm not a murderer. It is the other man or me in a fight, and I don't stop to think—is it a sin to do this thing? And after it's over, what's the use of disturbing the mind? The killing of a bad man shouldn't trouble one any more than killing a rat or an ugly cat or a vicious dog."

All his victims, from first to last, were gunmen, men of violence, if not "bad men." They died with guns in their hands, often after firing the first shot. Given the choice of "him or me," Hickok never hesitated, in any Christian confusion of aims, to choose the other fellow. Compassion and forbearance were too expensive west of Kansas City.

A good example of the meaningless nature of gunplay on the border was to be found in the homicidal annals of December 1867. Late on the afternoon of December 22, dusty and thirsty from a long ride, he walked into a crossroads saloon in Jefferson County, Nebraska. It was a rough place, with planks and barrels for a bar and the whiskey drawn straight from the keg. A dozen herders were lounging in the place, propping themselves against the sod walls on cracker boxes.

Four of the men—Seth Beeber, Jack Slater, Frank Dowder, and Jack Harkness—decided they didn't like Hickok's looks. Perhaps they were offended by the fastidious frown with which he surveyed the accommodations.

The quartet began making loud remarks about Hickok's appearance, probable antecedents, and proclivities.

Hickok tried to ignore them.

Emboldened by his evident desire to avoid trouble, they came closer and turned nastier in their comments. Hazing a stranger, particularly if he were slightly citified, was a recognized rural sport. They were so intent on amusing themselves that they did not notice Hickok's eyes change to a chilly gun-metal gray, which was a sure sign that a cold, purposeful rage was gathering inside him.

Hickok ordered a drink. He raised it to his mouth to cut the dust of a long ride. Even in this prairie boozing den it was unthinkable that anyone would come between a man and his drink. One of his would-be tormentors, however, suddenly pushed Hickok just as he was about to swallow a mouthful of the stuff. The whiskey splashed all over his face and dripped down his mustachios. Hickok was shoved so hard his head banged against the rudimentary bar and his flat-topped black sombrero rolled on the floor.

Hickok whirled around and landed a backhander in the face of the man who pushed him, which sent the man reeling into a corner of the room.

"Now cut it out before this gets serious," he growled.

Instead the herders went for their guns.

Hickok shot and killed the man on his left but was wounded in the right shoulder by one of his companions. His right arm was useless. In a flash Hickok drew his other gun with his left hand and cut loose again with ambidextrous precision. The other three men went down, all with bullets in their heads. Even with the bullets flying around and shooting with his left hand, Hickok was so sure of his aim that he went for the head. A man shot in the torso can keep firing, even if fatally wounded, but a bullet in the head usually put him out of action.

When they drew up the casualty list a few minutes later, it was found that Beeber, Slater, and Dowder all were killed instantly with bullets in their brains. Harkness, sprawled in the corner after shoving Hickok and being backhanded in return, had his right cheek and part of his jaw shot away but survived. Ten years later his maimed face was still to be seen around Kansas City, a poignant lesson in the futility of gunfighting.

Hickok arrived in Kansas City a week later and holed up in a hotel room for almost two months until his shoulder healed.

He had an even narrower escape in North Platte, Nebraska, while pursuing a gang which had been stealing government property. North Platte was the terminus of the Union Pacific Railroad then, a lively place with a temporary population of five thousand. A measure of order had been restored only after a vigilance committee got out their hemp and strung up some of the more violent characters hanging around town.

At least two desperadoes escaped the curative rope, and when they learned that Wild Bill Hickok had come to town they decided to make a name for themselves at his expense.

Watching him enter the restaurant, they evolved a rather cute plan for disposing of him. Unfortunately they discussed their plan in loud, blustering tones and were overheard by a German immigrant girl on her way to work as a waitress in the restaurant.

She had just brought Hickok his dinner when she saw one of the men coming in the rear door, the other through the street entrance.

The waitress told Hickok what was happening in a barely understandable accent, but he got the idea.

"Thanks, little girl," he said. "Please stand to one side at once."

Before they could catch him in their cross fire, and probably before they realized what hit them, Hickok went into action. He caught the man at the front door just as he was raising his revolver, cutting him down with the gun from his left holster, then pivoted in one easy motion and shot the man coming in the rear door with his right-hand gun. Both

men were killed by shots spaced so closely together it
sounded like a single report.

The two nameless gunmen were dumped into a prairie
grave; Hickok was given the thanks of the vigilance committee and went on his way. Luck, too, it would seem, was
an ingredient in the career of a successful gunfighter.

Between hunting down lawbreakers, the government saw
to it that he earned his one hundred dollars a month by
assigning him as a scout and dispatch rider to the various
army forces, commanded in 1867 by Major General Winfield
Scott Hancock, trying to prevent a large-scale outbreak of
the Indians in western Kansas. That year public opinion had
demanded that an attempt be made at a peaceful settlement
with the Indians. The Medicine Lodge treaty was arranged
with the Southern Plains tribes, the hard-fighting Cheyennes,
Arapahoes, Kiowas, and Comanches, providing reservations
in the Indian Territory and promising that white settlers
would not invade the country between the Arkansas and the
Platte.

Hickok and most of his fellow plainsmen were convinced
that no piece of paper, signed, sealed, and beribboned though
it may be, would bring peace to the Indian country. They
were soon proved right. The younger Indians repudiated
their elders' word, and white settlers repudiated their government's.

Warrior bands of the Cheyenne attacked settlements and
stage stations along the Smoky Hill River. In return General
Hancock ordered the burning of Indian villages along the
Pawnee Fork.

Hickok was a scout in the summer campaigning that ensued, having been requisitioned by Hancock. The general
was a Civil War hero, had commanded a corps in the Army
of the Potomac, but he didn't understand Indian fighting.
The tribesmen, in brief, made a fool of him, luring him into

long, futile pursuits and attacking wherever his cumbersome columns could not reach. There would be no Gettysburg on the Great Plains, as a long line of Union generals was to learn, and very few of those muralistic charges so beloved of veteran cavalry generals. But the generals experienced in the formal campaigning of the East—aside from a few senior officers like Phil Sheridan, O. O. Howard, Nelson Miles, and George Crook—were a long time learning that they had to adapt their methods to the hit-and-run style of the Indians. The high-level blundering naturally made the job of Hickok and his fellow scouts all the more hazardous and difficult.

Hickok was employed largely in carrying dispatches from General Hancock's headquarters to the various columns in the field. Since a lone rider could be seen for miles on the plains, he had to ride by night and spend the days hiding in ravines or clumps of brush. Once he had a very close call with a band of Arapaho braves who rode into a gully where he had been holed up. He killed two of the tribesmen and then rode like hell for the head of the ravine. Out in the open he found himself between two larger bands of Arapahoes, for whom the braves in the ravine had been scouting. They spotted him and gave chase, but Black Nell managed to outrun them and Hickok made it back to Fort Hays without a scratch.

Late that summer Hickok was attached to the 7th Cavalry, whose commander was that ardent glory hound Lieutenant Colonel George Armstrong Custer. In some ways the two men resembled each other, particularly in their thirst for renown; one went down in history as the most famous of the Indian fighters, the other as the most celebrated of the gunfighters. Both were killed in the same year, in a manner peculiarly befitting the way they lived, in circumstances which would have delighted the playwrights of ancient Greece. Both affected shoulder-length ringlets and colorful garb, and there was no lack of the picturesque around Custer's headquarters with Hickok in his fancy beaded buckskins and Custer in his red scarf, specially tailored uniforms, and whorls of gold braid.

Hickok became something of a favorite in the Custer household at Fort Hays. To Colonel Custer he was "one of the most perfect types of physical manhood I ever saw." Furthermore, wrote Custer in *My Life on the Plains,* he was "entirely free of bluster or bravado . . . Wild Bill was a strange character, just the one which a novelist might gloat over. He was a plainsman in every sense of the word, yet unlike any other of his class.

". . . Of his courage there could be no question. It had been brought to the test on too many occasions to admit of a doubt. His skill in the use of the rifle and pistol was unerring, while his deportment was exactly the opposite of what might be expected from a man of his surroundings . . . He seldom spoke of himself unless requested to do so. His conversation, strange to say, never bordered on either the vulgar or blasphemous. His influence among the frontiersmen was unbounded, his word was law, and many are the personal quarrels and disturbances which he had checked among his comrades by the simple announcement that 'this has gone far enough,' if need be followed by the ominous warning . . . that the quarreller 'must settle it with me.'"

In none of the shootings in which Hickok was involved, Custer said, was there "a single instance in which the verdict of twelve fair-minded men would not be pronounced in his favor."

Custer's pretty wife, Elizabeth, was even more impressed by Hickok, to judge from her almost giddy description in her memoirs, *Following the Guidon,* in which she wrote:

"Physically, he was a delight to look upon. Tall, lithe, and free in every motion, he rode and walked as if every muscle was perfection, and the careless swing of his body as he moved seemed perfectly in keeping with the man, the country, the time in which he lived. I do not recall anything finer in the way of physical perfection than Wild Bill when he swung himself lightly from his saddle, and with graceful, swaying step, squarely set shoulders, and well-poised head, approached our tent for orders. He was rather fantastically clad, of course, but all that seemed perfectly in keeping with the time and place. He did not make an armoury of his waist, but carried two pistols.

"He wore top-boots, riding breeches, and a dark blue flannel shirt with scarlet set in the front. A loose neckerchief left his fine, firm throat free. I do not remember his features, but the frank, manly expression of his fearless eyes and his courteous manner gave one a feeling of confidence in his word and in his undaunted courage. He was the 'mildest mannered man that ever scuttled ship or cut a throat.' While on duty carrying despatches, he let no temptation lure him into the company of the carousers who acknowledged him as their king. His word was law and gospel in that little town, for even where no laws are respected, the word and will of one man, who is chosen leader, is often absolute . . .

"Wild Bill reminded me of a thoroughbred horse. Uncertain as was his origin, he looked as if he had descended from a race who valued the body as a choice possession, and therefore gave it every care. He not only looked like a thoroughbred, but like a racer, for he seemed even in repose to give evidence of great capabilities of endurance—of fine 'staying powers,' in his own vernacular. The days of the Greeks are slowly returning to us when the human form will be so cared for that no development it is capable of will be neglected . . ."

When Custer and the 7th Cavalry undertook a long reconnaissance into the Sioux country, Hickok was one of the scouts attached to his column—the "most prominent man among them," Custer said—as it moved out from Fort Hays to Fort McPherson on the Platte, then to the headwaters of the Republican, to Fort Wallace, and finally back to Fort

Hays after covering about a thousand miles of hostile territory. Hickok was detailed mainly to ride back to Fort Hays at intervals with Custer's reports on everything the column encountered. Since the country was swarming with hostiles, the courier service was much more dangerous than scouting and riding with the column.

Once Hickok and another scout named Jack Harvey were riding back to Fort Hays. About thirty miles west of Hays they came across a man who had been wounded and scalped but was still breathing. He told the scouts that his party of six men had been attacked by about fifteen Indians. His companions had disappeared, probably had been run down and slaughtered by the war party. A few minutes later the man died.

A dust cloud boiled up on the horizon, and Hickok and Harvey decided they'd better take cover in a hurry. They hid in a small ravine nearby just as the warrior band came back to the scene of their murder. The Indians examined the fresh tracks with interest, then raced along the lip of the ravine, hoping to catch sight of the newcomers. Just as they spotted Hickok and Harvey, the scouts opened fire and knocked several braves out of their saddles. The Indian band fled, not knowing exactly how many white men were in the ravine. Hickok and Harvey continued on down the ravine, which widened into the sandy bed of a dry river. The scouts thought they were safe now and could circle around to the south and reach Fort Hays. The Indians, however, had come back to the ravine and could be seen plunging down the steep slope toward them. Hickok and his partner sensibly took to their heels, being outnumbered at least six to one. The Indians evidently hoped to run them down before they could reach Fort Hays. The scouts' weary mounts began to falter.

Hickok decided on a bold maneuver. He and Harvey suddenly wheeled their mounts and charged straight back at their pursuers. They counterattacked with revolvers blazing away. The Indians were so surprised that they turned and ran for their lives. The two men made it back to Fort Hays without further interference from the Indians.

By the time winter closed over the prairies it was obvious that General Hancock, who carried a pontoon train with one of his unwieldy columns, would never be able to bring the Indians under control. He was sent back East to take up more suitable garrison duties. His successor was a man whose ability more than matched his prestige—Major General Philip M. Sheridan, young, aggressive, and hardheaded. In the closing year of the Civil War the hard-driving Sheridan had commanded the Cavalry Corps of the Army of the Potomac, had shattered Jeb Stuart's brigades at Yellow Tavern, cleaned out the valley of the Shenandoah with ruthless energy, and finally harried Robert E. Lee to the surrender at Appomattox. Sheridan, who had served on the frontier in his youth, had no illusions about proceeding against the Indians as he would against a civilized army. He was falsely credited with the slogan, "The only good Indian is a dead Indian," but it pretty well summed up his views. He did not waste his time reflecting that "the Plains Indians are the best light cavalry in the world," as so many officers kept saying in palliation of their failures, but set about plotting their defeat. Against six thousand warriors in the four dissident tribes, Sheridan had only a total of twelve hundred cavalry and fourteen hundred infantry, later augmented by the 19th Kansas Volunteer Cavalry, which was mustered into the federal service.

Sheridan hoped to make up for his inferiority in numbers by establishing an intelligence system which would enable him to strike at Indian concentrations before they could attack him. He enlisted several hundred scouts, Hickok among them, for service in the Department of the Missouri, a command which embraced Missouri, Kansas, New Mexico, eastern Colorado, and the Indian Territory. General Sheridan listened to anyone—scouts, settlers, Indian agents, plainsmen, friendly tribesmen—who could tell him anything about the movements and intentions of the restive Cheyenne, Arapaho, Kiowa, and Comanche tribes. He also tried to pacify the dissidents by liberal issues of beef and other rations. But the Indians were intent on war.

In July of 1868 the tribesmen broke loose along the border from the Arkansas to the Republican. The Cheyennes suddenly departed from their reservation near Fort Dodge and went on the warpath against a settlement of peaceful Kaw tribesmen near Council Grove, then massacred scores of white settlers in the vicinity. Large bands of Comanche and Kiowa warriors joined them in devastating the white settlements in the valleys of the Saline, the Solomon, the Smoky Hill, and the Republican. The Kansas frontier was at the mercy of the raiding bands until Sheridan could manage to pin down the elusive war parties. In September Sheridan sent a force of fifty scouts—not including Hickok—under Colonel George A. Forsyth in pursuit of Roman Nose and his Cheyenne raiders. Roman Nose turned on his pursuers September 17 on the Arickaree fork of the Republican. Forsyth and his scouts dug in on a small island in the shallow Arickaree and held off several hundred of Roman Nose's followers while a couple of his men slipped through the Indian lines and brought out a rescuing column from Fort Wallace.

Sheridan decided upon a winter campaign. It had never been tried before and brought an outcry of protest from his officers. But Sheridan reasoned that "the soldier was much better fed and clothed than the Indian," who hibernated in his winter lodges, improvidential always, half starved, ill-clad, debilitated by disease. He would catch the somnolent redskin, for once, at a disadvantage. One column under Custer, with Sheridan accompanying it, would strike for the Cheyenne villages in the valley of the Washita (which it did at dawn, November 27, killing Chief Black Kettle, 103 of his men, and an unreported number of women and children);

another would come up from Fort Bascom under Colonel A. W. Evans, and a third column would set out from Fort Lyon in eastern Colorado under General Eugene A. Carr. All three columns were to converge on the Indian winter camps around the headwaters of the Red River as their ultimate objective.

Hickok was assigned as a scout to the 5th Cavalry, with its headquarters at Fort Lyon. Several times he carried dispatches from the Colorado garrison to General Sheridan at Fort Hays during the autumn of 1868. In his *Memoirs*, General Sheridan wrote of the difficulty of finding bona fide scouts among the braggarts who lounged around frontier saloons. There were "plenty of so-called 'Indian scouts,' whose common boast was of having slain scores of redskins, but the real scout—that is, a guide and trailer knowing the habits of the Indians—was very scarce and it was hard to find anybody familiar with the country south of the Arkansas, where the campaign was to be made. Still . . . we managed to employ several men, who, from their experience on the plains in various capacities, or from natural instinct and aptitude, soon became excellent guides and courageous and valuable scouts, some of them, indeed, gaining much distinction." The general singled out Buffalo Bill Cody as a scout of great "endurance and courage" during his service with the 5th Cavalry in the same outfit as Hickok. Sheridan had no citation for Hickok, although he served quite as valiantly as Cody, presumably because Wild Bill fell out of favor with the army several years later for killing several troopers from the 7th Cavalry.

Soon after Hickok arrived at Fort Lyon he was sent out on a long solitary prowl northward to investigate reports that the country was alive with Cheyenne war parties, and he became involved in one of the most desperate incidents of his scouting career. He was returning to Fort Lyon on Sunday afternoon, September 10, 1868, when he came across a partly

burned wagon and several corpses on the grassy bank of
Kiowa Creek.

Less than an hour later he rode into the settlement of
Gomerville, about fifty miles southeast of Denver, which was
built around a sawmill on the creek. A short time before
Hickok arrived a courier had galloped in with the news that a
wagon train had been attacked, evidence of which was the
burned wagon Hickok came across up the creek. The men of
the settlement and from surrounding ranches decided to form
a company of militia and take after the Cheyenne band immediately. Hickok accepted command of the expedition.

With thirty-four men armed with everything from Henry
repeating carbines to smooth-bore muskets, Hickok scoured
the country between Kiowa Creek and the Republican River.
Not a sign of hostiles could be found. On the way back to
Gomerville, on the eighth day out, Hickok climbed to the top
of a table-shaped mesa with several companions to get a panoramic view of the countryside. The tableland was located
on the banks of Sand Creek, only a few miles from where
Colonel J. M. Chivington and his Colorado volunteers in 1864
attacked the defenseless lodges of the Cheyennes and killed
more than a hundred men, women, and children.

Almost immediately Hickok and his friends were spotted
on the mesa by a Cheyenne war party. Down below, not
more than a mile away, the plain was covered with tribesmen, several hundred of them in full regalia.

Hickok ordered the whole group to come up to the top of
the mesa and dig in for a siege. It was close to three o'clock
in the afternoon; the Indians had three or four hours of daylight in which to attack the settlers. "Immediately," Alva
Gomer wrote later, "Wild Bill ordered the men to fortify the
camp. With their spurs, with tin cups and with spoons and
tin plates, they scooped out a place in the soft sand large
enough to make a hiding place for all the men as well as for
most of the horses and mules, though a good many of these

latter were killed before the entrenchments were thrown up sufficiently high to protect them. It took hours to make the trenches, since half of the men had to stand guard to keep back the savages, while the other half used their improvised shovels or scooped the sand out with their hands. In all, about twelve holes were dug, large enough to afford shelter to the entire force of men and such of their horses as remained alive."

The mounted Cheyennes pressed their attack for all they were worth but found that frontiersmen, most of them crack shots, were harder to deal with than a cavalry patrol of that size. "Hickok carried a gun loaded with buckshot, with which he kept the Indians busy all afternoon. He was a crackshot, and so long as the Cheyennes remained within range, Wild Bill, Riley, Garrison and the other crackshots picked them off rapidly. Tiring of this, the Indians retired beyond gunshot, evidently deciding to starve out the defenders."

The besieged settlers were almost out of food and water; their ammunition was running low, and obviously they wouldn't be able to hold out much longer. They decided someone had better ride for help. Hickok nominated himself. None of his companions offered any vigorous objections.

When darkness finally enveloped the mesa, Hickok mounted Black Nell and plunged down the slope. He had to run a gantlet of fire as he passed between two bands of Indians, but his mare carried him swiftly beyond pursuit.

The historian of this affair, Alva Gomer, was a fourteen-year-old boy at the time it happened. He gathered an account of the fight on the mesa from the men involved, and quite probably it was as accurate as could be expected under the stress of events. His arithmetic may be questioned, however, when he states, ". . . I was awakened by the sound of a galloping horse. It was Wild Bill coming down the road to the mill. He had made the forty-five miles across rough country in less than three hours . . ." A ride of that distance, over broken and unfamiliar terrain, at night could hardly have been accomplished in three hours. In any case, Hickok arrived safely in Gomerville that night of September 18.

"In a few words he told his story," Gomer continued. "He wanted reinforcements and he must have them right away. Immediately riders began to scour the country to gather such men as were available. It was imperative that they should get back to the table mountain where the men were corralled before the break of day, or the entire outfit would be massacred . . . I shall never forget the ringing words of Wild Bill as the gallant little relief party started on its daring ride in the face of death. 'Follow me, boys!' he cried. 'This is a ride for life.'"

A score of men followed Hickok, Gomer recounted. "Before break of day they reached the table mountain. Wild Bill led them on with a storm of yells in order to deceive the Indians as to their numbers. If the Indians were to hold the ground, the rescue party would be lost. For this reason it had been necessary to get there before the light of day would disclose their small number to the Indians. But the Indians had had enough. They fled precipitately on hearing the yells. Thus, by a daring coup, Wild Bill saved thirty-four lives that would otherwise have been sacrificed."

With the thanks of Gomerville for leading its men safely through the encounter with the Cheyennes—well deserved if, as Gomer said, he brought the whole party out alive—Hickok returned to Fort Lyon. The garrison was preparing its expeditionary column to strike for the Indian Territory in conjunction with the columns from New Mexico and Kansas.

Hickok acted as guide for the vanguard under General Penrose, who struck through the Raton Mountains with three hundred men while General Carr followed with the main body. Winter campaigning in the mountains was tougher than the military commanders had expected. Wagons had to be slid down the slopes by wrapping their wheels in chains.

The going was so slow and difficult that supplies were used up faster than anticipated. Penrose's vanguard stumbled on through blinding snowstorms. General Carr's command, meanwhile, was having difficulty following their trail and catching up with them. Buffalo Bill Cody was Carr's chief of scouts.

Penrose's vanguard, guided by Hickok, made its way down the Cimarron, then struck south toward the Canadian. While Custer's 7th Cavalry was conducting its slaughter over on the Washita, the troopers from Fort Lyon were wandering through a countryside entirely deserted, desolate, and blizzard-swept.

Penrose finally camped on Polladora Creek, hoping that General Carr would catch up with him soon. His men were down to quarter rations; his mules were dying by the scores. The whole command nearly starved to death before a squadron sent out ahead by General Carr with a fifty-mule pack train loaded with supplies found them. The two forces were then reunited.

Hickok and Cody had "a jolly reunion around the campfires," Buffalo Bill wrote later.

Their jolly mood, it appeared from subsequent escapades, carried over the rest of the campaign, which ended without a shot being fired and was much like a powerful haymaker landed in empty air. General Carr picked five hundred of his healthiest men and with a score of scouts, including Hickok and Cody, proceeded south to the Canadian River. The rest of his force was left in a winter camp.

Carr and his troops halted a dozen miles from a new supply depot called Fort Evans, established for Colonel Evans and his 3rd Cavalry expedition from New Mexico.

Hickok and Cody undertook a private reconnaissance and came up with a valuable piece of information. A bull train loaded with Mexican-brewed beer was en route to Fort Evans from the west. "Wild Bill and I," wrote Cody in his autobiography, "determined to 'lay' for this beer. That very evening it came along, and the beer destined for the soldiers at Fort Evans never reached them." Cody, tantalizingly enough, did not record just how he and Hickok managed to hold up a whole supply train and ride off with its cargo, but presumably they had willing assistance from the troopers of the 5th Cavalry. The beer, said Cody, "went straight down the thirsty throats of General Carr's command." Apparently it was a highly profitable transaction for the two hijackers. "It was sold to our boys in pint cups, and, as the weather was very cold, we warmed it by putting the ends of our picket pins, heated red-hot, into the brew before we partook of it."

A monumental beer bust ensued. Cody said it was "one of the biggest jollifications it has ever been my misfortune to attend."

The jollification somehow resulted in bad blood between the American and Mexican scouts attached to Carr's command. The Mexicans apparently were excluded from the social affair. A feud was just beginning to develop when Hickok and four other scouts were ordered to ride to Camp Supply with dispatches for General Sheridan. When they returned they found that the Mexican-American feud was still simmering. "The Mexicans," Cody said, "often threatened to clean us out, but they postponed the execution of the threat from time to time."

The blowoff, as might be expected, occurred around the whiskey barrels of the sutler's establishment. Charged up on cheap whiskey, the Mexicans and Americans came to blows —but fortunately no gunplay—and assaulted each other with enthusiasm. By the time that soldiers came over from headquarters and reluctantly separated the contestants the sutler's store was a tangle of canvas, boards, broken barrels, and unlucky brawlers, all reeking of spilled whiskey.

A cursory investigation satisfied General Carr that Hickok and Cody were the principal aggressors in the brawl. "It is possible," Cody conceded later, "that both Wild Bill and I had imbibed a few more drinks than we needed that evening." There wasn't much the general could do in the way of discipline, however, as he was a blind man in that rugged country without the services of his scouts.

"There are plenty of antelopes running around this country, and we need a fresh supply of meat," General Carr said. "I suggest the two of you work off your excess energy by replenishing our commissary."

Late that winter the cavalry expedition returned to Fort Lyon without having fired a shot in anger. About the middle of March 1869 Hickok was given dispatches for Fort Wallace and quickly learned that, with the coming of spring, the Indians again were in a troublemaking mood.

He made the journey to Wallace without incident and was returning to Fort Lyon without having seen an Indian sign. He was growing a trifle careless, riding by day and sleeping by night, instead of vice versa as was standard practice for dispatch riders in Indian country. Shortly after noon one day he killed a buffalo a few miles from the mesa where he and the Gomerville settlers had fought off the Cheyennes about six months previously. On a gravel bar in the creek bed he built a driftwood fire—another careless gesture—and broiled himself a pair of choice buffalo steaks.

Hickok was just using his sleeve as a napkin after this repast when a roving band of seven Cheyennes, attracted by the smoke, appeared on the bank above the stream and descended on him with a wild burst of yells.

Hickok's revolvers came out in a flash and accounted for four of the warriors. The other three raced toward him with their lances. One rode up close enough to hurl his lance into Hickok's right hip just as Hickok shot him in the head.

The scout fell to the ground, badly wounded, but afterward claimed that he managed to kill the other two braves before they could escape.

in the summer of 1865 Dave Tutt and Hickok were good friends and frequent companions.

Enter Susanna Moore, maid of the Ozarks. Hickok had met her, too, while on a mission to Arkansas. She was a good-looking blue-eyed brunette who lived with her family in the Boston Mountains of what is now Searcy County.

Hickok stayed with her pro-Unionist family while prowling around that section with some of his fellow scouts. Romancing the mountain girls apparently was part of his job of collecting information, or maybe he was only following his natural inclinations. Susanna Moore, at any rate, fell in love with him.

She was a creature of strong emotions, like most of the mountain people. One morning when Hickok's band sallied forth to battle with a Confederate patrol near Gordon's Fort, Susanna insisted on riding along as a guide. Riding with the Confederates was a girl named Agnes Masterson, with whom she was on the unfriendliest terms, partly because their families were on opposite sides of the political fence. While the Union scouts and the Confederate patrol began shooting up the countryside, Susanna Moore and Agnes Masterson engaged in single combat. They fired at each other with single-shot pistols, but both missed. The girls jumped off their horses and flew at each other, shrieking and clawing, pulling hair and scratching each other's faces. They had now fought their way to the edge of a cliff and were flailing away toe to toe. Susanna suddenly grabbed her opponent and threw her over the cliff. Agnes Masterson would have been a goner except that she landed on top of a cedar tree and was rescued by her friends a short time later when the engagement was broken off and the Confederate patrol withdrew.

Susanna obviously was not a girl to be trifled with. Yet Hickok trifled. Susanna, perhaps, was a bit too possessive for a man intent on free-lancing his way through life.

Binding up his wound as best he could, Hickok rode slowly toward Fort Lyon. A few miles from the fort the next morning some woodcutters spotted him coming down the trail from the north. They reached him just as he was about to topple out of his saddle and carried him to the fort's hospital. Cody, who was at Fort Lyon when his friend was brought in, said Hickok had managed to wrench the spear out of his hip and was still clutching it. Later Hickok gave the spear to Cody, who treasured it to the end of his life.

Hickok's wound, inflicted by a broad-bladed spearhead, refused to respond to treatment by the army surgeon and kept suppurating.

He decided to go home, for the first time since leaving almost fourteen years before, as soon as he was able to travel. He arrived in Troy Grove early in April and submitted to the ministrations of his mother, his younger sisters, and the local doctor. On arrival, his sister Lydia later told a newspaper reporter (in an interview published in the Chicago *Record*, December 26, 1896), he "said nothing of his wound for several days, though he had Dr. Thomas dress it and care for it. We learned of it only when he asked for some lint to put a fresh bandage on it.

"Later it became necessary to lance the wound and scrape the bone. The doctor came one evening to perform the operation, but Bill would not take chloroform. The doctor made four cuts outward from the wound, making a cross with the lance. I was holding the lamp and began to feel myself growing faint. 'Here, give it to me,' said Bill. He took the lamp and held it while the doctor scraped away, never flinching once during the operation."

His wound began to heal. And once the excitement of homecoming began to wear off he felt the onset of boredom and restlessness. He was thirty-two years old; the past decade had been filled with constant action and adventure, and perhaps it was a little trying to attempt to explain to the womenfolk just how their gentle boy had turned into a man-killer.

The mild scandal over his flight from Troy Grove, when he feared that he had killed a fellow teamster, was recalled with irksome humor by his fellow townsmen.

After a month of lounging around the old homestead Hickok decided to visit one of his boyhood friends, Herman Baldwin, who now lived in Chicago.

Baldwin met Hickok at the LaSalle Street Station, and the two old friends adjourned almost immediately to a saloon in the St. James Hotel, where liquor might ease the strain of closing the gap between their lives.

Perhaps unwisely—but quite in character—Hickok had ventured on the excursion to Chicago wearing his fanciest buckskins and moccasins, beaded and fringed in the height of frontier fashion. Undoubtedly he expected that this costume would excite the admiration of the populace. Instead there were snickers and guffaws and rude references to the "long-haired squawman."

Hickok and his friend decided to visit a nearby pool hall for a quiet game of billiards. Here they found a half dozen loafers draped around the place and looking for a bit of excitement. They gathered around Hickok and Baldwin after sizing up the two newcomers and deciding the odds were not unfavorable.

"Say, leather-britches, where did you come from?" one of the hoodlums asked Hickok.

"I come from a part of the country where men mind their own business—a place you evidently never saw."

"You're a regular bull o' the woods, aren't you? I suppose everybody in your part of the country wears rawhide and picks his teeth with a Bowie knife."

"No," said Hickok mildly, "but everyone where I come from knows who his father was."

Highly affronted at this slur, the habitués of the pool hall quickly armed themselves with billiard cues and came flailing at Hickok. The cue was an unfamiliar weapon, but Hickok entered into the spirit of the jousting match with his usual enthusiasm. He and Baldwin seized their cues and laid about them with energy and precision. When the brannigan was over, their opponents were stretched out on the floor and Hickok himself was considerably the worse for wear. Next morning he returned to Troy Grove with his head swathed in bandages.

A few weeks later he received a letter from U. S. Senator Henry Wilson of Massachusetts, soon to be Vice-President. It read:

"A party consisting of several gentlemen, ladies and myself desire to spend a few weeks in the far West during the warm season, and I hope it will be our fortune to secure your excellent services as our guide. I have heard much concerning your wonderful exploits in the West, and of such a character, too, as commend you very highly for efficiency in the scouting service of the government.

"If it be possible for you to accompany our party as guide some time during the following month, please write me at once, care Willard's Hotel, Washington, indicating what compensation you will expect, and also from what point in Kansas we had best start on the tour. I shall leave to you the selection of a pleasant route, as your general acquaintance with the places of interest between the Missouri River and the Rocky Mountains better qualify you for deciding the trip that promises the most attractions . . ."

Hickok, being at loose ends, accepted the offer immediately. He replied to Senator Wilson that his fee would be five-hundred dollars, that it would be best to leave from Fort Hays late in June. Then he left Troy Grove for Hays City. It was the last time his mother or sisters would ever see him. In many ways, gentle as he could be in the company of those he liked and respected, he had become a stranger to them, given to brooding withdrawals and polite evasions.

The Wilson rubberneck tour of the Wild West, perhaps unexpectedly, turned out to be one of the more pleasant episodes of Hickok's career. Playing guide and nursemaid to a group of effete easterners would have irked many of his contemporaries, but for Hickok it was a delightful change from the uncouth types who peopled much of his life. Shortly after he met the Wilson party at Fort Hays, Mrs. Wilson put him at ease by saying, "You are with an unsophisticated crowd of Yankees who know just about as much about life on the Plains as they do about the dark side of the moon. Please keep a protective eye on us and see that none of us gets into any trouble."

Congressional junkets were then in their infancy, had not yet reached the heights of freeloading attained by later practitioners, but the senator and his friends did well by themselves. They wanted to "rough it" on the Plains—or claimed they did around dinner tables back East—but a minimum of discomfort and inconvenience was required. They traveled in spring wagons, with plenty of camp servants and a train of well-stocked commissary wagons that S. S. Pierce of Boston would have approved. The gentlemen of the party dressed themselves in the height of Washington fashion, cutaway coats, tight trousers, and silk hats, and kept flicking dust off their lapels with white silk handkerchiefs. The ladies, it must be said, were a little more sensible and wore traveling costumes of gray serge, with scarves and parasols to protect them from the dust and sun. Even in the heat of a prairie summer, however, they were armored to the point of suffocation in many layers of skirts and petticoats, chemises, whalebone corsets, bustles, waists, and drawers.

The Wilson party, as a matter of fact, was a sort of pioneering group for eastern and international society. In the next year or two it became all the rage to tour the West, shoot a few buffalo, patronize a few tame Indians, and sip iced champagne while taking in the splendor of a prairie sunset. Western tourism got its start that summer. In 1870 and 1871 such eminent sight-seers as James Gordon Bennett, the Jeromes of New York (who married into the British aristocracy and ultimately produced Sir Winston Churchill), the Earl of Dunraven, and the Grand Duke Alexis of Russia, whom Buffalo Bill taught to substitute a morning gargle in whiskey for tooth-brushing, toured the tamer parts of the Wild West.

Long after these glamorous caravans went on their way an army officer sardonically wrote (General H. E. Davies, *Ten Days on the Plains*) that their camp sites were marked for years afterward by a litter of empty champagne bottles. An archaeologist exploring the West in some future century, General Davies thought, might decide that the Plains were inhabited by a race which concerned itself with a curious ritual of drinking out of "black vases bearing the names of Mumm or Roederer."

Hickok's tourist excursion roamed westward in style, keeping well out of hostile country, taking in such sights as the forks of the Republican River, the Grand Canyon of the Arkansas, the old Sand Creek battlefield, Cheyenne Canyon, and Forts Lyon, Sedgwick, and Wallace. Under Hickok's knowing guidance they were treated to some spectacular scenery but no dangerous thrills. He entertained them occasionally with displays of his marksmanship and made a gallant (but entirely respectable) impression on the ladies. With considerable trepidation they tried some of the specialities of prairie cuisine, buffalo-tail soup, broiled cisco (a perch-like fish), salmi of prairie dog, stewed rabbit, filet of buffalo garnished with mushrooms.

The party returned to Fort Hays after five weeks, having suffered nothing worse than a few cases of sunburn and having to drink their wine at tepid temperatures when the ice gave out.

Before parting Senator Wilson and his fellow wayfarers gave a dinner at which Hickok was the guest of honor. The senator made a graceful little speech, complimenting Hickok on "the most pleasant trip I have ever made." Hickok, in return, allowed that temporary immersion in polite society had done him no harm.

Senator Wilson, on behalf of his friends, then presented Hickok with a brace of ivory-handled, custom-made army .44 pistols. Hickok came to prize them above all other possessions and subsequently wore them on dress occasions and used them in several not so dressy gunfights. These were the famous "white-handled guns" he carried to the end of his days.

CHAPTER 8

No God West of Hays City

Apprehensive over the rising hoodlumism, the minority of respectable citizens in Hays City insisted that Wild Bill Hickok stay around and take charge of law enforcement after he returned there with Senator Wilson's party. A pioneer resident of the place said of the pre-Hickok days, "The firing of guns in and around town was so continuous that it reminded one of a Fourth of July celebration from daylight until midnight. There was shooting when I got up and when I went to bed."

And an early historian wrote of Hays and the characters it attracted in the summer of 1869, "The town was lively but not moral. The streets were lighted from the reflection of the blazing lights of the saloons." In the saloons and dance halls "women gaudily dressed were striving to hide with paint and ribbons the awful lines which dissipation had drawn upon their faces. These terrible marks were not confined to the women, for many of the men had noses painted cherry-red by whiskey. To the music of violins and the stamping of feet the dance went on, and we saw in the giddy maze old men who must have been pirouetting on the very edge of their graves . . .

"This scene was duplicated in every saloon and in various dancehalls. Disturbances were frequent in all of them, and these were usually settled with six-shooters. There was no church, and on Sunday morning the chaplain came over from Fort Hays to read the Episcopal morning service from the freight platform. A large crowd assembled, only a few of whom bowed their head during prayer . . ."

Hays City was founded in 1867, a settlement of board shanties, tents, saloons, and dance halls, a few false-fronted buildings. It would have been merely a wide place in the trail had it not been for the extension of the Kansas Pacific, the Santa Fe trade, and the roaring business brought by soldiers from nearby Fort Hays. An offshoot of the old Santa Fe Trail brought wool and other products from New Mexico for storage in Hays' warehouses and eventual shipment east. Long trains of canvas-topped freight wagons, drawn by mules and oxen, came up the prairie trail, causing the occasional visitor with a poetic eye to remark that they looked like a great white fleet coming into port over the sea of grass. The mule drivers and bullwhackers accordingly behaved like a hell-bent horde of sailors loosed after a long voyage. To add to the turmoil, upward of two thousand soldiers from Fort Hays—including the hard-living 7th Cavalry—found what passed for pleasure in the town, which was only a mile or two from their barracks. A brawl between Custer's troopers and a mob of bullwhackers was the bloodiest spectacle this side of Shiloh.

Early in 1869 it was regarded as the most violently lawless town on the frontier. Early in January that year three Negro soldiers, troopers from the 10th (all-Negro) Cavalry, were taken from the jail and hanged in a midnight lynching spree. A few weeks later Colonel A. E. Nelson, the commandant at Fort Hays, had to send a squadron into the town and arrest fifty men to halt a riot, the exact cause of which was never determined. Boot Hill, needless to say, was soon well populated. Many years later this unhallowed burying ground was uncovered by workmen digging basements in what is now a neat and respectable residential district in the vicinity of Eighteenth and Fort streets. Seventy-five bodies were exhumed, most of them still wearing boots, a few in crudely fashioned coffins but the majority simply dumped into the ground. It was one of the largest Boot Hills in the West.

With the meeting of the north-south trails and the east-west rails, a clash between the wild men of Texas, New Mexico, and Arkansas and the slightly tamer, commercially minded men of the Middle Border was inevitable. The free spirits of the South simply were unable to comprehend why the sodbusters and businessmen of the Kansas trail towns weren't willing to let them run wild, shoot up the street lights, each other, and occasionally a heavy-footed citizen in exchange for spending all their pay in the stores and saloons. Why did those moneygrubbing Jayhawkers have to hire professional gunmen to deal with their fun-loving guests? Call them sheriffs or marshals, give them a tin star and the authority of the law—they were still killers from the southern viewpoint. Between the herders and drovers of Texas and the more settled people of Kansas, too, there was still considerable hostility carried over from the Civil War, a mutual feeling that accounts had not yet been balanced, which the harsh and continuing effects of Reconstruction did nothing to alleviate.

The day of the gunfighter was now beginning, a score of years during which the most durable and prolific of all American legends bloomed. Few mythologies have had so short and vivid a life. Much of the shooting, no matter how skillfully it has been glamorized by succeeding generations in various entertainment mediums, was over such squalid concerns as the services of a whore, a marked card, a spilled drink, a casual insult or affront. Much of it was done by juvenile delinquents in chaps and spurs, with no social workers to protect them from the ruthless town marshals. The marshals were answerable only to their own consciences, which in many cases had suffered from atrophy. In the post-war years, in the towns where the cattle trails met the railroads, the unruly young Southerners once again experienced a Yankee determination to keep them under control. North of the Kansas line and Parallel 36, as Emerson Hough (*The Story of the Outlaw*) saw it, they were brushing against a different way of life, "brisk, bustling, with plenty of Yankee energy and Yankee cash to stock ranches, build cities, string railroads, start packing plants and factories." The only way they could express their resentment at the encroachments of civilization was with bursts of fire from their six-guns.

"The frontier sheriff now came upon the western stage as he had never done before," Hough wrote. "The badman also sprang into sudden popular recognition, the more so because he was now accessible to view and within reach of the tourist and tenderfoot investigator. These were palmy days for the wild West."

Wild Bill Hickok was designated sheriff of Ellis County, in which Hays City was located, at a special election in mid-August of 1869. From his first day in office he showed the populace that he intended to stop the wanton killing and aimless rioting. He patrolled the streets carrying a sawed-off shotgun, wearing two revolvers, with a Bowie knife tucked in the sash around his waist. Stalking through the saloons and dance halls, his grim and unbending figure had a pacifying effect on most of the troublemakers. "His reputation," wrote Eugene Cunningham in his near-classic *Triggernometry*, "reacted for him and against the man encountered. Facing the terrible Wild Bill the average rough was inclined to be nervous. And in any gun battle split-seconds may be of terrific import."

Except for sporadic challenges to the new sheriff's gun-fighting reputation, Hays City became a much safer place to live, and the correspondent of the Topeka *Commonwealth* was soon able to report, "Hays City under the guardian care of Wild Bill Hickok is quiet and doing well."

A roving correspondent of the St. Louis *Republican* described Sheriff Hickok for his readers: "In physique he is as perfect a specimen of manhood as ever walked in moccasins or wore a pair of cavalry boots—and Bill is a dandy at all times in attire—a regular frontier dude. He stands more than six feet tall, has a lithe waist and loins, broad shoulders, small feet, bony and supple hands with tapering fingers, quick to feel the cards or pull the trigger of a revolver. His hair is auburn in hue, of the tint brightened but not reddened by the sunlight. He has a clean, clear-cut face, clean-shaven except for a thin, drooping, sandy-brown mustache, which he wears and twirls with no success even in getting an upward twist at either end. Brown-haired as he is, he has clear, gray eyes. He has a splendid countenance, amiable in look, but firm withal. His luxuriant growth of hair falls in ringlets over his shoulders. There is nothing in his appearance to betoken the dead shot and frequent man-killer, except his tread. He walks like a tiger and, aroused, he is as ferocious and pitiless as one."

The St. Louis newspaperman described an incident in which "Wild Bill came near furnishing, in his own person, the subject for a first-class funeral." Hickok was patrolling Front Street, Hays City's ramshackle Rialto, when "a small man, an Irishman by the name of Sullivan, jumped out in front of Bill with a cocked revolver, exclaiming: 'I've got you! Hold up your hands! Now I'm going to kill you, you——!' Up went Bill's hands. Sullivan then started off into a gloating dissertation about killing him, while Bill stood before him as rigid as the Apollo Belvidere." While Sullivan jabbered away, Hickok's hand was snaking toward his right holster. Suddenly he drew and fired, punctuating one of Sullivan's sentences.

"He talked his life away," Hickok remarked, holstering his revolver.

The once-garrulous Sullivan reposed under the anonymous soil of Boot Hill by nightfall.

Under less exasperating circumstances, however, Sheriff Hickok often managed to avoid ending arguments with a heavy .44 slug. "It was not his desire to bring on trouble or to kill anyone," wrote Frank A. Root and William E. Connelley in *The Overland Stage to California*. "One of his favorite ways in bringing a fellow to terms was clubbing with his guns. When occasion required, he could pound with ease an unruly cowboy or lawless thug until his face resembled a raw beefsteak." It was doubtful, however, whether his subjects appreciated these ministrations. Having one's face cubed into raw beefsteak could be a lot more humiliating than merely being shot; it was an insult to be pulped by a lawman's fists or guns, almost indecent, in fact. Fist fighting was not for Texans. "A Texan," according to Cunningham, "rather *disdained* so ineffective a method of dealing with an enemy. He was used to men, red and white and brown, who had to be killed to be settled."

Sheriff Hickok could be tolerant of and helpful to people who were in trouble rather than looking for it. He could show one face over the barrels of his double-action pistols, another to a luckless kid having a little trouble growing up.

One such beneficiary was Harry Young, the author of *Hard Knocks*, who gave Hickok high marks, as few others did, for gentleness and consideration.

Young, in his tender and foolish years, wandered into Hays City with forty dollars in his pockets. He immediately spent most of it buying champagne for a pioneer B-girl in one of the dance halls. Hickok had been watching Young and his money being separated with a sardonic eye. Late that night when the youth stood on the sidewalk outside the deadfall, ruefully fingering his last dollar and a half, Hickok came up to him with a sympathetic grin.

"What now?" Hickok asked the youth.

"Guess I'll have to go to work."

"Ever driven a six-mule team?"

Young shook his head.

"I'll show you the ropes," Hickok said, leading him into a nearby saloon. Hickok patiently taught Young how to tie the "government hamestring" on a mule's collar and harness a team to its wagon.

Next morning he took the youth out to the corral boss at Fort Hays. The latter tossed Young a collar and told him to tie the hamestrings. Young passed the test, and the head muleteer turned to Hickok with the comment, "You certainly drilled him well." Young drove mule teams around Fort Hays for six months and met a number of Hickok's other protégés, likewise rescued from less worthy endeavors. It was Hickok's own crime-prevention program.

Hickok could also back down gracefully under pressure which might prove fatal. His strict enforcement of the law incurred the wrath of one of the town's leading saloon-keepers, Jim Curry, a very tough citizen who had formerly driven a locomotive on the Kansas Pacific and scouted for the army.

A witness to their confrontal was C. J. Bascom, who many years later described it in a newspaper article (Kansas City Star, June 15, 1913): "A short time after Wild Bill was made marshal [sic] of Hays, Curry started his saloon and restaurant. As the proprietor of this institution he was under the constant surveillance of Wild Bill. One day Bascom went into his saloon to get his lunch and was invited by Curry to take a walk. They went to the most famous saloon ever established in Hays, or in fact, in any town along the Kansas Pacific. The proprietor of this saloon was Tommy Drum, a

Scotchman, a man always on the square and one who required no portion of the eternal vigilance bestowed by Wild Bill. Bascom and Curry found Wild Bill playing cards in Drum's saloon, sitting with his back to the door, but so far back that he anticipated no trouble from the position. But his judgment was at fault.

"Curry slipped up behind him and pressed his cocked revolver against his head, saying, 'Now, you son of a gun, I've got you!' Bill did not move a muscle. He showed no concern. He realized his danger but said in a casual way, 'Jim, you would not murder a man without giving him a show.' Jim replied, 'I'll give you the same show you would give me, you long-haired tough!' Everyone present knew the peril in which Bill stood, and the suspense was awful. Tommy Drum's oath was 'By the boot!' He was running about the saloon in great perturbation exclaiming, 'By the boot . . . by the boot!'

"Bill was really the only cool, self-contained man in the room, and remarked, 'Jim, let us settle this feud. How would a bottle of champagne all around do?' The manner in which Bill had taken the whole incident, and the unconcern with which he made this remark relieved the tension, and all burst out laughing. Tommy Drum opened a pint bottle of champagne for every one present. Curry and Bill shook hands and the feud between them was over."

Hickok bought back his life with a conciliatory gesture and a few pints of champagne on that occasion. But Jim Curry, for all his hotheadedness, was a fairly reasonable man, not a homicidal psychopath, such as many who made the mistake of challenging Hickok. For such creatures as were bent on assassination Hickok had a seventh sense that brought his guns out in a flash. He never hesitated or paused to inquire into motives—the slightest indication of hostility and his guns went into action. A lawman who was determined to stay alive had to have the jump on his opponents; he was a minority of one, with no friends, a few sympathizers, and rarely a deputy to back his play. Too often, as so many of his contemporaries proved by their deaths, a momentary benevolence could prove fatal. Hickok did not intend to die of an excess of benevolence.

Certainly few in Hays City appreciated his efforts to keep a lid on the town. As Bascom said in his Kansas City *Star* article, "Bill was ruling the town with an iron hand. It was something unusual and unexpected. They did not know just what to think nor how long this rule would last." The town-taming peace officer was indeed something new to the frontier; until now the constabulary of the various border towns was expected to maintain a passive attitude, cluck disapprovingly at murderous antics, and haul away the bodies. Hickok was the pioneer of strict law enforcement, and the Earp and Masterson brothers, Pat Garrett, Billy Tilghman, etc., came along several years later, down a trail broken by Hickok.

Thus many had to be convinced the hard way of Hickok's earnest intention to keep the peace. Bascom told of two soldiers from Fort Hays, armed and belligerent, who stopped the new sheriff one day on Front Street. "One of them said, 'So you are the long-haired son of a gun that *Harper's Magazine* talks so much about. I enlisted for the purpose of coming out here and doing you up.' He drew his revolver, and the other men stood by to help." Hickok talked his way out of that situation, but others required more drastic measures.

Shortly after that incident Hays City was troubled by the presence of one Bill Mulvey, who had frequently terrorized his home town of St. Joseph, Missouri, and had come West in search of more ferocious amusements. Mulvey was quiet enough when sober, it was observed, but overindulgence brought on an urge to fire his guns in all directions and watch the citizenry scampering for their lives.

One day Mulvey cut loose on Front Street while Hickok was in another part of town, knowing the sheriff would quickly be attracted to the scene. "I'm taking over the town,"

139

Mulvey bellowed. No one cared to dispute the point while Mulvey was brandishing his pistols.

Hickok hurried around the corner to be confronted by Mulvey with both guns ready for action.

"You're under arrest," Hickok announced.

"What for?"

"Disturbing the peace."

"Looks like I've got the winning hand," Mulvey said, waving his pistols triumphantly.

Hickok glanced at the guns and admitted, "I guess I can't beat that pair."

"I'm running you out of town," Mulvey announced. "Turn around and start marching for the town limits."

Hickok glanced over Mulvey's shoulder and cried out, "Don't shoot him, boys; he's only fooling around!"

It must have been an old trick even then, but it worked on the whiskey-fuddled Mulvey. His attention was diverted just long enough for Hickok to draw and shoot him through the head. Without further ado Bill Mulvey was removed to Boot Hill and buried with his entire estate—boots, guns, and a half-empty bottle of whiskey.

So far Hickok had been meeting liquored-up amateurs on the streets of Hays City. In October of 1869, however, a full-fledged gunfighter stepped on stage with a long string of victims on his record. His name was Jack Strawhan, and his gun was notched like a corncob. Like Bill Mulvey, he came to Hays City with the avowed purpose of putting away the vaunted Wild Bill Hickok. One of many claimants to the title of "fastest gun in the West," Strawhan had many of the town's sportsmen betting on him to fulfill his boast.

Strawhan and Hickok had met before, under circumstances that still galled Strawhan and determined him on vengeance. Some months before Hickok had paid a brief visit up the line at Ellsworth. Strawhan was on a drunken rampage and had the town terrorized. The sheriff and his deputy asked Hickok to help them take him into custody.

The three men advanced on Strawhan with drawn guns, and Strawhan knew he would be killed if he tried to shoot it out. Strawhan dropped his gun belt but put up a violent struggle when Hickok and the other two officers put the arm on him.

The jailhouse at Ellsworth—usually the first municipal building erected, of necessity—was still under construction. So Strawhan was manacled to a post, in public view, and kept there until he sobered up. Hungover, parched for a drink, Strawhan took his cure with very bad grace under the rude stares of the citizenry and swore he would kill Hickok for his part in the humiliation.

Now Strawhan had come to Hays City to keep his promise. He kept watching Hickok on the streets and in the saloons but never making an overt move, knowing that Hickok's guns would come out at the first hint of a provocation.

One day late in October Hickok was standing at the bar of Tommy Drum's saloon with several friends. Strawhan had been stalking him that day, and now he slipped through the side door of the establishment. Hickok, as usual, was alert. His back was to Strawhan, but he was watching everything that went on through the mirror behind the bar. He observed Strawhan's furtive movements while pretending to be absorbed in the conversation of his companions.

Hickok waited until Strawhan drew his heavy navy Colt, then fired at the man who had every apparent intention of shooting him in the back.

Strawhan hit the floor with a bullet over his right eye.

According to some accounts, including that of Buffalo Bill Cody, Hickok whirled and fired with one of his .44 revolvers. Others said Hickok fired over his shoulder, a very awkward maneuver. The more likely version was that he had slipped one of the two .41 Derringers he often carried in his waistcoat into his hand as he watched Strawhan sidle up to him. The distance between them was only about ten feet when Hickok fired, well within the effective range of the miniature pistols.

The sheriff bought a drink for the house while the undertaker was being summoned.

Hickok was suddenly, and temporarily, a popular man in Hays City. That night the brass band paraded out to serenade him.

When it came around to the election on November 2, however, the voters repudiated Hickok's ironhanded rule of the town. They elected his deputy, Pete Lanahan, to the sheriff's office by a vote of 114 to 89.

Hickok stayed on to serve out his term, which ended January 1, 1870, but various miscreants refused to allow him to leave his office in peace and dignity. A professional pugilist named Patterson came to Hays City to open a gymnasium and awaken enthusiasm for what was then known as "the manly art of self-defense." It was not easy to persuade the gun-bearing populace that fists were preferable to firearms in settling a dispute. Patterson needed publicity. First he rigged up a ring and gave a public demonstration of the efficacy of fisticuffs with several of his more advanced pupils as targets. Hays City was still unimpressed.

Patterson, who may or may not have suffered from occupational head noises, then conceived what seemed to him to be a splendid idea to attract attention. He would challenge Sheriff Hickok.

One evening he stepped up to Hickok in a crowded saloon and said, "I hear you're supposed to be the toughest man on the border. I say you're not, Hickok. I'm the best fighter in these parts and I can prove it."

"Where will the shooting commence?" Hickok inquired.

"No shooting, Hickok. I know you're supposed to be the best pistol shot on the Plains. Any puny little weakling can shoot another man with a gun. It takes a real man to fight it out with his hands."

Hickok bowed and said, "Shall we step outside, Professor?"

A crowd gathered around them in the street outside Tommy Drum's saloon. Patterson assumed the scientific posture of the trained pugilist. Hickok stared at him in amazement for a moment, then "sailed into the Professor like a red-hot ball from a columbiad." In a few minutes Patterson was battered into insensibility by Hickok, who had never heard of the Marquis of Queensberry. Patterson left town a few days later to set up his gymnasium in another locale.

In the process of bringing a measure of law and order to Hays City, Hickok aroused the enmity of the troops stationed at the nearby fort, particularly the 7th Cavalry, which had a regimental leaning toward rowdyism and liked to be situated near a wide-open town where saloons and whore houses could be wrecked and mass brawls staged without unseemly interference by the residents. The tragedy of the Little Big Horn six years hence cast a collective halo over Custer's hard-riding horsemen, but, glorification aside, many of them were a bad lot, jailbirds and desperadoes in uniform, sufficiently callous to massacre Indian villages like Black Kettle's on the Washita. Civilians unfortunate enough to live in their vicinity found them not much more preferable to the savages they were being protected from.

This applied to some of the regiment's officers as well as the men, particularly to the commanding officer's younger brother, Captain Tom Custer. Tom Custer not only had some of Colonel Custer's vainglorious traits but, unlike the latter, was a violent drunkard. The colonel was always bailing his brother out of trouble, just as his superiors were frequently called upon to rescue him for the consequences of his arrogance and disobedience. When the Sioux chief Rain-in-the-Face was a prisoner of the government, Tom had his henchmen hold him down while Tom beat and kicked the Indian.

143

Tom Custer expiated some of his sins, perhaps, by dying at the head of C Troop, 7th Cavalry, at the Little Big Horn. And Rain-in-the-Face, coming across his body on the battlefield, tore out his heart and liver and ate them, or so he claimed afterward.

During Wild Bill Hickok's reign in Hays City, Tom Custer got out of hand while Colonel Custer was sojourning at Fort Leavenworth. Roaring drunk, he rode through town shooting at lights and windows. One of his favorite tricks was to ride into a saloon to the dismay of fellow patrons. Once he rode his mount into a pool hall and tried to force his horse to jump up on a table. When the horse balked Custer shot him then and there.

Hickok was a friend of Colonel Custer's but he couldn't tolerate any more trouble from his younger brother. Next time Tom Custer came whooping into town Sheriff Hickok caught up with him, yanked him off his horse, arrested him, and stood by while the justice of the peace fined him for disturbing the peace.

No one had ever treated the spoiled young man like this before, unfortunately, and he meditated revenge.

On New Year's Eve—Hickok's last night in office—Tom Custer and three brawny sycophants from his troop rode into Hays City to settle accounts with Hickok. The town was already bulging with soldiers and civilians stoking up for a bleary welcome to the new year. Custer and his three assistants stationed themselves in Paddy Welch's saloon and waited for Hickok to show up.

Hickok strolled into the crowded, dimly lighted saloon. Before he could belly up to the bar the three soldiers pounced on him, two of them jumping him from the rear and pinning his arms back while the third slowly drew his gun. There was a desperate struggle during which Hickok managed to free himself, only to find that he had been disarmed. Custer's

144

troopers were bearing down on him as the other patrons scattered for cover.

For a moment it looked as though Hickok was finished. Paddy Welch, behind the bar, proved himself a friend in that instant. He tossed Hickok a loaded revolver. The moment it landed in his palm Hickok began firing.

When it was all over, gun smoke enveloped the scene. The only sound was that of bodies thudding against the floor.

The smoke cleared, revealing Hickok still on his feet . . . three dead soldiers on the floor.

Captain Tom Custer lit out for Fort Hays. His big brother wasn't available, being at Leavenworth for the holidays, so he went to Phil Sheridan, now a lieutenant general commanding the whole frontier army, with his complaint that Wild Bill Hickok was mowing down the fun-loving troopers of the 7th Cavalry. Little Phil exploded in wrath. He had been friendly to Hickok when the latter served in his scouting force, but he wasn't going to stand for a trail-town sheriff shooting up his troops. He issued an order for Hickok to be brought in "dead or alive." Highhanded, yes, but there was "no law west of Abilene and no God west of Hays," and Sheridan was willing to fill the vacuum.

Someone at the fort, probably one of Hickok's friends among the scouts, rode into Hays City that night and warned Hickok to get out of town, unless he felt capable of taking on the whole 7th Cavalry. Hickok thought he ought to stick around until midnight, when his term officially expired, but his friends, among them John W. McDaniels, persuaded him not to be a stickler about the terms of his agreement with Ellis County. McDaniels was the engineer on a Kansas Pacific freight train scheduled to pull out for Kansas City. He hurried Hickok over to the yards and into the cab of his locomotive just as a mob of horsemen headed out of Fort Hays for the town. "I made passenger time with that freight getting clear of Hays that night," McDaniels said later. A few hours later, at Ellsworth, Hickok dropped off the freight, lucky to be alive and able to celebrate the new year of 1870.

The rest of that winter Hickok shuttled back and forth, along the line of the Kansas Pacific, between Ellsworth, Topeka, and Kansas City, an aimless and jobless period in which he spent most of his time lounging around barrooms, cardrooms, and hotel lobbies. He was just about the most famous—or notorious, depending on the viewpoint—character on the border that winter. In less than five months as sheriff of Ellis County he had gunned down eight men. It was considered a privilege to buy him a drink, lose money to him at the poker table, listen to him yarning about the Indians.

Ellsworth, on the Smoky Hill River, was beginning to come into its own as a trail town—a fact attested by the number of thugs, sharpers, and prostitutes arriving on every train. The whores worked their way west much as their European sisters worked their way east, beginning in Paris and ending in Port Said. When they were young and pretty they paraded through the parlors of the plushy, mirrored bordellos of Chicago and St. Louis, then they slid down the line a bit to Kansas City or St. Joe, and finally, raddled and shopworn, abandoned by their pimps, they drifted out to the end of the line where men could not be choosy, Hays City, Ogallala, Abilene, Wichita, Dodge City, Trinidad, Pueblo. The dance-hall girls, who were in a separate class, since their favors were not so openly on the market, and in many cases not for sale at all, were somewhat more attractive.

The dance-hall girl has become a romantic figure in movie and television reconstructions of the Old West—a high-spirited lass capable of holding her own against the rough-necks who sought her favors. For a grimmer and more real-istic picture of how the girls came West, it is instructive to read Miguel Otero (*My Life on the Frontier*) on the subject. Otero, before he became governor of New Mexico, was familiar with all the Kansas trail towns and a clear-eyed observer and historian of their earliest days. In his now often neglected memoir he wrote:

"Wholesale trafficking in female human flesh . . . during those frontier days was more horrible than the atrocities committed by the wildest Indians. In order to keep the dance halls filled with girls, the owners would stake some woman to go back East and bring in a fresh lot of girls. They would be induced to come West under the pretext that they could obtain work in some hotel or private family at much better wages than they were receiving in their home towns. But when they reached their destination, they would find themselves forced to accept a life of debauchery, or be thrown into the street in a strange town, there to starve to death among the riffraff.

"It was no uncommon sight to see a group of dance-hall owners, badmen and pimps gathered at the depot to meet the train on which their victims, a cargo of fresh young girls, were coming to their inevitable ruin. They gathered on such occasions for the purpose of being on the ground and seeing with their own eyes whether their orders had been properly filled.

"In order to expedite delivery, assignments were generally made on the depot platform by the smiling procuress who had conducted the party—much as a horseman would pick his horses or mules at a country fair. It was never long before the entire cargo had been initiated into the necessary accomplishments of the trade, drinking, smoking, snuff-dipping, as well as the art of roping the improvident sucker . . ."

The newly recruited girls could expect little in the way of western chivalry, such as she may have read or heard about back East. A visitor to Ellsworth in its early days (quoted in Floyd B. Streeter's *Prairie Trails and Cow Towns*) said its population consisted of "the tall, long-haired Texas herder, with his heavy jingling spurs and pairs of six-shooters; the dirty, greasy Mexicans with unintelligible jargon; the gambler from all parts of the country, looking for unsuspecting prey; the honest emigrant in search of a homestead in the great free west; the keen stock buyers; the wealthy Texas drovers; dead beats, cappers, pickpockets, horse thieves, a cavalry of Texas ponies, and scores of demi-monde."

Hickok put up at the Grand Central Hotel, which was more central than grand, and soon was embroiled in trouble. It involved the chief reason for his stay in Ellsworth, the transitory affections of a dance-hall girl named Emma Williams. Until Hickok came on the scene she had favored a local hoodlum named Bill Thompson, who fancied himself a gunfighter. Thompson was enraged when Emma indicated her preference for Hickok. It was said that Emma was beautiful, but then all women in western legend, like the heroines of tabloid murder stories, are beautiful; more important, she was available, and that was the main thing on the woman-hungry frontier.

Thompson decided a bullet was the only cure for his rival and followed Hickok to a restaurant the night of February 17, 1870.

Hickok was soon to adopt the sensible practice of always sitting with his back to a wall and with a view of all the approaches, but this night he sat with his back to the door.

He looked up as the waiter was bringing his soup. Suddenly and wordlessly panic transformed the waiter's face. Hickok dove under the table.

A second later Thompson, coming up behind him, cut loose with his revolver. There was considerable damage to the crockery, but Hickok was unharmed.

He drew a Derringer, fired up at the would-be assassin, watched him spin around with a bullet in his brain and crash to the floor.

Then he resumed his place and told the waiter, "All right, bring me another bowl of soup."

The coroner's jury, convened the next morning, quickly brought in a served-him-right verdict on the late Bill Thompson.

Later that winter, the charms of Emma Williams apparently having palled, he went to Topeka for several months. The state legislature was in session and the town was lively. Many of his old friends were sojourning there for the winter, a few as legislators, others hoping to influence the legislators, and still others looking for easy pickings in the gambling houses. The atmosphere of a frontier capital, boozy, easygoing, and congenial, suited him fine for the time being.

Hickok spent much of his time at the home of Buffalo Bill Cody and his wife, Louisa, who had settled there for the winter. Mrs. Cody related that she met Hickok for the first time at a dance in the ballroom of one of the hotels.

On being told that her husband was going to introduce her to Hickok, Mrs. Cody exclaimed, "What! You mean that killer?"

"Yes," Cody replied. "He doesn't dance much but he said he was going to dance with you if he broke his leg. I want you to look your prettiest."

"For a man-killer?" Mrs. Cody protested. "Why, Will, I would be afraid to death of him."

Mrs. Cody wrote in her memoirs that she changed her mind about Hickok the moment her husband brought him forward and "a mild-appearing, somewhat sadfaced man bent low in a courtly bow."

She confided later that "I was so happy to find mildness where I had been led to expect there would be the most murderous of persons. Instinctively I looked about for revolvers. There was none, not even the slightest bulge at the hips of the Prince Albert coat he wore. I was happier than ever. We danced, and I must confess that we danced and danced again."

Hickok also spent considerable time that winter with a

149

friend from his army-scouting days, Captain H. C. Lindsay, who now operated a livery stable in Topeka and served as a deputy sheriff. He often made the rounds of the Kansas Avenue saloons with Lindsay.

On one such patrol in mid-March, in a saloon at Sixth Street and Kansas Avenue, they came across a man whom Hickok had booted out of Hays City a few months previously for stirring up more than his share of trouble. The bad man was in his cups.

Pot-valiant, he sneered at Hickok, "I hear the 7th Cavalry ran you out of Hays just like you did it to me."

Hickok shrugged and started to walk away.

"Wait a minute," the other man said. "You ran me out of Hays; now I'm going to run you out of Topeka."

He started to draw his gun, an unfortunate gesture interrupted when Hickok pulled out his own revolver and rapped him over the skull with the barrel.

"Now," said Hickok, after assisting the man to his feet, "you have just enough time to catch the night train for Kansas City. Go to Lindsay's livery stable and have yourself driven to the station. Tell the driver to report to me when he gets back. And if I ever see you again I'll put this gun to the use it was intended for."

Lindsay refused to arrest Hickok, despite the latter's argument that he had breached the peace. Next morning Hickok went into police court and insisted on being tried for disturbing the peace. The Topeka *Commonwealth* reported, "Wild Bill Hickok was fined $5.00 and costs yesterday for punching the head of some unfortunate mortal, whose name we did not learn."

Early that spring something far more worrisome than stray characters with a grudge began to trouble him. His eyes had been bothering him for some time, and whenever he looked into lights of any kind they were edged with "halos as bright as January sundogs." Even the comparatively mellow lamplight hurt his eyes. Hickok worried over his eyesight but kept it to himself. What use was a blind gunfighter? If his enemies heard about it they'd come streaking toward him like buzzards.

Out of the blaze of prairie suns and the eye-searing glitter of mountain snows, Hickok hoped the trouble would clear up by itself, but it didn't. He finally went to a physician.

The diagnosis was ophthalmia, an inflammation of the eyeballs. It could become progressively worse. The doctor suggested return visits and a change to gentler occupations.

CHAPTER 9

South of the Railroad

For Wild Bill Hickok the period between the spring of 1870, when he learned that his eyesight was failing, and mid-April of the following year was a season of bitter discontent. Added to his doubts about the future was his failure as a pioneer Wild West showman (described in a subsequent chapter) and bad luck at the poker table. His fortunes ebbed to the point, in fact, where early in 1871 he signed on as an army scout again at Fort Harker. He had a strong sense of personal dignity and was convinced that he looked ridiculous wearing smoked glasses—a necessity to protect his eyes against sun and snow glare—while out on scout.

He was still at Fort Harker early in April when an emissary arrived from Abilene. The latter was Charles Gross, representing Joseph G. McCoy, the new mayor of the city. His proposition was that Hickok assume the office of city marshal of Abilene, the former incumbent having just been killed.

Hickok accepted forthwith; the job promised higher pay, added fame, and the excitement to which Hickok was addicted from the beginning to the end of his life.

He walked into the wildest of the Kansas cow towns at the peak of its career as the railhead of the Chisholm Trail—only Dodge City a few years hence possibly exceeded it in violence. Hundreds of thousands of Texas cattle bellowed from the surrounding prairie. Inside the town two thousand cow hands were running wild. One man, with the help of two deputies, was expected to keep a semblance of order, protect property, and be responsible for the lives of a thousand persons populating the town north of the railroad tracks, north of the saloon and red-light district.

Abilene had existed for exactly a decade when Hickok rode in to pin on the marshal's star. It was laid out in town lots in 1860. Asked for a suggestion on what to name it, the wife of an early settler proposed Abilene, a name out of the Bible, because it meant "city of the plain." The Kansas Pacific reached Abilene in March of 1867, and shortly after that the Chisholm Trail became the main avenue of the Texas cattle drives. Before that the four-pronged Shawnee Trail through Missouri and eastern Kansas had been used by the Texans. The Texas herds, however, were tick-infested and spread a cattle fever to the northern spreads, until the Kansas legislature passed a law forbidding Texas cattle to enter four eastern counties, forcing the drovers to seek railheads farther west. Thus Abilene, Ellsworth, Wichita, Newton, and later Dodge City came into being.

A young cattle dealer named Joseph G. McCoy, Illinois-born, came to Abilene a few months after the Kansas Pacific reached there. It was then a small settlement of log huts, sod houses, a store, and a saloon. Not very promising, except to the visionary mind of Joseph McCoy. He sank most of his money into a trainload of pine lumber from Hannibal, Missouri, and built a complex of loading pens, chutes, and corrals on the railroad tracks east of town. Then, with missionary zeal, he went to Texas to persuade the cattlemen to bring their herds up the Chisholm Trail, six hundred miles long,

153

two hundred to four hundred yards wide. The trail came up from the Rio Grande; crossed the Colorado River at Austin, the Brazos near Waco; passed through Fort Worth; forded the Red River, and proceeded through Indian Territory, crossing the Washita, the Canadian, and the Cimarron, before reaching the Kansas line at Caldwell.

Thousands of cattle started coming up the trail from then on, and Abilene prospered accordingly. Four hotels, ten boardinghouses, five dry-goods stores, and a dozen saloons were operating by 1870. The largest of the hostelries was the Drover's Cottage, built by Joseph McCoy from his stacks of surplus lumber; it had a hundred rooms, barn and corral space for fifty carriages and a hundred horses, and practically every big cattleman in the West signed its register one time or another. By 1879 "Texas Abilene," the cow pokes' playground, had sprung up south of the railroad tracks. The redlight district, also necessary for the accommodation of the influx from Texas, moved around like a gypsy camp—largely due to harassment from the "decent women in town." At first it was conveniently located, close to the heart of Abilene. Then in 1870, before Abilene was incorporated as a city, the board of trustees evicted the whores and they settled a mile outside the town limits, along Mud Creek, in a shanty town of their own. A few months later they were driven from Mud Creek, too, and scattered to other Kansas towns where the "decent women" weren't quite so intolerant of their fallen sisters. When the cattle trade boomed early in 1871 they were back again, gaudy, defiant, and prosperous. Outraged that the "soiled doves" again had found cotes in the middle of the town, more than a hundred women marched on the city council with a petition demanding "active measures for the suppression of brothels." The councilmen were in a terrible dilemma: it was bad business to kick out the whores; 't was equally difficult to shut off the nagging of their wives.

The councilmen settled the matter by setting aside a tract

in the southeast section of town as a red-light district and decreeing that prostitution must confine itself to that area. An Abilene merchant, Theophilus Little, later recalled, "These women built houses on this ground, and it was covered with them. Some of them were more than a hundred feet long. Beer gardens, dance halls, dancing platforms, and saloons galore were there. It was called the Devil's Addition to Abilene—rightly named, for hell reigned there supreme. Hacks were run day and night to this addition. Money and whiskey flowed like water down hill, and youth and beauty and womanhood and manhood were wrecked and damned in that valley of perdition."

After eating trail dust for six hundred miles—and surviving Indian attacks, gangs of rustlers, flooded rivers, drought, blizzards, prairie fires, and incessant toil—the cow poke was ready for anything, including that "valley of perdition," when he hit Abilene. Once released from the custody of the trail boss, with a year's pay in his pockets, he wanted a howling good time and no restraints on his high spirits. In appearance, habits, and temperament he was an appalling sight to the Kansans, vigorously as they strived to separate him from his money. A Topeka *Commonwealth* reporter described the typical cow hand as "unlearned and illiterate, with but few wants and meager ambition. His diet is principally Navy plug and whiskey, and the occupation of his heart is gambling . . . He generally wears a revolver on each side, which he will use with as little hesitation on a man as on a wild animal. Such a character is dangerous and desperate, and each one generally has killed his man. There are good and even honorable men among them, but runaway boys and men who find it too hot for them even in Texas join the cattle-drovers and constitute a large proportion of them. They drink, swear and fight; and life with them is a round of boisterous gaiety and indulgence in sensual pleasures."

On being paid off outside Abilene, the cow poke rode into

town and first had a few drinks to prepare himself for the ordeal of "duding up": a long soak in a hot bath, a thorough currying at a barbershop, and finally a visit to young and enterprising Jacob Karatofsky's Great Western Store for town clothes. Then he plunged into the pleasures of "Texas Abilene," the gambling tables, William H. Mitchell's Novelty Theater with talent "direct from Kansas City," the saloons, and dance halls. Above all, the dance halls. The Texan was an enthusiastic, noisy, and rollicking fellow on the dance floor who demanded a partner capable of standing up under his wild exertions.

Joseph McCoy, the true founding father of Abilene, looked upon "scenes of abandoned debauchery" in the dance halls with amazement and wrote in his *Historic Sketches of the Cattle Trade of the West and Southwest:* "With the front of his sombrero lifted at an angle of fully forty-five degrees, his huge spurs jangling at every step or motion, his revolvers flapping up and down like a retreating sheep's tail, his eyes lit up with excitement, liquor and lust, he [the cow poke] plunges into it and 'hoes it down' at a terrible rate in the most approved yet awkward country style, often swinging his partner off the floor for an entire circle, then 'balance all,' with an occasional demoniac yell near akin to the war whoop of the savage Indian."

Along Texas Street, or "Hell Street," as it was more popularly known on the other side of the tracks, the saloons were open twenty-four hours a day to accommodate the hundreds of cow hands milling around and throwing money away with both hands. They included such establishments as the Alamo, the Bull's Head, the Applejack, the Old Fruit, the Elkhorn, the Pearl, Jim Flynn's, Tom Downey's, the Lone Star, the Trail, and the Longhorn.

The most elegant, patronized by trail bosses, cattle dealers, high-rolling gamblers, and other moneyed types, was the Alamo. It fronted on Cedar Street, with three sets of double-glass doors that were folded back night and day. Several large paintings of nudes, voluptuous lasses lolling on velvet lounges, decorated the walls. The long bar was solid mahogany with brass fittings. "Here, in a well-lighted room opening on the street, the boys gather in crowds around the tables to play or to watch others. A bartender with a face like that of a youthful divinity student fabricates wonderful drinks. The music of a piano and a violin from a seated recess enlivens the scene and soothes the savage breasts of those who retire torn and lacerated from an unfortunate combat with the 'tiger.' The games most affected are faro and monte, the latter being greatly patronized by the Mexicans in Abilene, who sit with perfectly unmoved countenances and play for hours at a stretch. Your Mexican loses with entire indifference two things somewhat valued by other men—his money and his life."

Above the sounds of revelry, the blare of the dance-hall bands, the click and rattle from the gambling halls, the uproar from the saloons, was the frequent punctuation of gunfire. Most of it was all in fun, though a frightened non-Texan, dodging a spray of bullets, might find it hard to believe. The Texan best expressed himself in wild yells and reckless gunfire. J. B. Edwards, who delivered ice to the Texas Street saloons, wrote of his experiences in a pamphlet titled *Early Days in Abilene*. "When a man from Texas got too much tanglefoot aboard," he wrote, "he was liable under the least provocation to use his six-shooters. Not less than two were always hanging from his belt. If his fancy told him to shoot, he did so—into the air or at anything he saw. A plug hat would bring a volley from him at any time, drunk or sober."

How to keep the lid on Abilene, save it from being ripped apart, while harvesting fortunes from the cattle trade, was the question that confronted the solid citizens of Abilene. The Texas mob had to be kept under control, of course, but could not be offended by overly stringent law enforcement.

There was money to be made from the cow pokes as well as buying and forwarding cattle to the eastern markets.

Yet the Texans quickly showed they would resent even the minimum of restraint. An ordinance was passed forbidding the carrying of firearms, but the visitors promptly shot up signs giving public notice of the new law. The first masonry building erected was the jail—a sight that naturally maddened the Texans. Its walls were barely up before a crowd of Texans tore them down, and the job had to be finished under an armed guard.

The first man arrested was the Negro cook of an outfit camped outside of town who got drunk and shot out a number of street lamps. He was taken into custody. Next day his friends from the same outfit rode in from Mud Creek and took over the town. They ordered all business establishments to close, blew the lock off the jail and rescued the cook, and then rode past the office of the chairman of the board of trustees, T. C. Henry, later the "wheat king of Kansas," shooting it full of holes.

Several local men were tried out for the marshal's post, but all were quickly cowed into submission. A professional was obviously needed. The chief of police at St. Louis was asked to send a pair of his tougher officers. Two hard-bitten city cops showed up at noon one day, were chivvied unmercifully by hooting and gun-waving groups of Texans, and fled on the night train back to St. Louis.

Abilene, the board of trustees decided, required a regular town-taming marshal. One of the top lawmen of the West, Tom Smith, of Bear River, Wyoming, was finally selected. Nobody would run him out of town. He was a forty-year-old Irishman, born in New York City, who had come West to work on the railroad. Abilene's officials liked him from their first glimpse of him, a tall, rugged, black-haired, and square-jawed man with a quiet voice and a considerate manner. Tom Smith didn't believe in gunning down the unruly and obstreperous; first he would try reason, then a blow from his mallet-like fist—but no gunplay.

"Bear River Tom" soon brought a measure of peace and respectability to the streets of Abilene, even those in Texas Town. Unlike most marshals, he patrolled the streets on horseback, which gave him a clear view all around and a psychological edge on people afoot.

"I must trouble you to hand me your gun," he would say politely to an overexcited cow hand. Generally, after looking into his steady blue eyes, they complied without an argument.

He was strict about enforcing the no-firearms-in-the-city-limits law, explaining, "I'd as soon contend with a frenzied maniac as an armed and drunken cowboy."

Smith was allowed to hire a deputy of his own choosing, James H. McDonald, an unfortunate choice as it turned out.

A desperado named Wyoming Frank decided to challenge Smith and took bets around the cow camps on Chapman Creek that he could successfuly defy the anti-gun ordinance. He rode into town on a Sunday morning, most of which he spent boasting and drinking in various Texas Street saloons, waiting for Smith to make his first patrol of the day.

They met in the middle of the street, Smith being dismounted on this occasion. Wyoming Frank, with many an obscenity, dared the marshal to draw on him. Instead Tom Smith steadily advanced on him, making no move to draw his gun but keeping those unnerving blue eyes fixed on his opponent's. Smith backed the rapidly deflating bad man into a saloon, suddenly sprang at him, and knocked him down with a nicely executed one-two. He then disarmed him.

"I give you five minutes to get out of town," he told Wyoming Frank, "and don't let me ever set eyes on you again."

The bartender turned over his gun to Smith a few minutes after Wyoming Frank slunk out of the place, saying, "Here's my gun, Marshal. I won't be needing it as long as you're the marshal of Abilene."

One night at the Old Fruit a Texan who refused to be parted from his six-gun threw a kerosene lamp at Smith. Smith knocked him out and carried him to the jail, slung over his shoulder. From then on the marshal had little trouble with the Texans, many of whom not only feared Smith but respected him. It was the gun-slinging marshals they hated, the "hired man-killers." Henceforth, as Wayne Gard wrote in his authoritative *The Chisholm Trail*, "On both sides of the railroad, he was undisputed boss."

Smith was the prototype of the upstanding, clean-living, fearless yet self-restrained lawman—the prime hero of western fiction, and much, much rarer than might be supposed. He was, in fact, a martyr to his own decent instincts.

Late in October 1870 a farmer named Andrew McConnell, a Scotsman, shot and killed his neighbor, John Shea, an Irishman, with whom he had been feuding. Sheriff Joseph Cramer tried to serve a warrant charging murder on McConnell but was chased off the property by McConnell. Discouraged by this encounter, Sheriff Cramer appealed to Tom Smith for help, Smith also being a deputy U.S. marshal for the district.

Smith and his deputy, McDonald, went out to McConnell's farm on Chapman Creek with the warrant on the morning of November 2. McConnell was holed up in his dugout with a friend named Moses Miles. Tom Smith "walked into danger so steadily that it vanished at his approach," as the late William MacLeod Raine wrote, but this time danger did not vanish. McConnell fired as soon as Smith entered the dugout. Although wounded in the chest, Smith grappled with Mc-Connell and tried to subdue him. Meanwhile, outside the dugout, Moses Miles was holding off Deputy McDonald.

Pouring blood with a Winchester slug in his lung, Smith somehow managed to drag McConnell out of the dugout. Miles turned his attention from McDonald to Smith, picked up an ax, and almost beheaded the marshal with it. Mc-

Donald fled without making the slightest attempt to interfere with the slaughter.

While a posse took off after McConnell and Miles (subsequently captured, convicted, and imprisoned), Abilene gave Tom Smith a first-class funeral. Some years later it erected a statue in his honor.

Abilene was without the services of a marshal for five months following Smith's death. Meanwhile, 1871 was shaping up as the biggest season yet for the cattle trade. 1871 was Abilene's bonanza year; six hundred thousand head were driven to the Kansas railheads, and Abilene was "an island in a sea of Texas cattle." She was also awash in Texas humans, an estimated five thousand cow hands having come with the herds, plus a number of desperate characters including Ben and Billy Thompson and John Wesley Hardin. They would all meet the new marshal.

The first order of business when Abilene was incorporated and Joseph McCoy took office as its first mayor was the appointment of a successor to Tom Smith. Many candidates were proposed, but McCoy's right-hand man, Charles Gross, insisted that only Wild Bill Hickok would be able to keep the Texans in line this year. Some of the councilmen were inclined to favor a man of less ferocious reputation, but McCoy pointed out that only a "strong man" would do. He investigated Hickok's record and came up with the statistic often accepted by historians. Hickok, he said, had killed forty-three men in gunfights, not including Indians and Confederates. Fifteen was more like it.

Tom Smith's death had shown that a marshal had to be prepared to use his gun as well as his fists, and McCoy, an entirely civilized man, was determined to put a stop to the senseless killings. The Texans were getting out of hand again in the absence of stern law enforcement. "We were used to seeing men killed because someone disliked their looks, the color of their eyes, the cut of their clothes, or the refusal of a drink, or because they danced too much with one girl."

So it was agreed that Hickok should take over the marshal's office. His pay was $150 a month, plus half the fines paid into the city police court.

When Hickok arrived in mid-April 1871 the town was getting wound up for a summer-long spree. In addition to the desperadoes coming up the trail from Texas there was a large delegation present from eastern Tenderloins, pimps, whores, crooked gamblers, thugs, con men, sharpers of all kinds. Every train from Kansas City brought in more light o' loves and light o' fingers. The Abilene *Chronicle* complained there were "a larger number of cutthroats and desperadoes in Abilene than in any other town of its size on the continent." Thirty saloons were now going full blast in Texas Town, and the Novelty Theater fittingly enough was presenting *Six Buckets of Blood, Or Who Stabbed the Captain.*

Three deputies—James McDonald, Tom Carson, and James Gainsford—were appointed to assist Hickok in his duties. Carson, the nephew of Hickok's old friend, Kit Carson, was young but reliable. So was Gainsford. McDonald, of course, was a holdover from Tom Smith's brief term of office. Hickok marked him down as distinctly unreliable after hearing Charles Gross' account of how McDonald had left Smith in the lurch out at McConnell's farm. McDonald had hastened from the murder scene without trying to help the dying marshal, Gross said, and went immediately to the barroom of the Drover's Cottage. "Leaning against the bar, with a drink of whiskey in his hand, he blubbered out his yarn. There being no one to dispute him, his story had to go. But I still recall the looks that passed between men who had been raised from birth to eat six-shooters. It was so rank that no one could say a word." Hickok soon dispensed with McDonald's services.

In a few days after his arrival Hickok was easily the most

unpopular man in Abilene. He enforced the no-guns ordinance almost as strictly as Tom Smith, but he wasn't so polite about it. The Texans found it all the more humiliating that the man who kept them in check dressed like a big-city dude in a Prince Albert coat, checked trousers, embroidered waistcoat, sometimes a cape lined in scarlet silk. Why, the long-haired dandy looked more like a play actor than a cow-town marshal; newcomers mistook him for one of the company at the Novelty Theater. The Texans had feared and respected Tom Smith; they feared and hated Wild Bill Hickok.

"Talk about a rule of iron," wrote Mayor McCoy in his *Historic Sketches of the Cattle Trade*. "We had it in Abilene. We had to rule that way. There was no fooling with courts of law. When we decided that such a thing was to be done we did it. Wild Bill cleaned up the town and kept it clean, but we had to kill a few roughs to do it."

And the Abilene *Chronicle*, which was strongly anti-Texan, chimed in, "There is no use in trying to override Wild Bill, the marshal; his arrangements for policing the city are complete and attempts to kill police officers or in any way create disturbance, must result in loss of life on the part of violators of the law."

Whatever else they thought of him, the Texans found Hickok a formidable figure. Paschal Brown, a cow hand quoted in Cunningham's *Triggernometry*, described him as he came out of the Bull's Head one afternoon. "He wore a low-crowned, wide black hat and a frock coat. When I came along the street, he was standing there with his back to the wall and his thumbs hooked in his red sash. He stood there and rolled his head from side to side looking at everything and everybody from under his eyebrows—just like a mad old bull. I decided then and there I didn't want any part of him."

Paschal Brown's fellow Texans were not all inclined to submit so readily to Hickok's "ironhanded" rule of Texas Town, which they regarded as a private preserve, an autonomous colony, a bit of Texas on Kansas soil. One night Hickok roughed up several visitors who were brawling in a saloon. Out at their camp the next day they decided, with the help of their fellow riders, to invade the town, seize Hickok, and string him up to a telegraph pole.

Hickok was tipped off regarding their intentions an hour or two before they came whooping and hollering into Abilene.

He met them in the middle of the street outside the Last Chance Saloon. Although there were twenty or thirty men in the group that planned to lynch him, Hickok confronted them alone. He leveled a Winchester repeating rifle on their leaders.

The cow pokes were taken by surprise, having expected to hunt him down rather than meet this bold confrontation.

His Winchester aimed at their leaders, Hickok gave one brief command: "Hide out, you sons of bitches."

"Hide out" in modern speech meant simply "get lost."

The mounted mob hesitated for a moment, then scattered for safety on one impulse. One of them said later, "Every fellow in our crowd thought Bill meant him, and they all proceeded to 'hide out.' There was confusion for a minute; the leaders wheeled their horses; and in the mix-up, each tried to get the lead going the other way. To them it seemed a long time before they got strung out. There was no thought of resistance to Bill's order, and soon every member of the band was hitting the trail for camp as fast as his horse could carry him. So ended the attempt to hang Wild Bill."

There were complaints from those who thought the late Tom Smith was far superior to Hickok as a peace officer that the latter did not enforce the anti-firearm ordinance as effectively as his predecessor. It was true enough that Hickok did not maintain the man-on-horseback vigil initiated by Smith and that on the surface his overlordship of the brawling streets of Texas Town was more casual, but whenever trouble arose he was usually on the spot in a hurry. Homer W. Wheeler, who retired as colonel of the 5th Cavalry and with whom Hickok served at Fort Wallace a few years before, came to Abilene on a cattle-buying mission. In his memoir, *Buffalo Days*, Colonel Wheeler recalled, "One of my cowboys tried to run the town in good old western style, shooting off his gun and declaring that 'he was a wolf and it was his night to howl.' Hickok arrested him and placed him in the lockup. The cowboy had my revolver, which was returned to me. When I left Abilene, this cowboy was serving his sentence."

His nominal employers, the City Council of Abilene, found their new marshal equally as stern a figure as the Texans they hired him to keep under control. Hickok had little or no respect for the dignity of their aldermanic office.

One of his duties was to attend meetings of the City Council, not only to account for himself and his deputies, but to act as sergeant at arms and maintain order. It was also his task to round up a quorum when necessary. This was more arduous than might be expected because the councilmen were always slipping away to their business establishments. They were making money hand over fist and begrudged the time required to transact the city's business. This lack of civic spirit, not to mention their duty to the electorate, was exceedingly irksome to Hickok.

The Council session of May 8, three weeks after Hickok became marshal, was particularly annoying. At the beginning of the meeting it was found that they were lacking a quorum by one member. Hickok went out on the streets and grabbed the first Council absentee he came across. The councilman protested but was marched to the chamber at gun point. Later in the session the same member was found to have sneaked off.

Hickok found him in his store, mumbling over his accounts. He slung the maverick politician over his shoulder, carried him to the Council chamber, and dumped him in his chair.

Hickok watched over the remainder of that meeting with his gun in hand and his eyes sweeping around the table with a menacing glint. Some of the members wondered whether they didn't need protection against their protector.

CHAPTER 10
Thompson, Hardin & Co.

With trouble always around the corner or just down the block Hickok stalked Texas Town's streets catfooted, ready to pounce before a situation could get out of hand. He didn't patrol the streets constantly, preferring to make his general headquarters at the Alamo while his deputies walked their beats, but he placed himself on public view several times a day with monitor-like promenades of Texas Street and the red-light district. He liked to gamble but drank sparingly. Liquor-dulled nerves could cost him his life in a tight spot, and he had to stay in training so long as thousands of trail hands crowded into Abilene.

He took endless precautions against being bushwhacked. Outside the Alamo he always carried a sawed-off shotgun, which the cow hands respected more than anything on earth, or a Winchester repeater. In addition to his double-action revolvers he tucked a pair of Derringers in his waistcoat and a Bowie knife in his sash. He always walked down the middle of the street and made a wide turn at the corners. On entering any kind of establishment he kicked back the door sharply to make certain nobody was hiding behind it, and once inside he kept his back to the wall, facing all the room's occupants.

Through his prestige as a gun handler—and the iron will behind it—a wide-open town swarming with violent men was prevented from erupting into anarchy. He couldn't relax for a moment. During the eight months he spent as marshal of Abilene the possibility of sudden death followed him like a shadow. He knew there were scores of trigger-happy youths ready to risk their lives against the hope of gaining renown as "the killer of Wild Bill Hickok." And he heard reports that certain cattle barons, who hated Kansas marshals almost as much as their hired hands did, were encouraging Texas gunfighters to try their skill against Hickok.

Several times, while he bunked at the rear of the Elkhorn Saloon, his sleeping quarters were riddled by fusillades late at night. The attempts at assassination failed; not only that, they encouraged him to maintain a constant state of alert. He went to sleep with a revolver in one hand and his sawed-off shotgun in easy reach. And before going to sleep he used an old crook's trick to guard against being taken by surprise, crumpled up newspapers and scattered them around the floor. A rustling newspaper makes a fairly effective burglar alarm.

An Abilene old-timer recalled Hickok's oddly stealthy appearances—almost manifestations—around the town. "He *slid* into a room, keeping his back to the wall, watching the whole crowd like a hawk. He looked like a man who lived in expectation of getting killed."

John Conkie, who was the jailer at Abilene for several months during Hickok's regime, had a vivid memory of those tense weeks when Hickok was keeping the lid on the city's volatile and transient population. Conkie too was one of the few people in town who took an objective view of the new marshal. He characterized Hickok as "fearless and cool in the face of danger . . . always showed good generalship . . . always had a semblance of law to support his quick and accurate gunplay . . . He was not naturally quarrelsome; on the contrary, he was rather slow to anger and seldom aggressive.

"Probably no man was ever more hated by cowboys and desperadoes generally than was Bill . . . His suspicious nature was so aggravated by the constant threats against his life that at times he became tyrannical and overbearing and nearly lost confidence in his best friends.

"When expecting serious trouble, he always carried a sawed-off shotgun; and it was a very common sight in Abilene in those days to see Wild Bill sitting in a barber's chair getting shaved, with his shotgun in hand and his eyes open. Yet his popularity among his friends and acquaintances was so great that he could get more stake-money than any other poker player I ever knew.

"He was probably the least understood and most abused of all the noted frontiersmen of his time. Hickok, although a dangerous enemy, was a faithful friend and would always respond to the cry of distress. We called him 'Wild Bill,' but his iron will would bend in sympathy to the sigh of a child. Perhaps his early training and environment made him a typical frontiersman, a fearless peace officer and one feared by lawless characters. In a word, he was a mixture of frontier recklessness, coolness and rare generalship in positions of great danger not likely to be equalled again in the changing West."

One reason for the lack of understanding undoubtedly was that he held himself aloof from the churchgoing and respectable permanent residents of Abilene as well as its less well-mannered floating population. He shunned church suppers and dance-hall orgies alike. He seemed to look upon almost everyone as his potential murderer. Most people considered him a loner, a misanthrope. Some of the solid citizens who tried to cultivate his acquaintance as one of the border's leading celebrities were brushed off with something close to contempt. His only associates were the big gamblers, the "sporting men" who dropped in from Kansas City and St. Louis, the men who ran the best saloons and the biggest games in town. The big money had an undeniable attraction for him; he had the money hunger that characterized his generation, from President Grant to the trickiest financier of the "Flash Age."

Because of his predilection for the company of the high-rollers, the aristocracy of the local night life, many historians considered that he stacked up poorly in comparison with Tom Smith, his undeniably virtuous predecessor. Hickok, wrote the late William MacLeod Raine (*Guns of the Frontier*), "believed in a wide open town. A gambler and a drinking man, his alliances were with the vicious rather than the decent element . . . All he asked of the parasites was that they operate in such a way as not to annoy him." Hickok made no secret of the fact that he considered the proprietor of the Old Fruit, for instance, quite as respectable as the merchant who trimmed the cowboy with shoddy goods at high prices.

There was another aspect of Hickok's behavior in Abilene that was not calculated to win the approval of the staid and stodgy. That was his taste in female companionship. He was exceedingly polite, even gallant, toward all women, but he generally spent his time with those who were not received in the politer society north of the tracks. It was said that in his fear of assassination he "refused to sleep in the same room with another man, never fully trusted any woman," but he was on intimate terms with a number of what were delicately referred to as "the demimonde," or women, in the police-court phrase, with "no visible means of support."

One of his friends in Abilene was Mattie Silks, whose admirers described her as a "vest-pocket edition of Lily Langtry" and who later in the seventies became Denver's leading madam. In Abilene she operated a high-class establishment which was patronized by the wealthier cattlemen. She was in her early twenties in those days, a small, shapely blonde with a gorgeous complexion and a quick temper.

Later, when she fought the only recorded pistol duel between women in the West, she claimed that Hickok taught her how to handle a gun. Judging by the results of the duel, however, she was not a credit to her instructor.

Hickok and Mattie Silks presumably were on platonic terms in Abilene. The love of Mattie's colorful life was a Texan named Corteze Thompson who lived off the proceeds of Mattie's establishment, although he would fly into a homicidal rage if anyone was indelicate enough to refer to him as a pimp. "In the South, where I come from," Cort Thompson would explain, "nobody works but niggers."

After a bad night at the gambling tables Thompson would rush over to Mattie's, pound on her door, and howl, "Money! Cash money! Shower down or I'll shoot up the joint and wreck the ballroom floor!"

The celebrated pistol duel took place in Denver's Olympic Gardens on August 25, 1877, at the climax of a champagne party being given by Mattie for the upper crust of whoredom. Somewhat overserved, Mattie accused a rival madam, Katie Fulton, of making a play for Cort Thompson. Honor, it was decided, could be satisfied only by invocation of the code duello.

Thompson, preening himself over the situation, agreed to act as referee. The two women stood back to back, each with a pistol in her hand. At the referee's command they each took three paces, then turned and fired. Mattie and Katie both missed. But the bullet from one of the pistols—most witnesses said it was fired by Katie—struck Cort Thompson, puncturing his neck. It was widely agreed that this was poetic justice. But it was only a flesh wound and Thompson survived the duel over his affections, though much annoyed at the ironic outcome, and continued the Denver variation of the Frankie-and-Johnny theme.

Aside from teaching Mattie Silks how to use a pistol, as she claimed, Hickok was more directly involved with several other women in Abilene.

Susanna Moore, of all women, made her reappearance in Hickok's life during his first months there. Six years had passed since Hickok last saw her in the post-war turbulence of Springfield, during the days preceding his gunfight with Dave Tutt. She apparently had been one of the reasons for the enmity between the two men. In any case, Hickok was still attracted to her.

What brought her to Abilene—unless it was a summons from Hickok—was never made known. In those days gossip about a man's sex life was a dangerous pastime, particularly a man like Wild Bill Hickok. It was even more dangerous to commit such speculations to writing. Little survives regarding his warmed-over affair with Susanna Moore or why they got back together after what must have been a bitter disagreement over her relations with the late Mr. Tutt.

All that is certain is that they lived together for a short time, sharing a cottage south of the tracks.

Then Susanna went her way, voluntarily or otherwise.

Subsequently Hickok fell for a beautiful young woman named Jessie Hazel. Her address was in the Devil's Addition, down in the red-light district. Despite her profession, Hickok took a passionate interest in Jessie. It may not have been love, in the north-of-the-tracks sense, but Hickok wanted it understood that Jessie was his girl after hours. Naturally it dismayed the respectable people of Abilene that their marshal should take up with a "woman of the town." Perhaps it even dismayed him a trifle that he should fall for the likes of Jessie. But a man who lived in expectation of sudden death couldn't be too particular; the flesh had its consolations in those hours when he shut out the bright lights and rowdy music of Texas

Street and holed up for the night. Jealousy over Jessie Hazel and her transient affections subsequently played a part in the only gunfight in which Hickok became involved during his employment in Abilene.

Considerably less objectionable to Abilene's respectable people were his relations with a lady who came to the city in August. She was Mrs. Agnes Thatcher Lake, a handsome and well-preserved widow, some years older than Hickok and the proprietor of Lake's Circus—probably the first respectable woman Hickok had anything to do with in some time. On the death of her husband two years earlier she had taken over operating the circus with a brisk efficiency. One of her aides was James A. Bailey, later a partner in Barnum & Bailey. She was a personage in the circus world, an accomplished equestrienne, animal tamer, and tightrope walker, almost a three-ring show by herself.

Hickok and Mrs. Lake had met almost two years ago when her show played Hays City. He had come to her rescue with a gallantry which Mrs. Lake still fondly remembered. The City Council of Hays had decided to assess her fifty dollars for the privilege of giving performances on the edge of town.

Hickok, slamming his fist on the Council table, had denounced the city fathers as a "pack of coyotes" and told them:

"Instead of charging Mrs. Lake for a license, you ought to vote her an appropriation for coming to this Godforsaken hole."

The Council decided to forego the license fee rather than contend with Hickok's wrath.

Now, in Abilene, Hickok established himself in her favor by standing guard at all performances and protecting the show from ruffians who might think it amusing to take a shot at a lion or an acrobat. The comely widow, from all accounts, fell in love with Hickok, probably unaware of his obsession with Jessie Hazel. Old-timers (quoted by Cunningham in *Triggernometry*) said she "fell with a crash, clean through to the basement." An earlier biographer (Connelley, *Wild Bill and His Era*) talked with a friend of Hickok's who said Mrs. Lake "tried her best to get him to marry her and run the circus."

Hickok's friend asked him why he did not accept the proposal, to which Hickok replied, somewhat unromantically, "I know she has a good show, but when she is done in the West she will go East, and it is the West for me. I would be lost in the States. No, it won't do."

Hickok's friend also recalled, "I know she was keen for it. She wrote to him after leaving Abilene. I know, for the letters came in my care under seal to the cottage." Mrs. Lake was so determined on marriage that "Bill induced his friend to tell her that he was already married—had a wife in Illinois. In this way only was he able to avoid marrying her without giving offense."

Mrs. Lake was a persistent woman, however, not too discouraged over Hickok's skittishness about getting married, and she was later to become an important part of his life.

Considering that Hickok was involved with women at almost every stage of his career, it is curious, if not inexplicable, that rumors and hints have long been circulating that Hickok was not as manly a chap as he pretended to be. Freudian explanations have been sought for various facets of his behavior, his habit of wearing his hair in a shoulder-length mane (then not at all uncommon among plainsmen), his predilection for costumes that bordered on the gorgeous, his long avoidance of marriage. Even his preference for shooting opponents in the head—which was practical in that a man with a bullet in his head was less likely to retaliate than a man with a bullet in his torso—has been cited as indicating a tendency toward sexual abnormality, for reasons too complex to be grasped by one unversed in psychiatric jargon. The conclusion that Hickok was a latent or potential homosexual, from such scant evidence, seems highly unwarranted. What

THOMPSON, HARDIN & CO.

more the man could have done in his rather short life to prove that he had no such tendencies is difficult to say, unless he had devoted all his time to well-publicized fornications. The insinuation of homosexuality to various prominent persons has become a popular indoor sport. All the cozier, perhaps, because such accusations are all but impossible to refute. It is noticeable, however, that people eager to pin the homosexual label on someone else are often exhibiting tendencies in that direction themselves.

Aside from the feminine complications in his life that summer, Hickok had plenty to worry about in the line of preserving law and order. Five thousand trail hands were camped in the vicinity of Abilene, one day twenty-five hundred of them were counted in the saloons of Texas Street, and a spontaneous combustion of violence could be expected at any moment. Somehow, thanks mostly to his prestige as the deadliest shot in the West, Hickok kept the death toll down and the crimes confined to such relatively minor and inevitable offenses as drunk-rolling, cheating, pocket-picking, stealing, brawling, and the like, common to saloon and red-light districts anywhere.

His most vexing concern was a running feud with the Bull's Head and its proprietors, who were determined to eliminate Hickok from the scene, preferably in a plain pine box. The owners of this establishment were Ben Thompson, the gunman-gambler, and his outsize partner, Phil Coe, both of whom were Texans. Coe was fairly pacifistic for a Texan; at least he had never been known to kill anyone. He became troublesome only when drinking, on which occasions he was characterized by Theophilus Little, the Abilene merchant, as "a red-mouthed bawling thug, a plug-ugly, a dangerous beast."

Ben Thompson, on the other hand, was a man to worry even Wild Bill Hickok—a fellow virtuoso with the Colt .45s.

Thompson had nothing but contempt for cow-town marshals. "The fighting pimps," he called them. "They hide in the parlor houses whenever there's real trouble." He did not exclude Hickok from this graceless category.

Thompson was one of the few men who would have been a match for Hickok. More than a match, Bat Masterson thought. Masterson, who was a friend of both men and had seen them in action, wrote an authoritative series on his gun-fighting contemporaries for a magazine years after he had retired. Of Ben Thompson he wrote, "It is doubtful if in his time there was another man living who equalled him with a pistol in a life-and-death struggle. Thompson in the first place possessed a much higher order of intelligence than the average man-killer of his time. He was absolutely without fear and his nerves were those of the finest steel. He shot at an adversary with the same precision and deliberation that he shot at a target. A past master in the use of the pistol, his aim was as true as his nerves were strong and steady. Wild Bill Hickok, Wyatt Earp, Billy Tilghman, Charley Bassett, Luke Short, Clay Allison and Jim Curry were all men who played their part on the lurid edge of our Western frontier at the same time Ben was playing his, and it is safe to assume that none of them would have declined the gage of battle had he flung it down. However, I am constrained to say that little doubt exists in my mind that Thompson would have been the winner."

Even his friends said Ben Thompson exhibited "a craving to kill," particularly under the influence of alcohol. And he drank a lot, unlike most men who lived by the gun. "He never went to bed," a friend of his recorded, "without a full quart of 3-Star Hennessey brandy, and he always emptied the bottle before daylight." There was little of the swashbuckler in his appearance. He was a dumpy little fellow with mild blue eyes and a constabulary mustache and looked like a fairly prosperous grocer. "He was very neat in dress, and always took particular pains with his footwear, his small feet always being clad in well-fitting boots of light material, a common form of foppery in a land where other details of dress were apt to be carelessly regarded. He wore a dark mustache which, in his early years, he was wont to keep waxed to points. In speech he was quiet and inobtrusive, unless excited by drink." Despite his deceptively mild appearance, Bat Masterson said, "the very name of Ben Thompson was enough to cause the general run of 'man-killers,' even those who had never seen him, to seek safety in flight."

Thompson was born in England or Nova Scotia—the point is disputed—but was brought up in Austin, Texas. His father deserted the family when Ben was a boy, and he went to work at an early age as a printer to help support his mother and younger brother, Billy. When the Confederacy went to work, Ben joined a Texas regiment and was stationed at Fort Clark. He reacted poorly to military discipline. He and his fellow soldiers became dissatisfied with the rations they were issued, a situation Ben tried to remedy by raiding an army warehouse. A sergeant collared him and announced he would be court-martialed for stealing government property. Ben didn't think it was worth facing a firing squad for a sack of cornmeal and a side of bacon, so he shot the sergeant, then a lieutenant who came running to investigate the disturbance.

Thompson broke out of the guardhouse, fled from Fort Clark, and re-enlisted in another regiment at Eagle Pass. In a few weeks he was involved in another scrape. Ben took on a whole roomful of Mexicans in a saloon across the border at Piedras Negras, shot and killed three of them before escaping over the river. Again he was forced to desert and re-enlist elsewhere, this time with General Kirby-Smith's army up along the Red River. He settled down to a spell of honest soldiering. Kirby-Smith's forces were involved in real fighting, not garrison or border-guard duty, and there were legitimate targets to shoot at—Yankee infantry bent on invading the Red River valley. Thompson performed so heroically at the battle of Sabine Crossroads that he was given a battle-field promotion from private to captain.

After the collapse of the Confederacy, Thompson skipped to Mexico with Kirby-Smith and other diehards. He joined up with another lost cause, the Emperor Maximilian's, whose throne was shakier than the Confederate dollar. The imperial forces were soon overcome by President Juarez's republican armies. Thompson fled the country shortly before Maximilian was executed by a Juarista firing squad.

Like many ex-Confederate soldiers, Thompson was too restless to settle down in Texas and undergo the rigors of being reconstructed. He became a leading figure among the professional gamblers who met the cattle drives in the various trail towns. Usually he was accompanied by his younger brother, Billy, who was described as "handsomer, larger and louder" than Ben. There was a striking difference between the two brothers, according to frontier historians. Ben usually had a good reason for shooting a man, but Billy took a psychopathic delight in the act of killing. Many of the shootings in which the Thompson brothers were involved had a common pattern—Billy starting a fight and Ben, always his protector, stepping in to finish it with fatal results for the other parties.

Ben Thompson's contempt for the law was supreme; he regarded it as outrageous when the community tried to protect itself against him. Once when a murder warrant was issued against him down in Texas, by people who should have known better, he rode his mustang into the courthouse and without dismounting addressed the bench: "Here I am, gents, and I'll lay anything there's no charge against me. Am I right? Speak up, gents; I'm a little deaf." The clerk of the court finally managed to croak out the dimissal, "No charge, Ben." Thompson tipped his hat and clattered away.

Another thing Ben couldn't stand, in addition to being curbed by the law, was losing at the gambling tables. He regarded it as his God-given right to come away the winner. Sometimes when luck was against him he would suddenly give a savage snort of laughter and rake in all the money on the table, his and everyone else's. Nobody dared resent this cavalier termination of the game. Then, to show he wasn't motivated by pure greed, he would take all the money and dump it on the bar and buy drinks for the house until it was gone. Once in Leadville, Colorado, he dropped two-thousand dollars in cash and his eight-hundred-dollar diamond stud at a faro layout. Brooding over this misfortune, according to a newspaper account, Thompson "got drunk and turned over the gaming tables, shot out the lights, ran the crowd out of the place, pounded one man up with a six-shooter, wound up cleaning up the street with a Winchester."

He recognized gambling as a probably fatal compulsion with him and told his biographer (W. M. Walton, *Life and Adventures of Ben Thompson*): "Sooner or later a gambler meets an untimely death. Every time a man sits down at a table to gamble he takes his life in his hands. Fatal difficulties arise from cause and no cause; men are killed in their own quarrels and those of others. Yet I continue in that way of life. But so help me God I never have and never will assist, encourage or influence any youth or man to engage in this hell-earning business, which I will probably follow until I am dead."

These pious thoughts, however, were not uppermost in Thompson's mind when he hit Abilene in the spring of 1871 and opened the Bull's Head with his brown-bearded friend, Phil Coe, as partner. Ben saw a chance to clean up and went about making the Bull's Head the fanciest sucker trap in Abilene. He and Coe bought the most elaborate faro layout on the market and set it up in a back room. Business was booming in no time. The cow pokes favored the Bull's Head because it was owned by Texans, while most of the other saloons and gambling houses were operated by Yankees.

Soon enough the Bull's Head's success was heartily resented by its rivals. Ever after Texans claimed that its competitors decided to drive the place out of business, using Marshal Hickok as their chief prod. It was rumored that Hickok was to eliminate Thompson from the scene with a timely blast from his six-guns.

Even without this disgruntlement in the background, Thompson and Hickok would never have found it possible to cherish each other as friends. Thompson detested Yankees as Hickok hated the Rebs. Hickok was always the lawman, Thompson always the lawbreaker. They detested each other on sight. "One or the other," it was widely predicted, "will leave Texas Street in a box."

The Bull's Head gave further offense to the citizenry in the matter of its sign, an obscenely exaggerated painting of a Texas longhorn. A delegation called upon the proprietors to point out that their sign was offensive to "decent people," an insult to whatever virtuous women might walk down Texas Street—unlikely as that was. Thompson and Coe replied that they were well pleased with the sign and its advertisement of Texas virility and these wheyfaced moralists could go climb a tree, or something equally unbecoming. The delegation carried their complaint to the authorities, who ordered Marshal Hickok to do something about that sign. Hickok, with a shotgun crooked in his arm, stood by while alterations were daubed in on the bull's anatomy.

Even after the censors had almost converted their bull into a steer, Thompson and Coe continued to prosper at the Bull's Head. There were charges made before the City Council that the Bull's Head patrons were being trimmed outrageously in crooked games, that cowboys had been drugged and rolled in the back room, that the faro layout was rigged so that nobody had a chance to win unless the proprietors whimsically chose to allow it.

The Council showed a sudden and unusual concern for the cow hands in their midst. First it revoked the Bull's Head's liquor license, hoping to force it out of business. Thompson and Coe continued to operate at a profit from their gambling enterprise.

Hickok took the next step against the Bull's Head himself. He ordered that the faro layout be hauled from the back room, where so many strange misfortunes seemed to have befallen various customers, and installed in the front of the establishment, where Hickok could keep an eye on the proceedings. Thompson and Coe, cursing mightily, complied with the order. A few days later, when Bull's Head patrons broke the faro bank with an extraordinary run of luck, some credence was given the suspicions that Thompson and Coe had been "improving their luck" in the back room.

Ben Thompson was furious. He proclaimed to anyone who would listen that Hickok was discriminating against him, that he was the hireling of the Yankee saloon and gambling-house owners. It appeared to some that Thompson's argument, boiled down, was that "Hickok is protecting the other crooks but not us."

It would probably have seemed to a newcomer that a show-down between Hickok and Thompson, the two readiest gun slingers in town, was inevitable. Not so to the more knowledgeable, who understood that gunfighters had no stomach for facing each other in deadly combat. If the gunfighters had ever organized a trade union, their first rule would have been: No member shall fire upon another member. (One of the few exceptions to this fraternal understanding was the shoot-out between Luke Short and Jim Courtright, which was fatal to the latter, in Short's Fort Worth gambling house.)

Unwilling to challenge Hickok himself, Thompson thought he saw a way out of the impasse when he heard that John

Wesley Hardin, the eighteen-year-old "man-killer from the Hard Water Fork of Bitter Creek," was coming up the Chisholm Trail with a cattle drive. Hardin was a gun-crazy kid, unlikely to have acquired that trade-union prejudice against bucking another gunfighter. Thompson was pretty sure he could talk young Wes Hardin into taking care of Wild Bill Hickok.

Thompson was right about one thing—Hardin was just about the most reckless pistoleer north of the Rio Bravo, the No. 1 hero of the Texas cow hands. The young desperado already had a string of killings, and coming up from Texas added several more victims to his list. On the Kansas border an Osage had demanded a steer for allowing Hardin's outfit to cross. Hardin gunned the Indian down without further palaver and left his body tied to a steer's carcass as a warning to other Osages with ambitions to collect a toll from the cattle drives. While the outfit was camped on the prairie outside of Abilene, Hardin and one of his friends got into an argument with a group of Mexican trail drivers, shot and killed six of them.

Not unnaturally Hardin was feeling about nine feet tall when he rode into Abilene June 1 with the Clements brothers, who constituted his personal claque. Hardin would strut into a saloon with the Clements boys and listen appreciatively while they told admiring fellow cow hands, "Thirty men that kid's downed. He's chain lightning and eleven claps of thunder with the six-shooter! He'll fight at the drop of a hat and drop the hat hisself!"

No one listened to this bellicose talk with greater interest than Ben Thompson.

He took Hardin aside at the first opportunity, told the quick-triggered stripling all about Hickok, how the marshal of Abilene hated Texans and went around shooting innocent cowboys in the back. He also pointed out, in case Hardin wasn't steamed up enough, that the man who killed Wild

Bill would be proclaimed a Lone Star patriot to rival the heroes of the Alamo.

But Wes Hardin had a higher boiling point than Thompson had reckoned. He looked the older man in the eye and inquired, as he reported many years later in his autobiography, "If Hickok needs killing so bad, why don't you kill him yourself?"

"I'd rather get someone else to do it," Thompson was quoted as replying. (Thompson told Fred Sutton, a veteran peace officer and co-author of *Hands Up!*, that Hickok was the only man he ever feared, that Hickok "had two hells in his eyes.")

Hardin shrugged and walked away from his compatriot. Cagey old Ben didn't give up hope though. Hardin was defying the no-guns ordinance, strolling around town with both six-shooters in plain view. Hickok couldn't permit that without abdicating all claims to enforcing the law in Abilene. His enemies were willing to bet that Hickok's sense of pride and Hardin's cockiness would prove a combustible combination the first time they met.

As for Marshal Hickok, hearing the news of Wes Hardin's arrival and open flouting of the firearms ordinance, he was plainly in a sweat. The first night Hardin was in town Deputy Tom Carson got into an argument with the Texan over his guns and was told to go chase himself. Hickok had no yearning to shoot it out with Hardin. Neither his failing eyesight nor the slightly slower reflexes of his thirty-four years recommended going up against the hellion from Bitter Creek. And if he succeeded in downing Hardin, the town might well boil over with several thousand Texans rioting over the death of their idol. Furthermore, Hickok was rather proud of having ruled the streets for six weeks without having to shoot anyone.

On the other hand, if Hardin were allowed to keep on strutting around in full armament, everybody else would start wearing their guns.

Hickok wisely decided on diplomacy as the first step. He arranged to meet Hardin in a "neutral" saloon. They sat down over a bottle and talked amicably. Hickok found the young man somewhat less harum-scarum than he had expected. He seemed fairly reasonable aside from an inordinate pride in his calling.

Hickok showed Hardin a number of handbills which had come into the marshal's office from Texas, offering various rewards for Hardin's arrest. He tore up the flyers and said he didn't intend to do anything about them. Then he added:

"Let me give you some advice. I'd advise you not to pay attention to Ben Thompson. Don't let him influence you."

He also suggested that it would make things "easier" all around if Hardin didn't go armed while in Abilene. In return, he said, "if I can do you a favor while you're in Abilene, I'll be glad to do it."

They parted amicably, but Hardin kept his guns on. He'd heard a rumor—probably from Ben Thompson—that Hickok was going to shoot him in the back if he got the opportunity, and though Hickok seemed square enough for a Kansas marshal he didn't intend to take any chances.

According to Hardin, in an account written long after Hickok was dead and unable to contradict him (in his autobiography, *The Life of John Wesley Hardin*), he and Hickok met later that night in another saloon.

Hickok, he admitted, had the drop on him.

"What're you doing with those pistols on?" he quoted Hickok as saying.

"Taking in the town."

"Well, take 'em off. You're under arrest."

The marshal, Hardin said, could have shot him then and there and claimed the rewards. Hardin continued:

"I said, 'All right,' and pulled them out of the scabbards, but while he was reaching for them I reversed them and whirled them over on him with the muzzles in his face,

184

springing back at the same time. I told him to put his pistol up, which he did."

Two hundred Texans in the place were howling for Hardin to kill Hickok while he had the chance.

Hickok remained perfectly cool and unperturbed, although at any moment he could have been shot without a chance to defend himself. Not by Hardin, who obviously had a certain sense of honor in these matters, but by one of the drunks whooping it up all around him.

Deputies Carson and Gainsford came on the run, but Hickok waved them off.

Young Hardin turned to his bloodthirsty compatriots and yelled, "Don't touch a gun. I'll kill the first man who goes for a gun. This is my fight."

Marshal Hickok suggested it was time they had another drink in private. They strolled away together and went into a saloon up the block. Another peace conference was held. They agreed that it was a standoff between them; each man had had the drop on the other, and neither had taken homicidal advantage of his opportunity. Hardin, admitting to himself that Hickok seemed a likable man, agreed not to "embarrass" the marshal during the rest of his stay in Abilene. Still it was not agreed upon whether or not Hardin would be permitted to wear his guns.

Before the night was out, however, Hardin broke his promise not to "embarrass" the marshal. He got in a row in a restaurant with a man who was loudly denouncing Texans. Hardin shot and killed the Texas-hater.

He knew that now Hickok would certainly come for him with his guns out and high-tailed it out of town, riding thirty-five miles to his outfit's camp on the North Cottonwood. He did not come back to Abilene.

Hickok partisans have angrily denied, in particular, Hardin's claim that he got the drop on Hickok by reversing his guns. This trick was known as the "road agent's spin."

185

Presumably Hickok would have known all about such a maneuver and been on his guard against it. It was an old trick even then, usable only on neophytes. There is no record, not even a newspaper account, to suggest that Hardin's story was true. His only supporting evidence came from Texans who claimed to have witnessed the incident.

It was unlikely that an experienced peace officer would demand that another man hand over his guns, as Hardin's story had it. The usual method of disarming a man, particularly a notorious gunman, was to order him to unbuckle his gun belt and drop it to the ground, then step back from it. The officer would then pick up the belt and its weapons and march their owner away at gun point. It was regarded as unwise and unhealthy to allow a gunman to lay hands on his guns when you had the drop on him.

Yet it is undeniable that Wes Hardin came to Abilene, wore his guns, got away with a killing. It was also in character for Hickok—remembering how he handled Jim Curry in Hays City by sitting down with him over a bottle of champagne— to deal with Hardin diplomatically. This was not, of course, a display of cowardice as has often been suggested. A cowtown marshal had to know, above all, when not to shoot, and Hickok was old enough now to realize the true proportions of valor and discretion. The only man who could have regretted that was the unfortunate citizen who cussed out Texans in Hardin's presence, and he was dead.

CHAPTER 11

Gun Fight at the Alamo

By midsummer the town had quieted down considerably. Right in the middle of its biggest boom the cattle trade began to fall off. A post-war depression was gathering force in the East and was to culminate in the Panic of '73; unemployment was increasing in the eastern cities and meat purchases declined accordingly. Whole herds went unsold and faced a winter on the Kansas prairies. From one hilltop the eye could take in thirty to fifty thousand cattle in a panoramic sweep. Some cattlemen were driving their herds northward three hundred miles to the Nebraska towns, as Mari Sandoz wrote (*The Cattlemen*), "hoping for government greenbacks if there was no chance of gold coins counted out on a horse blanket at a trail campfire."

Ben Thompson improved matters considerably, from the standpoint of the local bourgeoisie, by leaving for Kansas City late in July to meet his wife and children coming up from Texas. He intended to come back, but their buggy overturned while the Thompsons were out for a drive. Ben's leg was fractured, and Mrs. Thompson's arm was broken so badly it had to be amputated. Meanwhile, Phil Coe, his partner, sold out his interest in the Bull's Head to Tom Sheran but hung around the establishment as a professional gambler.

By September 2 it was so peaceful even in Texas Town that the City Council discharged Hickok's deputies, leaving Hickok the sole peace officer in town.

The Council also passed an ordinance closing the dance halls and the red-light district. Marshal Hickok was ordered to see to it that their denizens left town. He must have gone about it with vigor, for the Abilene *Chronicle* reported on September 14 that "almost every eastbound train carried away a vast multitude of sinful humanity. Prostitutes, pimps, gamblers, cappers, and others are finding their nefarious occupations no longer profitable." The Council also passed an anti-gambling ordinance, which was most displeasing to Hickok. Naturally the respectable people believed this applied only to the professionals in Texas Town. Hickok, however, decided it must apply to both sides of the tracks. One night he raided the home of a banker, where a sociable game of whist was being played for modest stakes, and dispersed the players, threatening those who protested with a night in jail.

Hickok was in a bad mood those days. His infatuation with the beauty of the Devil's Addition had turned out badly. The fickle Jessie Hazel predictably would turn to some other man sooner or later, probably sooner, but Hickok's humiliation was intense when she showed a preference for one of his bitterest enemies in Abilene, Phil Coe. Besides being the cordially detested Ben Thompson's partner, Coe was Hickok's leading rival as the dandy and lady-killer of Texas Town. Most people thought he cut an even more dashing figure than Hickok; he was six feet four, handsome, had a suave manner when sober and in his right mind, and had a lot more money to throw around than the marshal.

188

Coe had one amazing peculiarity for a Texan and a professional gambler: he almost never carried a gun.

On an afternoon that caused a great clucking of tongues all around Abilene, Hickok heard that Jessie was openly consorting with Coe. This affronted not only whatever feelings Hickok had for the girl but his roosterish pride. Hickok stormed over to the Drover's Cottage, the fanciest drinking spot in town, and found the pair sharing a bottle of champagne in the hotel parlor. A violent scene ensued and might have ended in shooting, except that Coe, as usual, was unarmed. Some said Hickok slapped Jessie so hard that she fell to the floor. Coe, whose gallantry stopped short of suicide, did not interfere.

Now, in autumn, Jessie and all her harlot sisters had migrated elsewhere, but the bitterness between Hickok and Coe was undiminished. Later the Junction City *Union's* correspondent reported that Coe had threatened to kill Hickok "before the frost."

Abilene, meanwhile, was getting ready for one more big spree before the season ended and the town was locked in for the winter. Cattlemen and cow hands, those still left in and around Abilene, planned on celebrating their departure with the customary splurge. The Dickinson County Fair was also at its height. On October 5 the town was almost as lively as during the midsummer boom.

To Marshal Hickok, bearing the solitary responsibility for law enforcement, October 5 was anything but a holiday. He announced that the firearms ordinance would be strictly enforced and warned the cow hands to stay on their own side of the tracks. Hickok didn't want any mingling of the Texans and the sodbusters in from their prairie farms to attend the county fair. It was hard to say which group hated the other more. The cattlemen regarded the farmers as a pack of Jayhawkers, "nesters" who were ruining the frontier with their windmills and barbed-wire fences. To the farmers the drovers were a lot of highhanded ruffians who didn't hesitate to devastate their land with the trampling herds and make their towns unsafe with the disorderly cow hands. Kansas and Texas, in brief, wanted a quick divorce, which was soon to be provided when the railroads extended into Texas and made the cattle drives unnecessary.

The drinking and carousing got under way early in the evening of October 5. One of the cow hands' favorite sports was to seize any fairly prosperous citizen found on the street, hoist him to their shoulders, and carry him to the nearest saloon, where he was plunked down on the bar and commanded to buy drinks for the whole mob. All this in a spirit of rough geniality—no harm done except to the victim's purse. Young Jake Karatofsky was thus borne into the Apple-jack Saloon and released only after buying a round or two from the lush profits of his Great Western Store. Marshal Hickok permitted this form of merriment, uncomfortable as it may have been for sobersided citizens, and to show there was no hard feeling himself bought a round for one of the roving mobs of celebrants at the Alamo. But he cautioned them to keep their celebrating in bounds, fearful that as the evening went on and more barrels were drained the situation might get out of hand.

Shortly after dusk the merchant Theophilus Little, leaving his office to go home, observed the mob careening through Texas Street as though the world were coming to an end at midnight. "They went up and down the street with a wild rush and roar, totally oblivious of anything in their path. It was a drunken mob. I hurried home, got my family inside the house, locked the doors, and told my folks not to step outside."

The respectable people battened down against the storm, hoping that one man would somehow keep it under control. None offered their services to Marshal Hickok in preserving order.

Shortly before nine o'clock Hickok pushed his way through the riotous mob in Texas Street over to the Novelty Theater for a brief conference with Mike Williams. The latter was a friend of his, employed as a special policeman at the theater.

"No matter what happens," Hickok shouted in Williams' ear, "I want you to stay on this side of the street. Understand?"

Mike Williams nodded.

Hickok then returned to his station at the Alamo, where they were considering closing the double-glass doors against the roistering throng and calling it a night for the first time in the history of the establishment.

Shortly after nine o'clock Phil Coe, with a full cargo of liquor aboard, surrounded by a group of equally boisterous friends, came out of the Bull's Head. He was wearing a revolver for the first time—so his friends said—since coming to Abilene. What his purpose was, if any, will never be known. There was a report that "an inner circle of Texans, engaged in the saloon business and gambling halls, had conspired to kill Bill on the night of the roundup, and that in selecting the man to carry out the decree the lot had fallen on Coe." If such a conspiracy had been formed, however, it seems more likely that a professional gunman would have been hired for the job, rather than carelessly assigning it to the inexpert Coe. When he went out on the street with a gun at his side, openly defying the law, Coe probably hoped to stir up trouble for Hickok by encouraging the mob to run riot and smash up the town—the Texans had no more use for it.

Coe and his friends went careening over to the Alamo, where Hickok was known to have stationed himself.

Coe let out a Rebel yell and fired a shot in the air outside the Alamo.

Hickok came out of the Alamo drawing his guns. He saw Coe with the smoking revolver in his hand.

"Who fired that shot?" he demanded somewhat unnecessarily.

"I did," said Coe, grinning.

"Why?"

"I shot at a mad dog."

It was a silly answer, calculated to infuriate Hickok. Anyone shooting at a dog in that mob would have been certain to hit one or more Texans.

So Coe and Hickok, with a wild-eyed crowd all around them, finally came to a showdown. They were standing less than ten feet apart. Coe fired first, his bullet scorching a path through Hickok's coat but inflicting only a flesh wound.

Hickok came out with both of his double-action revolvers and fired them simultaneously. He always shot for the head, but in this extremity his aim was low. Coe went down with two bullets in his abdomen.

"I've shot too low," Hickok exclaimed in disgust, studying the outsize figure of Coe thrashing the dust of Texas Street in the lamplight from the saloons.

The crowd fell back, shocked into its senses at Coe's quick comeuppance.

Just at that moment, disobeying Hickok's orders that he stay on his own side of the street, special policeman Mike Williams came running out of the shadows. Hickok mistook him for a Texan coming up to avenge Coe; perhaps he only saw him out of the corner of his unreliable eyes; at any rate, he fired immediately. This time his aim was, unfortunately, better. Williams went down with two bullets in his head. Between his failing eyesight, Williams' disobedience of his orders, and the extreme tension of the moment Hickok had killed a man of whom he was very fond. "In battle Hickok's reactions were lightning-quick," wrote William MacLeod Raine, "but one finds back of them at times a hint of panic." Under the circumstances, surrounded as he was by hundreds of belligerent Texans, Hickok might have been forgiven more than a "hint of panic."

Hickok still did not realize that the second man he had shot in the space of less than a minute was his friend Mike Williams. Through the gun smoke he told the crowd, "If any of you want the rest of these pills, come and get 'em."

The crowd dispersed. Hickok bent over the body of his second victim and saw that it was Williams. He carried his friend's body into the Alamo and laid it on a poker table and wept over it.

Half an hour later, almost out of his mind with rage and grief, Marshal Hickok rampaged up and down Texas Street. He went into every bar and shouted, "Every one of you mount his pony and ride for camp—and do it quick!" He tore along Texas Street, knocking down men who made a show of defiance or were slow to obey his orders to clear out of town. Nobody was reckless enough to oppose his order to close down Texas Town and put a sudden end to the celebration. Groups of horsemen galloped across Mud Creek and out to their camps on the prairie as though the devil were on their heels. "That night the desperate heroes of border strife hid in cellars and sunflower patches, or on swift ponies found their way to their cattle camps," wrote one observer. The lights went out in every saloon and deadfall in Texas Town. By midnight the only figure stirring on its streets was that of Marshal Hickok.

Never again would the cow hands raise hell in Abilene. The town had known its last moment of excitement—until some eighty years later when General Eisenhower paid a visit to his boyhood home.

There was a pathetic footnote to the gunfight at the Alamo. Phil Coe was still alive when he fell into the street and was carried to the home of a friend near the schoolhouse. He lingered for three days in the greatest agony with two bullets in his abdomen. A belly wound was almost always fatal in those days; there was little that could be done for him. Some said Hickok paid a dramatic visit to Coe's deathbed, but the story does not ring true. Hickok was a good hater, held Coe responsible for Williams' death, and was never known to indulge in any sentimentality over a fallen opponent, no matter how great his suffering. Children who attended the school near where Coe finally breathed his last remembered for years afterward listening to his agonizing moans and thinking that "it would take forever for him to die."

From then on Abilene was quiet as a prairie-dog town in winter. A terrific autumn rain fell over the prairies, the worst that even the older Indians could remember, moving up through Kansas, Wyoming, and Dakota Territory. Then the wind shifted, a norther came whistling down, and the Great Plains were coated with a vast slick of ice. Then a three-day blizzard struck, killing thousands of unsold cattle, whole herds of buffalo, scores of hunters and plainsmen caught out on the plains.

Abilene burrowed in for a long, hard winter.

One thing its citizens were all but unanimously agreed upon: no more cattle drives. Their decision was published in the Texas papers: "We most respectfully request all who had contemplated driving Texas cattle to Abilene . . . to seek some other point for shipment, as the inhabitants of Dickinson County will no longer submit to the evils of the trade." Abilene had thrived for several years on the cattle trade, but it was in no mood for gratitude and did not take time to reflect that much of its prosperity would vanish with the drovers and their herds.

By the following summer it became evident that Abilene was just another tank town on the Kansas Pacific without the cattle trade. With bitter reproach Joseph G. McCoy wrote, "Four-fifths of her business houses became vacant, rents fell to a trifle, many of the leading hotels and rooming houses were either closed or taken down and moved to other points.

Property became unsaleable. The luxuriant sunflower sprang up thick and flourished in the main streets, while the inhabitants, such as could not get away, passed their time sadly contemplating their ruin. Curses both loud and deep were freely bestowed . . . The remaining inhabitants betook themselves to suing each other, with a vigor equalled only by the famous Kilkenny cats. Some of the best citizens became entirely bankrupt from the sudden stagnation of trade." During the summer of 1872, McCoy wrote, petitions again were circulated, this time "praying, inviting, begging the cattlemen to return with their herds, but alas! it was too late."

Late in 1871, however, the people of Abilene only wanted to see the backs of their noisy visitors from Texas. The same went for their gunfighting marshal. The City Council, on December 12, announced that it was dismissing Hickok, effective the next day, "for the reason that the city is no longer in need of his services."

Many of the citizens, in fact, were as eager to be rid of their flamboyant protector as of the rambunctious Texans. They still regarded Tom Smith as their martyred hero, complaining along with the pioneer iceman J. B. Edwards that "Wild Bill did not use his hands as his luckless predecessor had done; he used his hardware instead. His bravery has been described by oldtimers in Abilene as cruder than Tom Smith's. Many believed that Wild Bill without his guns would have been tame." They chose to disregard the fact that Hickok had used his guns only once, the night of October 5, during his eight months as marshal of Abilene and that it was doubtful whether even Tom Smith's fists could have kept the lid on the town that night.

With considerably more fairness Eugene Cunningham wrote, "Hickok had a tremendous job on his hands in Abilene. He has been variously described as a racketeering, cowardly officer, and as a very paragon of chivalrous bravery. The truth, of course, lies between these two opinions . . . Such fire-eaters as Wes Hardin did nothing to make life easy for them [the cow-town marshals]. A kid will take a chance where a grown man hesitates. And a kid's bullet is just as deadly as anyone's."

Dismissed without so much as a vote of thanks by the City Council, which doubtless resented his highhanded tactics as its sergeant at arms, Hickok headed out of Abilene that night. His farewells were few and brief. There was no one to see him off on the wind-swept platform of the Kansas Pacific depot as he boarded the eastbound train for Kansas City.

He had taken off his marshal's star that afternoon and presented it with an ironic bow to the City Council and would never again wear the badge of a peace officer.

CHAPTER 12

Hickok Treads the Boards

One of the oddest facets of the western legend was that it was being re-created, fictionalized, and enlarged upon almost at the moment the events on which it was based were taking place. Men like Wild Bill Hickok, Buffalo Bill Cody, and a few others brave enough to face an audience performed their heroics out West, then hastened East to act them out, with suitable embellishments, behind the footlights. The western, as America's own myth, monopolizes television and theatrical screens today and enthralls much larger audiences, but even back in the seventies the public was eager for western drama indoors, Wild West shows outdoors, and paper-backed literature printed in car lots. Dime novels under the signature of Ned Buntline and Prentiss Ingraham sold by the millions. Between 1869 and 1933 the rather startling total of seventeen hundred dime novels was written about Buffalo Bill alone. The real western bonanzas, it seemed, weren't to be found in some Godforsaken mining camp but along the Rialtos of eastern cities and among the busy printing presses.

An event hardly had time to happen before it was being dramatized, publicized, and glorified back East. Was it any wonder that an air of unreality, an atmosphere of self-consciousness, began to pervade the scenes of western history? An illiterate young ruffian barely had time to fan away the gun smoke surrounding him and his latest victim before a roving hack was offering to write his life story, complete with justifications and noble sentiments.

Even then the material was growing thin, and one hero was forced to borrow from the legend of another. In *Buffalo Bill,* the first of many dramatizations of Cody's supposed exploits, Ned Buntline, the dramatist, had Buffalo Bill fighting "Jack McKandkess, a border ruffian," with Bowie knives—a barefaced appropriation of Hickok's supposed massacre of the McCanles "gang."

But the public was avid for western entertainment, and not merely because of a fascination with the frontier and its expanding opportunities. In the seventies western violence, somewhat sugar-coated and sentimentalized, helped Americans taper off from the excitement of the Civil War years. As Mari Sandoz has pointed out, the ten-year period from 1866 to 1876 was an era that "demanded the gaudiest, the most exaggerated characters to continue, if not the violent heroic times and deeds of a very bloody war, at least such heroics as could be whipped up to feed the public's voracious, wolfish hunger."

Hickok was shrewd enough to realize, even way out West, that there was money to be made out of the life he had led and was leading. He not only wanted to live the legend but profit by it. Soon enough he began to see himself as a unique sort of institution, patented, trademarked, and copyrighted.

Hickok's first venture into show business was a Wild West show, the first of its kind. No matter how much debunking has been done on his career, not all of it unwarranted, even the more skeptical historians have conceded that he was the innovator of this type of entertainment. Admittedly it was a humble and unsuccessful beginning, but his conception was the seedling from which Buffalo Bill reaped several fortunes and from which grew the traveling outdoor extravaganzas that toured the country for half a century, presenting a blank-cartridge-riddled version of the West that never existed except in a showman's fancy. Hickok evolved the pattern on which Buffalo Bill, Pawnee Bill, the 101 Ranch, and other showmen merely expanded and imposed more businesslike methods.

Hickok got his bright idea in the spring of 1870, a few months after fleeing Hays City with the 7th Cavalry on his heels. His ambition was to uproot a bit of the West and transplant it to some eastern city for the delight and amazement of people curious about the fauna of the frontier.

He had done well at the gambling tables in Topeka, Ellsworth, and Kansas City that spring and had a bank roll of several thousand dollars. Hardly a Barnum-sized stake, but Hickok hoped that the show's novelty would catch on quickly, without a lot of money spent on advertising and press agentry.

He decided to call his show "The Daring Buffalo Chase of the Plains." It would open at Niagara Falls, on the Canadian side of the border, in July when the place would be swarming with tourists. Just how the show would be transported, supplied, housed, and financed were pettifogging details that could be left to a later date.

In May of 1870, Hickok went about getting his show together with his customary energy. His cast must include cowboys, Indians, and buffaloes to carry out the promise of its title.

First the buffalo. He went up the Republican to the buffalo feeding grounds in Nebraska with three cowboys who were to be part of his company. Enlisting the buffalo in his enterprise quickly proved to be the most vexing of his problems. It was quite easy to shoot a buffalo, but capturing him was extremely difficult. Nobody, in fact, had ever tried it before.

Hickok and his cowboys tried lassoing them, but the buffaloes ran with their heads so low it was impossible to get the loop around their thick furry heads. The only solution was to cut one buffalo out of the herd and then chase him until he was ready to drop. A rope was then fastened around his horns. By this laborious method six buffaloes, outraged, unruly, and rebellious, were finally corralled.

It took two weeks for Hickok and his assistants, hauling the buffaloes along by ropes, to get them to the railroad yards at Ogallala and load them into cattle cars. Everybody who witnessed the spectacle of Hickok cramming buffalo into railroad cars naturally thought he was a madman.

Hickok next recruited four hungry but fairly tame Comanches as members of the company. One of the Comanches had a pet cinnamon bear, another somehow had acquired a monkey, neither of which they intended to leave behind. Hickok allowed the Indians to bring along their pets.

Hickok & Co. set out for Niagara Falls late in June—the impresario himself, three cowboys, four Comanches, six buffaloes, a monkey, and a bear.

The show opened July 20, with four or five thousand people gathered around the wire enclosure in which "The Daring Buffalo Chase" was to be performed. There were no grandstands, no board fence around the enclosure, and therefore no admissions could be collected. Hickok had simply run out of money on arrival at Niagara Falls and would have to pass the hat and trust to the gratitude and generosity of the spectators to recoup his investment.

It was, on the whole, an exciting performance, although it did not proceed as planned. In the first place the buffaloes were reluctant to be chased; they had to be pushed into the arena and then just stood there, balking temperamentally, snorting and pawing the ground occasionally. Finally Hickok fired a gun and they took off in a wild charge. Round and round the enclosure they went, with the Comanches in pursuit. A few minutes later a pack of dogs attracted to the scene by the excitement, an equally joyous mob of small boys, and a number of adult spectators entered the enclosure and joined the chase. The arena was soon a dusty bedlam. Everybody but Hickok was having a wonderful time.

Then the situation got completely out of hand. With a concerted charge the buffaloes tore through the fence and thundered through the nearby residential section. Somebody unbarred the bear's cage to the delight of both the bear and the crowd. The bear had been sniffing at the wares of an Italian sausage vendor stationed nearby, seized this unfortunate in a fond embrace, and gobbled up his sausages. It took a number of spectators to pry the vendor from the bear, so ardent was the latter's friendliness. The monkey took this opportunity to break out of his cage, climb to the top of a wagon, and hurl everything he could lay his paws on at the crowd.

Hickok and his cowboys mounted up, rode after the buffaloes, drove them into a dead-end street, and finally herded them back to their corral.

"The Daring Buffalo Chase of the Plains" lasted exactly one performance. Hickok's assistants passed the collection plates, but most of the remaining spectators found they'd left their pokes at home or downright declined to contribute. The receipts totaled exactly $123.86, and Hickok was in the hole for approximately one thousand dollars.

To cap it all, when the dust had settled on this exhibition an English tourist came up to Hickok and inquired, "I say, my good man, are you an Indian or a white man?"

Hickok knocked him flat, saying, "That's the kind of man I am," and fled to the nearest saloon.

That wasn't quite the end of Hickok's misfortunes. The Comanches were clamoring to be sent home, although Hickok was flat broke. He finally managed to sell the six buffaloes to various Niagara Falls butchers. The proceeds were used to buy tickets home for the Comanches. Hickok and the cow hands were forced to beat their way back to Kansas City on the freights.

Hickok's next venture into show business came after his eight-month term as marshal of Abilene. He spent most of 1872, following that episode, in the gambling halls of Kansas City. Luck was not always with him, and outside of gambling there seemed to be few opportunities for an unemployed lawman of fierce reputation and failing vision. And then the authorities put a crimp in the gambling business when a reform ticket was voted into municipal office, and the police, in an abrupt about-face, made the gamblers feel decidedly unwelcome around Market Square. J. W. Buel, then a reporter for the Kansas City *Journal*, said Hickok described himself as "severely money-bound" during this period.

At this low-water mark, early in 1873, along came Buffalo Bill Cody, reeking of success and prosperity in a long, fur-trimmed coat like a European impresario's, Chicago tailoring, and a gold watch chain heavy enough to haul barges. His old friends, in fact, viewed Cody's affluence with something like consternation. A short time before Buffalo Bill had shown up at Fort McPherson in tail coat and silk hat. So great was the transformation that his old commanding officer, General Reynolds, bellowed at him, "Who in thunder are you?" And Buffalo Bill's old partner, Buffalo Chips White, was so enraged at the ex-scout's citified appearance that he would not be appeased or speak civilly to Cody until several bottles of champagne had been sluiced down his throat.

Cody wanted Hickok to join him in a touring dramatic company presenting an epic called *Scouts of the Prairie*.

Hickok, in reply to this offer, recalled his experiences of two and a half years ago with "The Daring Buffalo Chase of the Plains" and growled, "No more theatrical business for me. I lost my shirt the last time."

Cody pointed out that this time he couldn't lose anything

but his time, since the producers were handling all the financial arrangements.

And when Buffalo Bill remarked that Hickok would be paid at least a hundred a week for his efforts, maybe more, the latter's interest was plainly aroused.

Cody recalled in his autobiography that Hickok was not at all eager to expose himself to an audience and was certain he would make a fool of himself but admitted that he was flat broke and needed a new stake. Gambling would be curtailed around Kansas City for months, until the reform administration grew less watchful. So Hickok agreed to take up an acting career without even bothering to read the script of his first dramatic vehicle.

A less promising recruit for the American theater of that day could scarely be imagined. An actor in those times was expected to make large gestures, speak in thundering tones, and make himself at least twice normal size, dramatically speaking. If every word and movement were not clearly visible to the drama lovers perched in the uppermost gallery, they tended to become raucous and abusive. Theatrical lighting and acoustics had not been developed to the point where naturalism was at all possible. Hickok was flamboyant in dress and loved attention, but he was soft-spoken and had only contempt for the falsely heroic gesture. He was constitutionally incapable of understanding the demands of play-acting, of pretending. For a grown man to paint his face and strut before an audience seemed a disgusting fraud at best.

Nothing about the venture, except the prospect of a weekly pay check, could possibly have appealed to Hickok. He had a deeply ingrained dislike and distrust, like most westerners, of anything to do with the effete and mannered East and its cities. He was prepared to hate everything about his new profession and the people before which he would be required to practice it.

The only reason he accepted Cody's offer was despair over his present condition. At the age of thirty-six he was almost an old man by frontier standards. Even if the state of his eyesight permitted, his experiences as a lawman, being forced to flee from Hays City and having been curtly discharged by the city administration of Abilene, were hardly conducive to making the career of a peace officer at all attractive. Once a town was tamed down, its citizens had little use for a gun-fighting marshal and preferred something quieter and less menacing in the matter of law enforcement. He had no desire to take up scouting again and submitting at least partially to military discipline.

His only asset really was his reputation, and the only buyer at present was a catchpenny theatrical enterprise.

Scouts of the Prairie, the foundation of that enterprise, had already been exposed to public view and acclaimed a resounding failure, artistically speaking. The author was Ned Buntline, born Edward Zane Carroll Judson in an upstate New York hamlet and destined for a spectacularly unquiet life, a frisky fellow of many pursuits, adventurer on land and sea, drunkard, temperance lecturer, beggar, promoter, and jailbird. He ran away to sea at the age of fourteen, became a midshipman in the U. S. Navy six years later, and acquired an amazing tolerance for alcohol in the rum houses of the Spanish Main. His naval career was terminated amid a cloud of charges of insubordination and other crimes on the high seas. Styling himself Ned Buntline, he turned pulp writer and in 1847, at the age of twenty-four, produced a blood-drenched epic titled *The Black Avenger of the Spanish Main; or, The Fiend of Blood: A Thrilling Tale of Buccaneer Times.* Wandering from Canada to Mexico in search of story material, he acquired and abandoned a number of wives, the exact total of whom has never been accurately computed. In Nashville, Tennessee, he made off with the affections of the wife of a citizen named Porterfield. The latter challenged

him to a duel, which Buntline, a crack shot, won by placing
a bullet between Porterfield's eyes. A lynch mob broke into
the jail where Buntline was being held for this indiscretion
and strung him up in the public square. Somehow, according
to Buntline's account, the noose was fastened around his
heavily starched collar and he was cut down, still breathing,
by his friends. The only ill effect of this incident was a permanent crick in the neck.

Buntline toured the West as a temperance lecturer, a profitable side line not at all inhibited by his continuing devo-
tion to the bottle. He gave some of his most stirring lectures
on the curse of drink while swacked to the eyebrows and
barely able to stand up. Meanwhile, he was absorbing western lore, along with his whiskey, in all the frontier barrel
houses.

Somewhere along the line he got the idea of presenting
real-life plainsmen in a drama detailing their supposed exploits and for this purpose recruited Buffalo Bill and one of
his side-kicks, J. R. (Texas Jack) Omohundro. The play in
which they were to appear was apparently the least of his
worries. He dashed it off in four hours after locking himself
in a Chicago hotel room. The critics said *Scouts of the Prairie*
was a new low in dramaturgy, one remarking that it "could
have begun in the middle and gone forward or backward
just as easily as the way it was written." It was supposed
to be a straight melodrama, but audiences accepted it in the
only way possible, as a rip-roaring comedy.

The play was a mishmash of monologues by the scouts
telling of their experiences, interwoven with sudden bursts
of gunfire and Indian fighting whenever the audience became restive. One critic described it as "a three-cornered
fight between the scouts, the Indians and some characters
supposed to be whites." The leader of the white settlers,
played by Buntline himself, was "a human nightmare who
managed to keep drunk for several hours without a drop of

anything." Buntline even threw in one of his temperance lectures for good measure, and when a group of stage Indians tied him to a tree to burn him alive the audience broke out with cheers and applause. The second-act curtain came down with Gale Burg, Buntline's character, turned into a human torch.

"The third act," according to Henry Blackman Sell and Victor Weybright (*Buffalo Bill and the Wild West*), "was a rehash of the first and second, with resurrected Indians and constant shooting. Encouraged by shouts from the audience, which threatened to join in the battle at any time, the actors found lariats which had been overlooked before, and lassoed each other. Gale Burg died again, to the delight of the spectators, who felt he couldn't die too often. For weeks afterward it was said that dazed playgoers would shout, 'The Indians are upon us!' and explode in maniacal laughter."

Then, as now, audiences paid little attention to the outraged critics when presented with such ripe, unpremeditated humor as was offered by *Scouts of the Prairie*. The critics were unsparing in their denunciations. The man from the Chicago *Tribune* wrote of the opening late in 1872 at Nixon's Auditorium that Buffalo Bill "speaks his lines after the diffident manner of a schoolboy, fidgeting uneasily when silent," and that the leading lady, Mlle. Morlacchi, as Dove Eye, the Indian maiden, exhibited little more than "an Italian accent and a weakness for scouts." And the Chicago *Times* reported, "It is not probable Chicago will look on the like again. Such a combination of incongruous dialogue, execrable acting, renowned performers, mixed audience, intolerable stench, scalping, blood and thunder, is not likely to be vouchsafed to a city for a second time—even Chicago."

The show went on tour, visiting St. Louis, Cincinnati, Buffalo, and Albany, gathering the same kind of notices and equally large receipts in the box office. The best a St. Louis critic could say of the exhibition was that "Buffalo

Bill is a beautiful blonde." Cody's wife unexpectedly attended the opening in St. Louis. Spotting her in the audience, Cody was overcome by shame and blurted out, "Oh, Mama, I'm a bad actor." The audience applauded in total agreement.

Early in 1873 the troupe wound up in New York for a brief engagement at Niblo's Gardens—but not brief enough to escape the notice of the critics from the New York newspapers. The New York *Herald* thought "everything was so wonderfully bad it was almost good. The whole performance was so far aside of human experience, so wonderful in its daring feebleness, that no ordinary intellect is capable of understanding it." As for the acting, "The Hon. William F. Cody, otherwise known as Buffalo Bill, occasionally called by the refined people of the eastern cities 'Bison William,' is a good-looking fellow, tall and straight as an arrow, but ridiculous as an actor. Texas Jack is not quite so good-looking, not so tall, not so straight, and not so ridiculous. Ned Buntline is simply maundering imbecility." The New York *World* characterized the presentation as "very poor slop," whose only saving grace was Buffalo Bill and "a certain characteristic charm that pleases the beholders."

This, then, was what Wild Bill Hickok walked into when he came East at Cody's summons to take up a theatrical career early in the autumn of 1873. It was decided to reopen at Niblo's Gardens with a cursory rewrite job and without Ned Buntline. Hickok would play himself, and Buntline's character would be written out of the play. Several female characters were added in support of the doe-eyed Mlle. Morlacchi. And the management was taken over by the theater-wise John M. Burke, who billed himself as "Arizona John," though he had never been near Arizona. Burke was a former actor who had turned to theatrical press agentry and had served as the advance man when *Scouts of the Prairie* was on tour. He "had the imagination to see the place that Buffalo Bill should occupy in show business" and eventually helped Cody make several fortunes, which Cody dissipated with an airy grace.

Hickok came to New York suspicious of the whole venture, rightly convinced that he would make a fool of himself as an actor. As for New York itself, it appeared to be the metropolitan stew he had anticipated, swarming with outlandish foreigners, thieves, pickpockets, and supercilious dudes who seemed to find him ridiculous. Hell's Kitchen was tougher than any cow town and the Tenderloin a lot seamier than the Devil's Addition in Abilene. What the place needed, evidently, was a good, fast-shooting marshal, and what it had was a lot of fat, grafting cops with night sticks.

Possibly anticipating Hickok's confusion on arrival, Buffalo Bill had written him, "I am staying at the Brevoort Hotel, and you will land in New York at the 42nd St. Depot. To avoid getting lost in the big city, take a cab at the depot and you will be driven to the hotel in a few minutes. Pay the cabman two dollars. These New York cabmen are regular holdup men, and your driver may want to charge you more, but do not pay more than two dollars under any circumstances."

Hickok had these instructions firmly in mind when he landed in New York. When he dismounted from the hansom cab in front of the Brevoort, he handed the driver two dollars and turned to enter the hotel.

"Wait a minute," snarled the cabbie. "My charge is five dollars."

"Two dollars is all you're going to get," Hickok replied firmly.

The driver climbed down from his box, saying, "Well, you long-haired rube, I'll take the rest out of your hide."

There was a quick flurry of action, at the end of which a very lumpy cabman found himself sprawled in the gutter of lower Fifth Avenue. Hickok dusted off his hands and strolled into the lobby of the Brevoort. The manager, who had witnessed the scene outside, dashed up to Cody's room and shouted, "Say, Bill, I think the gentleman you've been expecting has arrived!" When the curbstone brawl was described, Cody agreed that it sure sounded like Wild Bill Hickok. In a few moments the two old friends were reunited. "Arizona John" Burke, in a memoir written for *Billboard* at the close of his long career, recalled, "Wild Bill arrived in New York dressed in a cutaway coat, flowered vest, ruffled white shirt, salt-and-pepper trousers, string tie, high-heeled boots, and a broad-brimmed hat."

He quickly became one of the town's celebrities and was followed around by crowds of admirers, mingled with a few scoffers—a circumstance he could doubtless have avoided by dressing less conspicuously.

He liked that part of it, the public adoration, but the necessity of appearing on stage, roaring out all sorts of nonsensical Buntline dialogue, was something else again. His friend Cody had a wide and well-defined streak of hamminess—or showmanship, to put it more gently—which allowed him to develop into an acceptable performer. Hickok had absolutely no talent for make-believe. He had to get by on his looks and his newspaper fame, which seemed to suffice for all but the more discriminating members of his audiences.

Even Buffalo Bill, the sponsor of his new career, was dismayed by Hickok's refusal to comply with any of the demands or traditions of the theater and wrote in his autobiography: "Although he had a fine stage presence, and was a handsome fellow, and possessed a good strong voice, yet it was almost impossible for him to utter a word. He insisted that we were making a set of fools of ourselves, and that we were the laughing-stock of the people."

Not content with lousing up his own performance, Cody continued, "Wild Bill was continually playing tricks on the members of the company, and it was his especial delight to torment the 'supers.' Quite frequently in our sham Indian

209

battles, he would run up to the 'Indians' (supers), and putting his pistol close to their legs, fire and burn them with the powder instead of shooting over their heads. This would make them dance and jump, although they were paid twenty-five cents each for performing the 'dying business.'"

This prankishness, of course, was an expression of Hickok's self-disgust at being trapped in this theatrical nonsense, a way of relieving his feelings and concealing the fact that he suffered from a bad case of stage fright, which afflicted him from the beginning to the end of his brief acting career. Some of the scenes would have caused a less aesthetic type than Hickok to cringe—one in particular in which he was called upon to shoot his way into a pack of Indians and singlehandedly rescue Dove Eye from her captors.

At the climax of this scene Hickok had to declaim one of Ned Buntline's less immortal lines:

"Fear not, fair maid! By heavens, you are safe at last with Wild Bill, who is ever ready to risk his life and die, if need be, in defense of weak and defenseless womanhood!"

With a speech like that to utter, Hickok naturally preferred to play this scene in comparative darkness. A stage-hand in charge of the spotlight, which was located in the gallery and beamed down on the stage, apparently divined Hickok's embarrassment during the scene. For several nights during the New York run, despite Hickok's vehement protests, he insisted on following Hickok around the stage with his beam of light. Hickok took to hiding behind the props and scenery while bellowing encouragement at Mlle. Morlacchi, which gave the scene a peculiar flavor indeed. Still the man in the spotlight gallery bedeviled him. One night he couldn't stand it any longer, hauled out his pistol, hurled it at the spotlight, and scored a bull's-eye. The audience thought it a delightful piece of business, those who escaped the flying splinters of glass.

Between stage fright and an inability to memorize Buntline's stupefying dialogue, Hickok often dried up completely on stage, at which point his stage partners, Buffalo Bill and Texas Jack, or the professionals in the company would attempt to cover up by ad-libbing, then asking Hickok leading questions which might prime his memory and get the plot moving again.

One of his early biographers (J. W. Buel, *Scouts of the Plains*) told of attending a performance at which Hickok made his entrance to thunderous applause. This so distracted Hickok that he forgot his lines completely. One of the actors, to get him back on the trolley, prodded him with questions, "Where have you been, Bill? What has detained you so long?"

Hickok groped for his lines. Inspiration came to him only after his gaze, roving around the audience, rested momentarily on a box in which a friend of his named Mulligan was seated with a party, and he blurted out, "I've just been out on a hunt with Mr. Mulligan, and we got corralled by a party of hostiles." Buel said the desperate ad lib "fairly brought down the house," since Mulligan was a prominent businessman.

"Thereupon," Buel added, "Bill, who is an excellent story teller and knows just how much ornamentation to give his recitals concerning Indians, related at some length all the particulars that a curious-loving audience could desire, and upon concluding the story there was an encore which shook the house like an explosion."

Buffalo Bill was often dismayed by Hickok's antics, the latter being completely unpredictable—and often slightly alcoholized—from the moment he strode out on stage.

In one of the play's early scenes Buffalo Bill, Wild Bill, and Texas Jack were supposed to be sitting around a campfire and telling stories while swigging out of a whiskey bottle. The bottle, of course, contained cold tea. One night, in an ornery mood, Hickok took the bottle in turn, swallowed cold tea, and then disgustedly spewed it out all over the stage, bellowing, "You must think I'm the worst fool east of the Rockies that I can't tell whiskey from cold tea. This don't count, and I can't tell a story unless I get real whiskey."

Buffalo Bill said he "tried to remonstrate with him, while the audience shook down the galleries with their cheers. At first I was greatly mortified, but it did not take long to convince me that Wild Bill unconsciously made a big hit."

The proceedings on stage came to a complete halt while Buffalo Bill hissed to the stage manager to get liquor in a hurry. The whiskey was produced after much frantic scurrying around backstage; Hickok took a long pull at the bottle and told his story "with excellent effect."

From then on Hickok insisted on having bona fide whiskey served during his performances. Buffalo Bill acceded, hoping it would induce Hickok to behave better. His performance improved, Cody conceded, but the whiskey tended to relieve Hickok of too many of his inhibitions. Mlle. Morlacchi, as Dove Eye, attracted his amorous attentions, and he "grew fonder of the heroine on stage than the script stipulated."

The young actress already was involved in a backstage triangle, which Hickok evidently aspired to turn into a quadrangle.

Texas Jack and the company manager, "Arizona John" Burke, were both in love with the comely young Italian actress. (She finally resolved the situation by marrying Texas Jack.)

With Hickok amorously pursuing Mlle. Morlacchi on stage, and Texas Jack and Burke glowering from the wings, the atmosphere backstage at Niblo's Gardens must have been rather tense for a time. Hickok's attention, in any event, was soon diverted elsewhere, and the leading lady no longer had to protect herself in the clinches with Hickok.

When the *Scouts of the Prairie* company went on a tour of various eastern cities in the spring of 1874, Hickok joined the troupe unwillingly, bound by his contract with the management. He asked both Cody and Burke to free him of his obligation, but he was a big draw at the box office—partly because of his name and partly because of his unpredictable antics on stage—and they refused. Frustrated in his yearning to go back West and have done with this foolish exhibition, he became more of a problem than ever to Cody and Burke.

The troupe was signed to appear at Titusville, Pennsylvania, then the center of America's first oil boom, a town filled with oil-field roughnecks and other boisterous but well-heeled transients. Cody and Burke foresaw trouble, particularly if Hickok could not be kept under control, and it was not long in finding them. The company arrived at their hotel, registered, and checked into their rooms. Then Cody, Hickok, and several others came downstairs to play billiards. They were halted outside the billiard room by the manager, who (Cody wrote in his autobiography) "stopped me and said that there was a party of roughs from the lower oil regions who were spreeing, and had boasted that they were staying in town to meet the Buffalo Bill gang and clean them out. The landlord begged of me not to allow the members of the company to enter the billiard room as he did not wish any fight in his house. To please the landlord, and at his suggestion, I called the boys into the parlor and explained to them the situation. Wild Bill wanted to go at once and fight the whole mob, but I persuaded him to keep away from them during the day."

That evening, however, while Cody was taking tickets at the theater adjoining the hotel, "the landlord came rushing up and said that Wild Bill was having a fight with the roughs in the barroom. It seemed that Bill had not been able to resist the temptation of going to see what kind of a mob it was that wanted to test the pluck of Buffalo Bill's party; and just as he stepped into the room, one of the bruisers put his hand on Bill's shoulder and said, 'Hello, Buffalo Bill, we've been looking for you all day.'"

As Cody later reconstructed the affair, Hickok daintily

removed the oilman's hand from his shoulder and politely denied that he was Buffalo Bill.

"You're a liar," the oilman roared.

"You're another," Hickok roared back.

Cody said that Hickok "instantly knocked him down, and then seizing a chair, he laid out four or five of the crowd on the floor, and then drove the rest out of the room. All this was done in a minute or two, and by the time I got downstairs, Bill was coming out of the barroom, whistling a lively tune."

Cody remonstrated with his friend, saying, "I thought you promised to come into the Opera House by the private entrance."

"I did try to follow that trail," Hickok replied with a defiant grin, "but I got lost among the canyons, and then I ran into the hostiles. But it's all right now, they won't bother us any more."

Thanks to Hickok's efficiency as a barroom brawler, Cody said, the company was not further annoyed during the stay in Titusville.

The natives were more friendly in most of the towns the *Scouts of the Prairie* troupe visited and consequently saw a more genial side to Hickok's nature. In Portland, Maine, the company stayed at the United States Hotel. Hickok retired to his room after the first performance around midnight, unusually early for him. Shortly after going to sleep, he was awakened by loud merriment in the room next to his. Clad in his nightshirt, Hickok went next door to upbraid his neighbors, fully prepared to do battle if they proved recalcitrant.

He found five of Portland's leading businessmen playing poker and tilting bottles, all in a friendly and jovial mood. Hickok was disarmed when they suggested he take a hand and a drink and forget about sleeping. Hickok shrugged and joined them at the poker table.

When the game broke up at dawn, Hickok was seven hundred dollars richer.

"Let this be a lesson to you, gentlemen," he said, rising and slapping a wad of greenbacks against his palm. "Never wake up a stranger, destroy his sleep, and then invite him to play poker with you. Good morning."

By the time the company reached Rochester, New York, Hickok was thoroughly fed up. They had a long run there and he became increasingly restive. One night a lamp in the bank of footlights exploded close to him, with a flash of light that seared his already sensitive and inflamed eyes. He had to undergo medical treatment and was forced to wear glasses with thick blue lenses when he wasn't appearing on stage. His secret fear that he would soon go blind grew more gnawingly insistent and, given his temperament, which impelled him to meet misfortune with belligerence, he was more of a problem than ever to his employers.

One night in Rochester he was standing in the wings, waiting to make his entrance, with Buffalo Bill's wife standing nearby. They were watching Texas Jack and Mlle. Morlacchi play an excessively sentimental love scene.

Mrs. Cody heard Hickok say, "Ain't they foolish? What's the use of getting out there and making fools of ourselves? I ain't going to do it any more."

A few nights later, apparently with severance aforethought, Hickok "resumed his old annoying practice of singeing the 'supers'' legs, and carried the trick so far that I remonstrated so sharply, that, without saying a word, Wild Bill doffed his buckskin suit and walked out of the theater, refusing to appear any more . . ." according to Buffalo Bill. Hickok was through with the life of a strolling player. To show there were no hard feelings, Buffalo Bill and Texas Jack chipped in a thousand dollars for Hickok's getaway money. He had, of course, saved nothing from his salary as an actor.

Instead of taking his new stake and heading for Kansas

City on the first westbound train, Hickok unwisely decided to go to New York first and try his luck at faro. He soon lost most of his money. Nor was his temper improved by reports he heard of a cheap-jack theatrical company which was playing in Binghamton, New York, offering a spurious version of *Scouts of the Prairie* and featuring an actor billed as Wild Bill Hickok.

Hickok regarded this as a counterfeiting of his own personality and went upstate in a stormy mood. He attended a performance at the Binghamton theater, sitting down front for a good view of the proceedings. There came a scene in which his imitator was shooting and slashing his way through a band of Comanches. Somehow it looked even more ridiculous when someone else was doing it. According to Buel (*Scouts of the Plains*), his temper boiled over and "he leaped upon the stage and, grabbing the manager, flung him bodily into the orchestra, and then knocked the personator of his character through the scenes, regardless of the knives and pistols and tomahawks carried by the Indians."

The curtain was hastily rung down, upon which "Bill unconcernedly resumed his seat and shouted to the company to proceed with the show." Fearful of another assault from the audience, however, the company refused to proceed with the drama until the police were summoned.

A solitary policeman came down the aisle, tapped Hickok on the shoulder, and announced he was under arrest. It was the first such experience for him and he found he didn't like it at all. Particularly irksome, as he explained later, was the fact that only one officer had been dispatched on such a perilous errand.

Hickok, Buel wrote, shook his head at the roundsman and said, "I would suggest that you send for assistance."

The policeman went out and found a brother officer, then returned to Hickok's seat.

"How numerous are you now?" Hickok inquired.

"There are two of us."

Honor was still not satisfied.

"Better get more help," Hickok told the cops.

This time the sheriff himself was brought to the scene. "Now will you accompany us to the jail, Mr. Hickok?" he was asked.

Hickok, deciding that his dignity was appeased, went along quietly.

Next morning a sympathetic judge listened to Hickok's explanation for violently interrupting the performance and fined him a nominal three dollars and costs.

Thoroughly disillusioned with eastern civilization, he then headed for the still wild West, never again to venture east of the Alleghenies.

CHAPTER 13

A Student of the Picture Cards

New excitement spread like a golden flame through the West in the summer of 1874. It was sorely needed, from the viewpoint of the men who lived on the excitement of booms and rushes, strikes and stampedes. The cattle boom was dying out in the railhead towns along the Kansas Pacific (although Dodge City's heyday was still two years in the offing), and buffalo hunting was growing less profitable after the massive slaughters of the past few years. The West was feeling the effects of the Panic of 1873.

Once again hopes were revived by the possibility of a big gold strike—this time in the Badlands of Dakota Territory. The Black Hills of what is now South Dakota were invaded by Colonel Custer and his 7th Cavalry, despite solemn promises and ironclad treaties given the Sioux that they would remain a sacred enclave to the tribesmen. It had long been suspected that gold veined the Black Hills, and that was a more than sufficient reason to break the white man's promise to the Indians, who believed they were the dwelling place of the Great Manitou.

Custer, with a thousand soldiers, two naturalists, two gold miners, and a geologist, had invaded the Black Hills early that summer for the ostensible purpose of finding a place to locate a military post there. The real reason was to determine the truth of rumors which had been circulating for more than a score of years that the creek beds of the Dakota Badlands were studded with nuggets. As early as 1861 a Sioux City Falls newspaper (the *Northwestern Independent*) had replied to anti-Dakota remarks of its contemporaries in Iowa by referring to them as "people in torn underwear who talk about the dent in a neighbor's silk hat." But, the editorial continued quite prophetically, "let them crow while they still have a voice. In less than two years Northern Iowa will see us rapping Dubuque over the knuckles with the Golden Key to the Black Hills, and shaking our dust and nuggets in the streets of Chicago!" That boast was fulfilled, not in two years but in fourteen.

One day late in July or early in August, Horatio N. Ross, one of the professional miners with the Custer column, panned out gold on French Creek, about four miles west of the present town of Custer.

Custer and his superiors tried to prevent the news from leaking out, but it was splashed all over page one of the Chicago *Inter-Ocean* of August 27, 1874:

GOLD!
THE LAND OF PROMISE!
Stirring News From the
Black Hills
THE GLITTERING TREASURE
Found At Last—A Belt
of Gold Territory
30 Miles Wide
THE PRECIOUS DUST
Found Under the

Horse's Feet
EXCITEMENT
Among the Troops

The rush was on, the last great stampede in the American West. "There would never be another like it," wrote Robert J. Casey in *The Black Hills,* "because presently there wouldn't be any more Old West. It was like previous booms in all its essential details. It was the same old melodrama with the same old plot and the same cast of characters and only slightly different scenery. But it differed in one important aspect. It was the first gold rush in which the fortune hunters could hope for something like modern conveniences. It was possible for them to ride most of the way to the Black Hills by train or steamboat. And there would soon be stage transportation from the present terminals."

Naturally this was an event from which Wild Bill Hickok, ex-lawman, ex-scout, ex-actor, and presently a professional gambler, could hardly afford to absent himself. Hearing the news from the Black Hills, he was off the mark with the swiftest of them, but he did not burden himself with a prospector's paraphernalia. Outside of his extensive wardrobe, a pair of Derringers, useful at poker-table range, was all the professional equipment he required. He had no intention, then, of grubbing around creek beds and mountain slopes with pick and shovel. The real money, he considered, was to be made separating the miners from their dust and nuggets after they had separated them from the earth. He would accommodate the sons of toil in comfortable surroundings, over the gambling tables, a safe distance from the rigors of prospecting and mining.

Hickok was now thirty-seven years old and not quite so wild a Bill. His eyes were bad; he had a touch of rheumatism, and rich living in the East had robbed him of some of the coiled-spring quality of his youth. But that didn't mean he was ready to hang up his gun belt and retire from the life of action and adventure. Hickok had merely become a trifle less willing to seek out trouble; he would still meet it more than halfway if it presented itself.

Word spread up the line of the Kansas Pacific that the ex-marshal of Abilene and the ex-sheriff at Hays City would be passing that way on his way to Cheyenne, Wyoming, the jumping-off place of the gold-seeking hordes. Also circulating in those towns where Hickok had briefly but vigorously established his six-shooter rule—perhaps hopefully—was the canard that he had turned play actor and toured the East with painted face because he no longer had the guts to face another gun.

And word bounced back from the trail-town circuit to Hickok himself that delegations of his old enemies would be waiting at the K.P. stations at Hays and Abilene to gun him down. Hickok promptly fired off telegrams to the editors of newspapers in those towns before boarding the train to Cheyenne. They read:

I SHALL PASS THROUGH YOUR PRAIRIE-DOG VILLAGES ON TUESDAY. I WEAR MY HAIR LONG AS USUAL.

The editors published this dispatch from the old town-tamer on their front pages.

Hickok's train rolled into Abilene, then Hays, at the appointed hour. Not a man took the opportunity of settling any old score with him. Instead, on the platforms of both stations, crowds of citizens gathered to cheer him on his way.

No civic reception awaited him in Cheyenne, however. Apparently he was not even recognized in the swirl of humanity in its dusty slab-sided streets. Celebrity counted for little when every man was fevered by visions of striking it rich. Later, as the invasion of the Black Hills was complicated by governmental prohibitions, the stampeders had a chance to look around them.

Cheyenne in the late autumn of 1874 was the staging base for the new gold rush. A decade before it had been a mere shantytown on the Wyoming steppe. In 1867 the Union Pacific pushed its way from Julesburg, and a considerable settlement of shacks, tents, and dugouts mushroomed to shelter the wild characters who came up the line on flatcars— "Hell on wheels," as the old settlers said—with a full complement of whores, pimps, barkeepers, gamblers, and ruffians. Cheyenne was assured of permanency when the line was extended from there to Denver. Freighting outfits made Cheyenne their terminal for the Montana and Dakota Territory traffic. It was a honky-tonk town, ready and waiting for the innocents from all over the nation who were confident they could scratch a fortune out of the Dakota gulches.

With so many suckers flooding the place, perhaps it was only to be expected that someone would try to trim Hickok while his identity was still not generally known. Apparently he did not wish to be recognized, for he wore his long wavy hair tucked up under his sombrero and wore his blue-tinted goggles even at night.

One of his first stops after arrival in Cheyenne was at the McDaniels Variety Theater, formerly the Planters House, a ramshackle complex of hotel, museum, barroom, theater, and gambling hall. It had "a general reputation for genial bawdiness," as an early Cheyenne historian put it. High-rollers who managed to attach themselves to an agreeable female found privacy in parlors wickedly furnished in red plush and were served champagne by waiters trained in discretion. The center of sociability, however, was the gambling concession in the Gold Room, operated by a man named Bowlby.

Hickok strolled up to the place as people were entering the theater for a variety performance. Admission was gained by tossing a silver dollar into a barrel at the entrance. Next morning the barrel would be rolled to the bank and its contents deposited. Anything theatrical was still anathema to the retired actor, so he continued on to the Gold Room.

Still suffering from a touch of rheumatism, he carried a cane fashioned from the butt end of a rosewood billiard cue which was "heavy as a Sioux war club." Hickok equipped himself with this shillelah both to ease the pain of walking and to protect himself; he had wielded the billiard cue with splendid effect in at least two brawls and now esteemed it as a weapon to be used in any situation short of gunplay. It would be useful in a few moments.

A fog of legend, claim and counterclaim, descended over what happened after Hickok stepped across the threshold of the Gold Room. One version, generally accepted, was written by Alfred E. Lewis (*Saturday Evening Post*, March 12, 1904), who got it from Bat Masterson, who was in Cheyenne during Hickok's stay there. The Lewis-Masterson version was fairly objective, Bat being a friend but not a violent partisan of Hickok's.

Hickok, still unrecognized in dark glasses and tucked-up hair, drifted over to the faro bank. He had one hundred dollars in his pocket and decided to devote the whole wad to bucking the tiger.

"I'll bet fifty dollars on the high card," he told the dealer.

King-tray came up, and Hickok's fifty dollars went into the bank.

He then risked the balance of his capital. This time deuce-eight came up, meaning Hickok had won. The dealer shoved twenty-five dollars at him.

"Why only twenty-five dollars?" Hickok demanded.

"The limit's twenty-five," snapped the dealer.

"Yeah," chimed in the lookout, a necessarily tough-looking citizen, "the limit's twenty-five dollars."

Hickok struggled to keep his voice and temper down and pointed out in a reasonable tone, "You took fifty dollars when I lost."

The dealer rewarded his forbearance by snarling, "Fifty goes if you lose, twenty-five if you win."

It was the rawest sort of swindle, handed out with insolence to boot. At least this pair of sharpers could have been polite about it. Hickok's temper went up like a rocket.

He raised his sawed-off cue and brought it whistling down on the heads of the dealer and the lookout, knocking both off their perches and out of action. A couple of bouncers came up on the run and were batted down before they could raise a fist or a gun. Then a number of other employees of the house closed in on the faro bank, while Hickok swung his walking stick in menacing arcs.

His glasses and hat fell off in the confusion, and someone yelled, "My God, that's Wild Bill Hickok. Watch out or he'll blow us all to Kingdom Come!"

Out the doors, stampeding in panic, went the whole mob, house men, customers, and all.

Hickok glanced down at the recumbent dealer and lookout, then at the stacks of money in the faro bank. Calmly and deliberately he stuffed all the currency in sight into his pockets. It had turned out to be a profitable evening after all, although purists might complain that he had improved his luck considerably with his walking stick.

He turned to leave the place. The Gold Room seemed to be entirely deserted. One witness said later that its occupants had "gone through the doors and windows in blocks of five."

Just as he passed the bar the bartender cautiously emerged from the floorboards and quavered, "Mr. Hickok, would you like a drink? It's on the house."

Hickok condescended to have a drink, tossed it off, and strolled out of the place.

His first caller the next day was Mr. Bowlby, proprietor of the Gold Room. He was accompanied by the city marshal. Both gentlemen approached Hickok in a placatory mood. Mr.

Bowlby stated that Mr. Hickok had walked off with about seven hundred dollars from the faro bank. The marshal murmured that, of course, nobody wanted any trouble with the celebrated Mr. Hickok. They were all gentlemen, weren't they, and couldn't the matter be settled amicably?

Mr. Hickok, however, believed that the house deserved to be penalized for trying to cheat him.

"I don't know as I ought to keep all the money," he added.

Mr. Bowlby nodded eagerly.

"In fact," Hickok continued, "I'd feel better about it if you would let me split it with you, Mr. Bowlby."

The marshal proclaimed this a generous offer. Mr. Bowlby agreed with considerably less enthusiasm.

"Then it's settled," said the marshal, linking arms with Mr. Bowlby and Mr. Hickok. "Now let's go down to the Gold Room and liquor up!"

During most of Hickok's unexpectedly extended stay in Cheyenne he behaved quietly and went about his business as "a student of the picture cards," as the local newspaper said. "Wild Bill still lingers with us," wrote the Cheyenne editor, not entirely pleased by Hickok's presence, "and makes a business of stuffing newcomers and tenderfeet with tales of his prowess and his wonderful discoveries of diamond caves, etc., which he describes as being located 'up north.'"

William F. Hooker in his reminiscences of early-day Cheyenne (*The Prairie Schooner*) said "Hickok was perhaps the best-known character in Cheyenne in the 'Seventies. He was a ministerial-looking person but was not a confidence man. He was just a plain gambler. . . Bill killed no one in Cheyenne; in fact, his days there were quiet and prosy . . . When he was in Cheyenne, he was on his last legs—had begun, as they say nowadays, to slow up . . ." Hooker also recalled that it was whispered around town that Hickok had "lost his nerve." Presumably this was because in his only recorded dispute while in Cheyenne, the affair at the Gold Room, he had saved ammunition and resorted to the walking stick; also, undeniably, he had lost some of his taste for violence. Henceforth, as he said, he would throw his weight around only if he was "put upon" and it was necessary as an act of self-preservation.

And this promise to himself he kept, not that he was entirely a peace-loving soul. While in Wyoming he made several excursions into the hinterland, the bare facts of which indicate he was still capable of making trouble. In Evanston he was arrested and fined for assaulting the sheriff, the cause of which disturbance was not recorded. During a junket to Laramie he became overexhilarated and was charged with disturbing the peace. The authorities requested that he leave town, which he did. But there was no gunplay in either of these incidents.

Quite probably he no longer trusted himself entirely with his guns. The accidental killing of his friend Mike Williams in Abilene had made a deep impression on him. How deep cannot be determined, but it is undoubtedly significant that following Williams' death he never fired another shot at another human being.

He had not lost his nerve, or courage, but his confidence in being able to hit exactly what he was aiming at. Most gunfights were over in a second or two and often took place with a large number of people standing stupidly, gawking with bloodthirsty curiosity, close to the line of fire. Even with his blurry eyesight he might be fairly certain of hitting his opponent in that flashing instant of action—but he could not be sure of not hitting, at the same time, one of the so-called innocent bystanders. He didn't want another Mike Williams on his conscience—or, if he didn't have a conscience, as so many of his contemporaries maintained, on his record.

Just how uncertain his eyesight was was illustrated by an incident at the Fair Grounds race track just before Hickok left Kansas City for Cheyenne. He and Ed Moore, a Civil War veteran, and several friends went to the races one day in August 1874. Moore (according to Connelley's *Wild Bill and His Era*) said Hickok remarked that he couldn't see at all without his glasses. One of the party noted that the right lens of Hickok's glasses was missing and "stuck his finger through the empty frame to prove to Bill that the glass was gone. Bill threw the glasses away in disgust . . ." Obviously Hickok's sight had deteriorated to the point where even the glasses didn't do much good.

Harry Young, the youth whom he had befriended in Hays by getting him a job as an army muleteer, kept bumping into Hickok all over the map. He told (in *Hard Knocks*) of meeting Hickok during this period and listening to him complain of his failing sight. Young quoted Hickok as saying, "Two steps before you stopped, I could plainly recognize you, after which I could see nothing but a blur. Don't mention this circumstance to anyone as I do not care to have it known."

Aside from disability, Wild Bill's "tameness" may have impressed the citizens of Cheyenne, as Hooker said, because he was never really as wild as he was reported to be. People who didn't know him expected Hickok to make an entrance with both guns out and spitting bullets. Most of the time, actually, he was quiet, courteous, even deferential. One witness to his gentler qualities was Mrs. Annie Tallent, renowned as the first white woman to enter the Black Hills, who was in Cheyenne at this period, her husband and his party having been chased out of the Badlands by the cavalry. A rather lengthy account of her casual meeting with Hickok is quoted in full below, from her book *The Black Hills, or Last Hunting Grounds of the Dakotahs*, not only because of what it reveals about Hickok but the impression he made on people who expected him to be an uncouth and swaggering desperado. Wrote Mrs. Tallent:

". . . One day while walking along the street in Cheyenne, there appeared, sauntering leisurely toward us from the opposite direction, a tall, straight, and rather heavily built individual in ordinary citizen's clothes—sans revolvers and knives, sans buckskin leggings and spurs, sans everything that would betoken the real character of the man—save that he wore a broad brimmed sombrero hat and a profusion of light brown hair hanging over his broad shoulders.

"A nearer view betrayed the fact that he also wore a carefully cultivated mustache of a still lighter shade which curled up saucily at each corner of his somewhat sinister looking mouth, while on his chin grew a small tuft of the same shade; and barring the two latter appendages, he might easily have been taken for a Quaker minister.

"When within a few feet of us, he hesitated a moment as if undecided, then stepping to one side, he suddenly stopped, at the same time doffing his sombrero and addressed us in respectable Anglo-Saxon vernacular substantially as follows:

"'Madam, I hope you will pardon my seeming boldness, but knowing you have but recently returned from the Black Hills I take the liberty of asking you a few questions in regard to the country as I expect to go there very soon. My name is Hickok.'

"I bowed low in acknowledgement of the supposed honor, but I must confess that his next announcement startled me.

"'I am called Wild Bill,' he continued, 'and you have no doubt heard of me.' He paused, then added, 'Although I suppose you have heard nothing good of me.'

"'Yes,' I candidly answered, 'I have often heard of Wild Bill and his reputation is not at all creditable to him. But,' I hastened to add, 'perhaps he is not so black as he is painted.'

"'Well, as to that,' he replied, 'I suppose I am called a red-handed murderer, which I deny. That I have killed men I admit, but never unless in absolute self-defense, or in the performance of an official duty. I have never in my life taken any mean advantage of an enemy . . . Yet understand,' he added, with a dangerous gleam in his eye, 'I never yet allowed a man to get the drop on me. But perhaps I may yet die with my boots on,' he concluded, his face softening a little.

"Ah! Was this a premonition of the tragic fate that awaited him? After making a few queries relative to the Black Hills, which I politely answered, Wild Bill, with a gracious bow that would have done credit to a Chesterfield, passed on down the street and out of sight."

Aside from a few delicious shudders and Victorian grace notes, Mrs. Tallent's report of her encounter with Hickok sounds plausible enough. He had come to a time when self-justification was necessary to him; the shooting days seemed to be over, for him at least, and he was wearying of a reputation for sheer homicidal efficiency. He was experiencing the first twinges of a yearning for respectability. With his 39th year approaching, he was already living on borrowed time for a gunfighter. A man had to realize when the salad days were over, quit when he was ahead.

And Hickok was intelligent enough to be aware that things were changing fast in the West. Soon there would no longer be a place for his kind, the adventurer, the gunman. It was only a matter of time before the whole cast of characters—gunfighters, badmen, road agents, professional gamblers, dance-hall queens—would no longer be tolerated, let alone admired. He had retreated before the steady march of respectability in Kansas, had seen the lace curtains and bay windows replace the swinging doors and the red lamps of the parlor houses. The advent of the respectable woman, who insisted on riding the cushions while her bawdy sisters came West on anything that rolled, who demanded her creature comforts as well as order and decency, was made possible by the extension of the railroads. The sledge strokes which drove in the golden spoke joining the railroads at Promontory Point were the death knell of masculine freedom out where the West began. As Duncan Aikman has written (*Calamity Jane and Other Wildcats*), "The construction towns faded into tank towns and track-walkers' stations or debris-caches on the desert. Their barbaric splendors were mourned. Their inhabitants scattered over the west to squat on mining claims or ranch land. They returned to 'the States' to lie about Indians and their good conduct, or, easing themselves into routine jobs on the new 'system,' settled down to being nagged by hastily summoned mates from the east who disapproved of the local climate, manners and groceries."

Even in 1875, way out in the territories, men were losing their grip, succumbing to female domination; the Ladies' Aid Society was more powerful than any gang of badmen. The new town-tamers were preachers, backed by the women of the community. Men were being enclosed by the female-ordained niceties—"Herbert, if you must smoke cigars, you'll have to do it on the porch or in the cellar from now on"— just as the prairies were being fenced in by barbed wire.

Drunkenness, lewd women, gambling, and gunplay, all would have to go. Any decent man could find his relaxation at an ice-cream social, a church bazaar, or a temperance meeting, couldn't he?

William F. Hooker (*The Prairie Schooner*) told of a cattleman who had prospered in Cheyenne at this time, despite an occasional tendency to drink himself silly. When he wobbled home, his wife would meet him at the door with a brace of pistols in hand. He would be marched at gun point to the barn at the rear of the house to sober up on a pile of straw, and he would stay in the barn for several weeks until Mme. Cattleman decided he had done his penance and was worthy of sleeping under her roof. It is hardly surprising that this indomitable lady has a stained-glass window dedicated to her memory in one of the Cheyenne churches.

In the raw frontier town of Laramie, on August 18, 1875, the editor of the *Daily Sentinel* was able to boast, "We don't believe there is a single New England village . . . that has as little crime, vice and immorality, as little drunkenness and rowdyism as Laramie City . . . We have lodges of Masons, Odd Felows, Rebecca, Sons of Temperance, Good Templars, etc. Nor are we destitute of taste in finer matters. There are from 20 to 25 pianos, twice as many organs and a silver cornet band."

The new hero of the western towns would soon be the shrewd businessman, the booster and joiner, whose sons and grandsons today let their whiskers grow and strap on gun belts in celebration of "Old Frontier Week," or some such, and pay curious reverence to the "badmen" their ancestors kicked out of town. Indubitably the Sons of Temperance won out over the Sons of Guns.

Hickok, as a member of the old breed, must have resented it all with an inward fury. He had always been on the side of law and order, but this was going too far. . . .

The gold rush, meanwhile, was piling up along the border of the Black Hills. Having opened the Pandora's box by verifying the reports of gold in the Dakota gulches, the government tried to slam the lid on the gold rushers by belatedly reminding everyone that a treaty with the Sioux forbade invasion of the Black Hills and that a Sioux war might break out if the treaty was not honored (which it did, in the summer of 1876, with the climax on the Little Big Horn). The so-called Gordon party of twenty-eight persons, including the above-quoted Mrs. Tallent, went in without government permission, staked claims along French Creek, and were escorted out by Major General George Crook's cavalry patrols. The army established a deadline beyond which whites were not supposed to venture, but small groups of prospectors evaded the cavalry patrols and went for the gold on their own.

Every day, through late 1874 and 1875, "came new mobilizations of eager adventurers to rave and fret at the cavalrymen they had failed to elude," wrote Robert J. Casey (*The Black Hills*). "The day came when pioneers more determined than cavalrymen were ranged along the Cheyenne frontier. And there were other rapidly growing mobs at Sidney and Fort Laramie and Sioux Falls City and Yankton and Fort Pierre. Rumbles of rising indignation among the Sioux tribes didn't cool them off any while they waited. They drew encouragement from their increasing numbers and began to boast of a day when they would pour into the Hills in spite of the military . . . and the generals were beginning to feel that the day might be fairly close at hand . . ." Hundreds of the "illegal argonauts" began slipping into the Badlands, fugitives from both the army and the Sioux. "That a lot of them were going to be found by their associates presently, dead and without their scalps, went without saying."

The government decided it was time to begin negotiations with the Sioux chieftains. A treaty commission in the fall of 1875 tried to buy the gold-bearing lands for six million dollars. Apparently its members still remembered the glorious days when tribal lands could be bought for a few red blankets and a handful of trinkets. Red Cloud, Spotted Tail, and Little Big Man, the Sioux leaders, were outraged by the government's offer and promptly demanded a hundred million dollars. Now it was the turn of the government's negotiators to display indignation. Neither side was inclined to much of a compromise between six and a hundred million dollars, and the treaty commissioners soon packed up and went back to Washington.

At that point the army decided to withdraw its protection from the Sioux lands and from the gold rushers itching to invade them. It solemnly washed its hands of responsibility, withdrew its patrols, and prepared for one hell of a war with the Sioux.

Until the Black Hills yawned open for the gold-seeking hordes with the spring thaw of 1876, Cheyenne was a mass of fretting, restless, and overeager people waiting for the rush northward. Among them, still, was Hickok. He had spent a year and a half in and around Cheyenne, living off the proceeds of faro and poker-table sessions and waiting for the day when the way to the new Golconda lay open.

Living by his wits and by his luck was beginning to tell on him. The pickings were rather lean by the winter of 1875–76, since most of the gold rushers were running low on funds.

Wild Bill evidently was now in a mood to be domesticated.

At this strangely fortuitous moment Mrs. Agnes Lake, the still-smitten circus proprietor, made her reappearance in Hickok's life. Hickok had wriggled out of marrying her before, but that was five years ago, in Abilene, when he was a lot less eager to be tied down. During the intervening years Mrs. Lake evidently had learned that his tale of having a wife in Illinois was merely the fictional device of a man determined to remain foot-loose.

So in February 1876 Mrs. Lake came to Cheyenne to visit her relative, S. L. Moyer, and his family. It seems fairly probable that she learned through Moyer that Hickok was in Cheyenne. Certainly the Cheyenne of 1876, winter-locked and desolate, was not the kind of place a lady would choose for a sojourn with distant relatives.

The details of how they came together again unfortunately are concealed behind the mid-Victorian sense of delicacy and discretion in such matters. Someone, however, with or without a little arch prompting from Mrs. Lake, approached Hickok with the tidings that Mrs. Lake was staying at the Moyer home. The rest was up to Hickok. A few years ago he probably would have grabbed his carpetbag and taken the first train out of Cheyenne, but now, a little lonely perhaps and with his best days behind him, and far less confident of the future, he made tracks for the Moyer home and presented himself to Mrs. Lake.

A lot of romantic phraseology has embroidered the culmination of this match, but the facts were that they decided at that first meeting to be married. Mrs. Lake was taking no chances on a skittish suitor: they would be married the next day. Who swept whom off whose feet was a secret contained between the two of them, behind the sliding doors of Mr. Moyer's parlor. Hickok was approaching his thirty-ninth birthday, and his bride, the mother of a grown and married daughter, was in her middle or late forties. Some said she was eleven years older than Hickok. She was, at any rate, an attractive woman, lithe and graceful from her years of bareback riding and performing on the trapeze. Undoubtedly there was a great deal of practicality involved in the marriage, but equally undoubted was the fact that there was a strong bond of affection between the two which was strikingly demonstrated in Hickok's subsequent letters to his wife.

The marriage was performed on March 5, 1876, at the Moyer home by the Rev. W. F. Warren, a Methodist minister. Only the Moyer family and a few friends of the bridegroom were present. That evening the Hickoks took the train for St. Louis, then went on to Cincinnati for a visit with the bride's daughter, Emma, and her husband, Gilbert S. Robinson.

The honeymoon lasted only two weeks. That, as it turned out, was also the duration of Hickok's married life.

They had agreed that after Hickok took his wife to her daughter's home and left her there he was to return to Wyoming and join the migration to the gold fields. Hickok was full of enthusiasm now, certain he would come back to Agnes a millionaire. He proposed—or so he told his new wife and in-laws—to lead a party to the Black Hills and then stake out claims for himself. That he had had no experience in prospecting no more deflated his hopes than a similar lack discouraged the other gold rushers. Or perhaps all along he intended to continue to be a "student of the picture cards" and get his share of the gold across mining-camp poker tables —a more familiar form of prospecting to Hickok. Mrs. Hickok, at any rate, was led to believe that he would toil with pick,

234

shovel, and pan and no doubt was pleased at the image of her husband unfamiliarly dripping with honest sweat.

Mrs. Hickok saw him off on the St. Louis train one evening late in March, watched his tall, confident figure mount the platform of a passenger car and disappear into the train. She would have to treasure that last glimpse through many years of widowhood, until the day of her death in 1917 in Jersey City, New Jersey. She never saw Hickok again.

CHAPTER 14

Calamity Jane and Other Fables

The West was broad in space but narrow in time, and it was so thinly populated that the cast of characters in one boomtown drama after another was almost interchangeable. Legends overlapped each other. Myths ran together like the colors in a slapdash painting. The process of amalgamation was only abetted by the fact that the people involved made an indoor sport of telling the tall tale, on themselves if possible, on someone else if necessary.

The Hickok legend overlay at least the edges of George Armstrong Custer, coincided frequently with that of Buffalo Bill Cody (a gem of press agentry), and became inextricably tangled with an even wilder bit of romancing—that of Calamity Jane, who was alleged to be an army scout, bullwhacker, pony-express rider, Indian fighter, frontier Florence Nightingale, camp follower, and mule-team driver at various stages of her career. The All-American tomboy. The hellcat in leather britches. The little girl from Missouri who could outshoot, outride, outdrink, outcuss, outfight, outchew, and outlie any of her male companions.

Legend has intertwined Hickok and Calamity Jane with a lover's knot almost as strong as the Atlantic cable. In films, in various forms of fiction, and in more than a few supposedly non-fictional works she and Hickok have been represented as sweethearts in matching buckskins, roaming the prairies together and fighting off hordes of Indians and other evildoers. As recently as 1958 a magazine article asserted that she was the mother of his child, that "as an 18-year-old girl she fell in love with Wild Bill Hickok the moment she set eyes on him. She saved his life, married him, gave him a divorce so he could marry another woman, and then became his mistress while posing as his partner." This account (in the *American Weekly*, June 1, 1958, by the much-respected Homer Croy) also stated that the marriage ceremony uniting Calamity Jane and Hickok was performed on a Kansas roadside; that the minister officiating was, of all wandering dominies, none other than the Rev. W. F. Warren of Cheyenne. The latter was the minister who married Hickok and Mrs. Lake in 1876, and—if this account were true—he must have been either a very nearsighted or exceedingly liberal-minded pastor to marry the same man twice.

The drab truth is that Hickok and Calamity Jane were intimate enough to exchange a handshake or a slap on the back— nothing more. In a searching examination of this much-rumored romance, Duncan Aikman (*Calamity Jane and Other Wildcats*) concluded that "the acquaintance was strictly casual and remained so. Mr. Hickok was the real thing in western derring-do and Calamity was merely a western spectacle. Mr. Hickok had killed no doubt upwards of a dozen in his various duties of self-defense, gambling punctilio and peace-officership, instead of the hundred or more who were sensationally attributed to him. But he had definitely and expertly killed them. Calamity, on the other hand, had talked exhaustively about being a scout and a rescuer of captains, but actually had been an amusingly rakish camp

follower and a kind-hearted demimondaine with an excep-
tional passion for plains life and male abundance. Wild Bill
was the sort of person to be grimly amused at such antics,
but to prefer for his intimacies solidity rather than hokum."

Hickok may not have been the most fastidious of men, but
a glance at any of the existing photographs of Calamity Jane
will indicate that she was not the sort to arouse any great
flare-up of romantic passion. She had a mass of coppery hair
usually tucked under a man's hat and blunt squarish features,
a squashy nose and heavy chin. Her voice was raucous and
her manner exuberant, when it was not downright riotous. A
contemporary historian wrote of her, "In appearance she was
large and thick, she wore men's clothing, chewed tobacco,
and was among the lowest of harlots, without a trace of refinement. Her temper was violent and when she went on a
tantrum the population took to the woods. In the writings her
good qualities have been magnified and her worst never dis-
closed. It was her boast that she never went to bed sober or
with a penny in her pocket." On the other hand, there were
many who swore she was an angel of mercy and a Molly
Pitcher of the prairies. Of all the thousands who knew her in
fifty-three or more years of life, few seemed to be able to dis-
cuss her objectively, without a sob tearing at the throat or a
sneer curling the lip.

None of the "facts" concerning her life up to the time she
was seen around Deadwood with Hickok are certifiable. Like
most living legends, largely self-created, she told a dozen different versions about every phase of her career. A pamphlet
titled "Calamity Jane, Written by Herself"—actually written
by a lady ghost writer—is not the solidest of documents. In
fact, the opening sentence is the only one that has not been
vigorously disputed: "My maiden name was Marthy Cannary; was born in Princeton, Mo., May 1, 1852; father and
mother natives of Ohio; had two brothers and three sisters, I
being the eldest of the children."

When Marthy, or Martha Jane, as she was christened, was thirteen years old, the family struck out for the Montana gold fields. Along the Overland Trail to Virginia City, Montana, she said, "the greater portion of my time was spent in hunting along with the men. In fact I was at all times along with the men when there was excitement or adventure to be had."

Both her parents died a year or two after they reached Virginia City. The girl struck out on her own, leaving the younger children to the uncertain charity of the neighbors. She became a camp follower in the railroad construction towns along the Union Pacific and around the cavalry garrisons, "started off on the trails hunting for the places where men were thickest." She consorted with soldiers, lumberjacks, section hands, miners, living with them as long as she pleased and then moving on. "In that country of rumors and the itch for marvels," wrote Duncan Aikman, "she was growing a reputation by these unfeminine dalliances."

She appears to have married a man named George White who took her to Denver and tried his best to make a lady out of her, dressing her sturdy frame in silks and satins and exhibiting her in more or less polite society. She couldn't take it for long; the company of respectable females, simpering, gossiping, flirting from behind their parasols, was more than she could stand. So one afternoon she left a note on the dresser for Mr. White and departed for less cluttered horizons.

In the next few years she hung out around Forts Bridger, Russell, and Hays, the rough and ready sweetheart of the cavalry. According to her own account, she often served in the ranks disguised as a man. Even the skeptical Mr. Aikman concedes it is possible that she served in the 1870 campaign against the Apaches in Arizona. On other expeditions she claimed to have gone along as a civilian packer with the wagon trains.

One cornerstone of her legend, however, has been thoroughly demolished. That concerns how she acquired the sobriquet of Calamity Jane. By her own account, she served in the campaign against the Nez Percés in Captain Pat Egan's company as a scout. Near the town of Goose Creek, Wyoming, Captain Egan's column was ambushed, she told her ghost writer. Her account continues:

"When fired upon, Captain Egan was shot. I was riding in advance, and when hearing the shot, turned in my saddle and saw the captain reeling in his saddle as though about to fall. I turned my horse and galloped back with all haste to his side and got there in time to catch him as he was falling. I lifted him onto my horse in front of me, and succeeded in getting him safely to the fort."

While riding tandem back to the fort, with Indian missiles whistling all around them, the wounded captain managed to gasp out, "I name you Calamity Jane, the heroine of the plains."

Captain Egan himself exploded this section of the Calamity Jane legend. His only connection with her was in the role of disciplinarian. A year or two after the supposed Goose Creek incident the captain heard a rumor around the post, Fort Laramie, that a woman dressed in a soldier's uniform was living in the barracks occupied by his company. To his further chagrin, he learned that for several weeks he had been returning the salutes of this creature, unaware that she was a woman. Captain Egan stalked over to the barracks and conducted an immediate investigation. He learned, to his horror, that *two* women were bedded down with his troopers, one of them Calamity Jane and the other a rare female associate of hers. Egan denounced them as "a couple of god-damned chippies" and ordered them booted off the reservation. Despite her claim that she had rescued him from the Indians and that he had bestowed her nickname, Egan said he'd never seen Calamity Jane before and never wanted to see her again.

Just how she acquired the sobriquet is not known, but it

brought her a celebrity more glittering than any of her rivals for the picaresque fame of the frontier, such ladies as Poker Alice, Madame Mustache, Big-Nose Kate, Pickhandle Nan, Rowdy Kate, and Kitty the Schemer. Her sobriquet, as Aikman said, "had a macabre splendor all its own and beyond them, undertones of violence and defiance, of gunplay and delirium tremens, of prairie thunder, mountain whiskey, hell, high water and sudden death, that the best of the others lacked."

Certainly she did her best to live up to her title. She strutted, bellowed, and whooped her way through the frontier towns; she embroidered on the rather sordid role of camp follower by claiming to be a better man than any she frolicked with, and she was likely to shoot up a saloon if anyone tried to downrate her publicly.

Nobody and nothing, of course, could have kept her away from the excitement of the Black Hills gold rush. She claimed to have accompanied the Custer column when it invaded the Hills in 1874, but there is no record of any service with the 7th Cavalry expedition, no published or documented recollection of anyone seeing her on that long reconnaissance.

She was well remembered around Cheyenne at the time, however, mostly for her drinking exploits.

She would swagger into a saloon and loudly announce, "I'm Calamity Jane and this drink's on the house." Cheers from the house, since she was now a recognizable celebrity.

A householder found her sleeping off a drunken stupor in his woodshed and unwisely suggested that she move elsewhere. "I'm Calamity Jane," she told the intruder. "Get the hell out of here and let me alone."

Another man, an easterner unaccustomed to the free and easy ways of the West, found her snoring away on his bed in a Cheyenne rooming house. She was fully clothed and sleeping off a Saturday-night drunk. The young man, shocked at this boozy apparition sprawling uninvited on his bed, timorously poked her awake and hinted it might be more ladylike of her to seek out her own pallet. "I'm Calamity Jane," she replied, "and I sleep where I damn please," and rolled over and went back to sleep.

Yet there were more charitable recollections of her too. She was remembered nursing sick children and ailing whores, staying at the bedsides of people stricken in the epidemics of diphtheria, cholera, and smallpox, at greater risk to herself than any imaginary flights of Indian arrows. In the reminiscences of Miguel Otero (*My Life on the Frontier*) he wrote, "There was one redeeming feature to those unfortunate women of the frontier: that was their charity. They were entirely unlike their male associates, the bad men of the frontier, who were constantly looking for a quarrel. These women in almost every instance took the part of the weak and would spend their last dollar to aid anyone in distress. Calamity Jane was no exception to the rule . . ."

The climax of her legend came with her meeting—brief and casual as it undoubtedly was—with Wild Bill Hickok. This tenuous connection with Hickok was worked for all it was worth by the dime novelists who capitalized on the stories about her, particularly after she was reported to have said with her last breath, in 1903, "Bill Hickok was the only man I ever loved."

If so, it must have been one of the most one-sided love affairs in western history.

They met, apparently, somewhere along the trail between Cheyenne and Deadwood in the spring of 1876. Hickok had just left his bride in Cincinnati and was leading a party of Colorado gold seekers into the Black Hills.

Wild Bill had hooked up with a Colorado gambler named Charlie Utter, who was described as having "a genius for personal pageantry, who made up for his inferiority to Mr. Hickok in stature by wearing mustachios and a mane even more luxurious; indeed if envious gossip is to be believed, by treating his lustrously blond ringlets to frequent applications of the curling iron." Colorado Charlie was considered an extremely dandified fellow, if not an eccentric, because of his habit of bathing every day, winter and summer, in a time and place when most men regarded a bath as something to be avoided in the interests of health. Thanks to his brief association with Hickok, Utter became known, quite without reason, as something of a badman and a dangerous gunman. Actually he was a mild-mannered fellow, much more interested in the ladies than in possibly fatal gunfights. He married one of the West's few lady gamblers, Eleanore Dumont, known as Minnie the Gambler. She dealt stud for him in an El Paso gambling house until 1904, when they embarked on a medicine-show tour of Mexico and Central America and found that selling nostrums to mestizo villagers was a lot more profitable than gambling in the States. Utter died before the tour ended, and Minnie the Gambler retired to Southern California with a modest fortune.

Apparently Calamity Jane joined up with Hickok's cavalcade at Fort Laramie or somewhere further up the trail to Deadwood. She had just suffered another dishonorable discharge from the U. S. Army. Accompanying General Crook's column in disguise, she joyfully went in swimming one day with a group of her favorite troopers. A young shavetail came along the riverbank where they were disporting themselves and was horrified to observe a female splashing around with the men; nothing he had learnd at West Point equipped him to deal with a nude female under these circumstances, so he galloped to headquarters with his problem. General Crook knew how to handle it: he ordered Calamity Jane out of camp by nightfall. Crestfallen, she headed for the Deadwood trail to join the gold rush. If she couldn't play vivandière to a troop of cavalry, she would join the miners and prospectors in their free-spending revels.

Calamity Jane was twenty-four, or possibly twenty-six, depending on whether you believe her or less partial observers of her career, when she threw in with Hickok, Colorado Charlie, and their companions. Hero-worshiper that she was, she dogged Hickok's footsteps. She amused him as a homeless pup would. Then and in Deadwood Hickok permitted her to belly up to a bar with him so long as she behaved herself. Calamity Jane liked to proclaim that she was Hickok's personal protégé and later more than hinted that they shared the same blanket roll, but they were no more than occasional drinking companions. "He was a married man and seemed to think much of his wife," said Ellis T. (Doc) Pierce, a Deadwood pioneer who knew them both fairly well, "and I never saw him associating with lewd women. I camped with Calamity Jane . . . and drunk or sober, she never made any talk to me about Bill, or even mentioned his name that I can remember. Now, anyone who knew that old girl will tell you that if she had a case on Wild Bill it would have been her main topic of conversation. Jane was great for notoriety . . ."

To the everlasting joy of the mythmakers, Calamity Jane and Hickok rode into Deadwood Gulch one afternoon in mid-April 1876, with Colorado Charlie and the others in their party trailing behind them like a retinue. It was a flashy entrance. The word flew down the gulch that Calamity Jane and Wild Bill Hickok were coming to town, and there were wild cheers along Deadwood's Main Street, particularly from the saloon entrances. "Tenderfeet on the outskirts of the crowd shuddered deliciously to meet this idol and allegory of dreadfulness face to face." But there were abstainers from this general rejoicing, "rival gamblers and rival would-be killers, thugs fearing a new city marshal of deadly accuracy, solid citizens desiring one," all of whom "appraised the famous stranger with dry curiosity." It was Calamity Jane's proudest moment. She had hooked her legend onto an even gaudier one. In front of witnesses, for once.

CHAPTER 15

Deadwood Days and Nights

Deadwood Gulch was a dead-end canyon notched in the Dakota wilderness, bordered by a rushing mountain stream and a steep rock wall. Its earliest residents lived on whiskey and beans, worked like demons to get at the Badlands gold before the main stampede began, endured a high rate of homicide and an even higher toll from the usual mining-camp diseases. In its first winter, 1875–76, it was the roughest place imaginable. "Deadwood," said Doc Pierce, Hickok's friend, "had only one narrow street, filled with stumps, boulders, lumber and logs, with hundreds of men surging from saloon to saloon—so you had to get acquainted with a majority of them, and have a speaking acquaintance. Whenever a gunman came to the gulch the word was passed along as quickly as it would be at a ladies' sewing society."

In February of 1876 Deadwood Gulch sheltered a few hundred men in shacks, cabins, and dugouts, but by the time the soft chinook winds thawed them out the canyon was mobbed with newcomers. And by midsummer it was estimated that twenty-five thousand people had crowded themselves into

245

the camps called Elizabeth City, Crook City, and Deadwood City, the largest and most notorious of these settlements in the gulch being Deadwood. "You can't count the people who are living in layers," as a Montanan said. Main Street was lined with buildings slapped together out of raw pine, a few stores, hotels, and other commercial establishments, but mostly saloons, gambling houses, and cribs where people were "shooting off their mouths and guns." The long, narrow street was jammed with horses, burros, wagons, mule and oxen teams, a traffic which churned up enough dust to keep Deadwood under a constant choking and stifling shroud.

About all that could be said for it was that the gulch was safe from the Indians. The mile-long opening into it was so narrow that two teams could barely pass and it could have been defended indefinitely by a handful of men.

And it was tough; it had attracted every able-bodied thug, whore, pimp, gambler, honky-tonk operator, gunman, and sharper in the West with an itch to improve his lot. All around the town miners were taking gold out in placer operations, much of which was weighed out, on pennyweight scales, twenty dollars to the ounce in the sucker traps of Main Street.

It was strictly an outlaw town; nobody had a right to be here, except the right established by force. The land it squatted on belonged to the Sioux, and the U. S. Government did not even recognize its existence. Yet it did exist and was to be one of the reasons for the Sioux uprising that spring which resulted in the massacre of Custer and two squadrons of the 7th Cavalry over in Montana.

J. S. McClintock, who operated a stage line there and later wrote grimly of its beginnings, thought it was a disgusting place, full of greed, murder, and mayhem. He denounced in particular the "many disreputable joints of which the Main Street of Deadwood was recognized as the mother lode. Such despicable institutions were not only tolerated but fostered if not liberally patronized by a part of the ruling officials of the new city. It was here, on the second floors of many saloons and gambling houses, as well as in more filthy dives in the so-called Bad Lands district down the street, where many incautious individuals were lured. They were entrapped through well-planned devices of entrapment aided and augmented by a glass or two. Mixed drinks were proffered seemingly with the best of motives by oily-tongued spotters capably assisted by a bevy of the pitiable female inmates of these veritable dens of vice.

"Once through the door and the fate of the unwary victim was settled so far as his personal assets were concerned. The more considerate of these deluded mortals, wakening to a realization of his unbearable condition, would take his departure to brood or rave to himself. Others, with less forethought, would enter into a noisy tirade of unbecoming language and proceed to inaugurate a roughhouse. The head of the damnable concern would then step from behind the scenes where he had been waiting to get a lion's share of the loot. With brass knuckles or revolver used as a bludgeon he would quiet the row in accordance with the established rule of priority rights by pounding the helpless, and now moneyless, sucker into a state of insensibility."

To a veteran of the Kansas cow towns, however, Deadwood was not nearly so dangerous a place as Abilene, Dodge, Hays, or Ellsworth during their climactic years. Wyatt Earp (quoted in Stuart Lake's *Wyatt Earp: Frontier Marshal*) thought that, "as compared to the Kansas cowtowns, Deadwood was a law-abiding community. There were plenty of tough citizens in the camp, with the usual run of saloons, gambling-houses and honky-tonks wide open twenty-four hours a day, and more crooked gamblers, thieves and outlaws than the cattle centers knew. On the other hand, the braggart bad men from Texas did not reach Deadwood in any numbers, and the few who did come soon learned that tactics employed in hurrahing the cowcamps meant disaster in the mining town, free and easy as that was. For one thing, there were no business influences which inclined Deadwood to leniency with the cowboys, such as they enjoyed in the Kansas trail terminals."

Doc Pierce, on the other hand, said, "Deadwood was then hog-wild; duels and gunfights in the streets, and often one had to duck or fall flat on the ground to escape a shower of lead."

Everyone, except the most fervent pacifists, went around heeled. The revolver was so ordinary a part of the male attire that it was known as the "Black Hills bustle."

Gunfighting talent was plentiful. Before Earp came to Deadwood, Bat Masterson, his deputy marshal at Dodge, turned in his star and lit out for the Black Hills. Bat took a good look at all the labor involved in gold mining and hurried back to Cheyenne, where he made a killing at poker and faro, then returned to Dodge City to be elected sheriff. Doc Holliday, then using the name of Tom McKey, was in residence for a spell, quietly doing the best he could in the Main Street gambling houses and managing somehow not to kill anyone while sojourning in Deadwood.

Other eminent pistoleers, catalogued by Earp during his stay, included Johnny Bull, Billy Allen, Tom Hardwick, Tom Mulqueen, Charlie Clifton, Boone May and his two equally deadly brothers, Charlie Rich, Johnny Oyster, Jim Levy, Charlie Storms, and Scott Davis. Some of them had not too long to live. Jim Levy was subsequently killed for claim-jumping down in New Mexico. Five years later Charlie Storms would be gunned down by the redoubtable Luke Short in Tombstone, Arizona. Tom Mulqueen was a little slow on the draw in Cheyenne a short time later. Charlie Clifton, an old bushwhacker from Missouri who once rode with Quantrill, soon cashed in his chips down in the Indian Territory.

Rich though Deadwood was in top-rated gunmen, few of them slapped leather in the gulch, probably because they were too busy scratching for an easy dollar; also the code of the gunfighters' union forbade one brother puncturing another without some very good reason, such as money. And money was to be had, not from each other, but from the hard-rock miners in the surrounding hills. One of the few shootings between professionals in Deadwood involved Charlie Storms and Johnny Varnes. The Leadville *News* reported late in September that they "fired several shots at each other . . . They only succeeded in wounding a bystander in the thigh."

In all this blaze of shooting stars Wild Bill Hickok, of course, was the premier celebrity. People actually cheered when he walked into a saloon. They crowded around him, offering to buy drinks, begging for the privilege to sit down at a poker table with him.

His first call on entering Deadwood with Calamity Jane and Colorado Charlie Utter, followed by lesser members of the phalanx, was at Nuttall & Mann's No. 10 Saloon on Main Street. There were two attractions there for Hickok, one of the proprietors, Carl Mann, being an old friend of his, and Harry Young, his ex-protégé from Hays City, being the barkeep of the establishment. Young recalled, "They dismounted and walked into the saloon, great crowds following them, until the room was packed. Mann cordially received them, asking them to make his saloon their headquarters, which they agreed to do. This meant money to Mann, as Bill would be a great drawing card. After the excitement of Bill's arrival had subsided a little, Bill looked at me a few moments, then said: 'Kid, here you are again, like the bad penny, but I am awfully glad to see you.' And turning to Carl Mann, he remarked, 'I first met this kid in Hays City, Kansas, and wherever I go he seems to precede me, but he is a good boy and you can trust him. Take my word for that.'"

Hickok and Charlie Utter set up light housekeeping in a

tent pitched near where the Chicago, Burlington & Quincy railroad station subsequently was built.

Young said flatly that "Bill's occupation at this time was that of a gambler," and all accounts of him in Deadwood place him almost constantly at a poker table or the bar at the No. 10 Saloon. He may have ventured out to the diggings a few times, but there is no record of his having filed a claim. By the time he arrived, in fact, most of the richer claims had been staked in the vicinity of Deadwood.

Venturing far from Deadwood soon became a rather foolish pursuit, since the Sioux had gone on the warpath with a vengeance. Across the Montana border they had gathered in the Yellowstone country to have it out with the U. S. Army, four of whose columns were converging on them. The ghastly result was the Little Big Horn and other less publicized battles. Word that Custer and his squadrons had been wiped out reached Deadwood late in June. Despite his trouble with Tom Custer in Hays City, Hickok was still a friend of the regiment's commander. George Armstrong Custer, along with his wife, had been one of the founders and builders of the Hickok legend. Together, one as the boldest of the Indian-fighting cavalrymen, the other as the most celebrated of the gunfighters, they had supplied the American public's postwar demand for heroes somewhat larger than life size. They had much in common, skill, flamboyancy, and an ability to attract attention. It was not altogether unfitting, from the detached viewpoint, that both should die in the same year, only five weeks apart in fact, in much the same poetically just circumstances. Then, too, it is well for legendary heroes to die when fairly young, untarnished, still vigorous and handsome, before sharp-eyed critics have too much of an opportunity to examine flaws and blemishes. Custer fading away as a toothless pensioner, Hickok yarning away his last years on a courthouse-square bench . . . they would have lost much of their historic luster, their legendary glamor, had fate permitted them to linger on.

Though Hickok did most or all of his prospecting at a poker table in the No. 10 Saloon, he gave Mrs. Hickok the impression in his letters home that he was out chopping away in the gullies with the rest of the stampeders. On July 19 he wrote Mrs. Hickok at the home of her daughter and son-in-law in Cincinnati:

> My own darling wife Agnes:
>
> I have but a few moments left before this letter starts. I never was as well in my life, but you would laugh to see me now—just got in from prospecting. Will go away again tomorrow. Will write again in the morning, but God knows when the letter will start. My friend will take this to Cheyenne if he lives. I don't expect to hear from you, but it is all the same, I know my Agnes and only live to love her. Never mind, pet, we will have a home yet, then we will be so happy. I am almost sure I will do well here. The man is hurrying me. Goodbye, dear wife. Love to Emma.

It was signed "J. B. Hickok."

At that, Indians or no, he might have been better off grubbing around the hills for gold. Being a famous gun slinger in a town like Deadwood was a risky proposition, although his lurid fame attracted the greenhorns to his table at the No. 10 Saloon and doubtless fattened his poke. The danger wasn't from his fellow professionals but from some kid drifting in with a yen to make a name for himself. The best way to do it was to kill someone with a big reputation. Some years later when the President of the United States personally offered Bat Masterson, broke and unemployed, the post of U.S. marshal in the new state of Oklahoma, Bat sensibly declined on the grounds that "I would be bait for grown-up kids who had fed on dime novels."

Hickok, too, was beginning to realize that fame, for a gunfighter, had its drawbacks. Wrote Harry Young in *Hard Knocks*, "Since I had last seen him, he seemed to have changed greatly and tried very hard to avoid notoriety, but unfortunately his past reputation was still a matter of public comment . . . Bill had attained much the same reputation as a prizefighter who has successfully sent all of his opponents down to defeat and become the acknowledged champion."

But Hickok also had more of a sense of bravado than fellow craftsmen, like Earp and Masterson, who lived to a peaceful old age.

He would head off trouble if he could—as he did in Abilene and Hays City—but he could not help but make the occasional grandstand play. Something to make people nudge each other and exclaim, "Here comes Wild Bill Hickok!" whenever he made an entrance. Something to make the rubes and tinhorns and tenderfeet gather around him in worshipful clusters.

One night at the No. 10 a friend of his burst into the saloon with the news that a group of Montanans, all ferocious in appearance, were boasting that they intended to wipe out Hickok. Everyone looked at Hickok to see how he would react to the threat. Doubtless the thought ran through his mind that men who bragged about what they were going to do with a gun rarely did it. He stood up from the table, loosened the revolvers in their holsters a trifle, and stalked out the door. A few minutes later he strode into the saloon where the Montanans were gasconading about their plans for Hickok. Six of them—so said witnesses friendly to Hickok—were lined up at the bar and listened meekly while he addressed them thus:

"I understand that you cheap, would-be gunfighters from Montana have been making remarks about me. I want you to understand that unless they are stopped there will shortly be a number of cheap funerals in Deadwood. I have come to this town to live in peace, not court trouble, but I do not propose to stand for your insults . . . Now line up against that wall . . ."

Knees knocking and teeth chattering, the Montanans obeyed his orders without the slightest show of resistance. Perhaps they expected a bullet in the back, considering that was how they had been claiming Hickok ran up his score. Hickok merely relieved them of their guns, then backed out of the saloon. From then on the Montanans talked small and walked humbly, at least while Hickok was around.

Perhaps it was that incident that prompted a number of citizens, merchants, and others with a stake in law and order to propose that Hickok be appointed city marshal.

Hickok didn't want the job, knew his eyesight wasn't good enough to handle the split-second situations he could expect to come up almost daily, and probably suspected that his reflexes had slowed to the point where younger gunfighters would have a distinct advantage. Wearing the lawman's badge would only increase the ambition of trigger-happy youths to gun him down.

Yet he couldn't bring himself to come right out and turn the offer of the marshal's post down. Instead he kept stalling. Probably he had an itch to rule the streets of Deadwood as he had Abilene, recover the old town-tamer's sense of power in holding down a boom town full of desperate characters. He must have recalled the terrible and wonderful hour in Abilene after killing Phil Coe (and Mike Williams, but that was an accident) and clearing the streets so that not a shadow moved on them except his own.

He may even have decided to take the job. But that will never be known. He wasn't given enough time to make a final decision.

Meanwhile, however, the report that Wild Bill Hickok was going to tame Deadwood sped around town and caused more alarm than rejoicing, especially among the people who were cleaning up big in Deadwood's first summer. There was too much money involved for them to view with equanimity the possibility that a tough marshal might clamp down on the local rackets. Hickok was known to be tolerant toward gambling and most forms of vice, but he could be expected to crack down on the crooked games, the drunk rolling, the panel houses, and the plain thuggery which separated the miners from their gold quicker and easier than any honest pandering to their weaknesses. Also they must have remembered that in Abilene, when the authorities decided on a cleanup, he had faithfully sent the whores and gamblers packing.

To the report that Hickok would be made marshal there was soon a counter-rumor that he wouldn't live long enough to draw his first month's pay. Tim Brady and Johnny Varnes, two of the local underworld leaders, were interviewing various gunmen who might be willing to rub out Hickok for a fee. The old pros didn't want the job, of course, but some foolhardy kid might be persuaded to take it on. . . .

Ever since coming to Deadwood, according to the testimony of various people who knew him, Hickok had been troubled by premonitions of death. He was a superstitious man, like many who lived as he did, and a supreme fatalist. He felt that he was marked for death—despite the rosily optimistic letters he wrote to his wife—and was equally certain that there was nothing he could do to avoid it. Deadwood was his appointment in Samarra.

J. W. Buel (*Life and Marvelous Adventures of Wild Bill*), who alone of his various biographers knew Hickok fairly well, said, "The very few intimate friends Bill had were well acquainted with his peculiar belief in spiritualism. He claimed to be clairvoyant, especially when danger threatened, and the many narrow escapes he had gave some evidence of the reality of his spiritual sight . . . Wild Bill asseverated that in all his fights he was surrounded by spirits, who kept him cool and collected while they made fools of his enemies."

Hickok, it seems, had wandered far from his father's Protestant orthodoxy.

And O. W. Coursey, the Black Hills historian who interviewed several of Hickok's companions on the journey from Cheyenne to Deadwood, gave this account of Hickok's feeling of doom:

"It is a strange anomaly that Wild Bill had a presentiment, or premonition, when he entered Deadwood Gulch that it would be his last one. As they came to the top of the upland divide (Break Neck Hill) and looked over into Deadwood Gulch, for the first time, Wild Bill said to Charlie Utter and his companions: 'Boys, I have a hunch that I am in my last camp and will never leave this gulch alive.' His companions scoffed at the premonition.

"'No, I am not dreaming,' replied Wild Bill; 'something tells me my time is up, but where it is coming from I do not know as I cannot think of one living enemy who would wish to kill me.'"

Harry Young, the bartender at No. 10, recalled that he met Hickok on the street two days before his death outside the 66 Saloon, and the following conversation took place:

Young: "Bill, you are not looking very well this morning."

Hickok: "I have a feeling that something is going to happen to me."

Young: "Bill, you are drinking too much."

Hickok: "No, that has nothing to do with it. I've had this feeling for two weeks."

Next day according to Coursey, the premonition of death still lingered with Hickok. Coursey wrote:

"On the evening before he was killed, he was standing up leaning against the jam of the door to the building in which he was next day assassinated, looking downcast, when Tom Dosier asked him: 'Bill, why are you looking so dumpy tonight?'

255

"Bill replied: 'Tom, I have a presentiment that my time is up and that I am going to be killed.'

"'Oh, poo, poo!' said Tom, 'don't get to seeing things; you're all right.'

"Bill started leisurely up Main Street, as if meditating."

That same evening of August 1, Hickok went to the tent he shared with Colorado Charlie and wrote his last letter home:

Agnes Darling:

If such should be we never meet again, while firing my last shot, I will gently breathe the name of my wife—Agnes —and with wishes even for my enemies I will make the plunge and try to swim to the other shore.

CHAPTER 16

Dead Man in Deadwood

Perhaps by the next morning, August 2, he had shaken off the premonitions which had been haunting him. He went about his daily routine, somewhat more cheerful than he had been the day before. He rose at noon, the gambler's dawn, and breakfasted with Colorado Charlie, did a few chores around the camp, and dressed himself carefully in the uniform of the day, his black cutaway, string tie, black sombrero, sixty-dollar calfskin boots, and the rest.

About 3 P.M. he set off, up Main Street, for the No. 10 Saloon, his regular place of business. The roadway was crowded as usual with horse-, mule-, and oxen-drawn transport. The sidewalks were jammed with miners, their pockets bulged by heavy pokes, in town for a midweek binge. Dust boiled up from the busy roadway, almost obscuring the scorching midsummer afternoon's sun. On the hillside looming over the town sunlight flashed on the water of the flumes supplying the mines above Deadwood. It was still a raw jerry-built town, unremittingly ugly, overcrowded, and over-violent. Someone said Deadwood looked like "a lot of lemon boxes in a backyard," but it wasn't supposed to be pretty; it was a place to get rich and clear out as quickly as possible. Wild Bill Hickok had passed all his adult life, except for his theatrical tour of the East and occasional stops in Kansas City, in places pretty much like this.

He turned in at No. 10, sauntered over to the bar, exchanged a few words with his friend Harry Young behind the bar, had his first drink of the day and the last of his life.

Then he sat down to play poker with three friends of his— Carl Mann, one of the proprietors of No. 10; Captain Frank Massey, a Missouri River pilot, and Charles Rich, a gunman-gambler of considerable reputation, all old friends of his.

Hickok, as usual, made a move to take the chair with the back to the wall. Either by prearrangement, or more likely on spur-of-the-moment inspiration, Hickok's three fellow players decided to euchre him out of the chair against the wall. Just for laughs. After a bit of good-natured jostling Captain Massey plunked himself into Hickok's customary place.

"Nobody is going to shoot you in the back," the river pilot said.

Hickok asked Captain Massey once again to yield the chair, but Massey refused—a refusal that he was to remember with more than one kind of pain.

They began playing about 3:30 P.M. Several times in the next half hour, according to Bartender Young's recollection, Hickok asked Massey to change places with him, but the other players laughingly said they weren't going to indulge Hickok in his "pet superstition" that afternoon.

Hickok hadn't sat with his back to people in a public place since Hays City, when only a fortuitous back-bar mirror had saved him from being shot in the back by Jack Strawhan. Perhaps it was nervousness over this circumstance that caused him to lose so heavily in that first half hour of play that he was almost cleaned out.

Shortly after 4 P.M. Captain Massey raked in a pot, and Hickok called over to Harry Young behind the bar to lend him fifty dollars to stay in the game.

"The old duffer [Captain Massey] broke me on the last hand," were the last words Young heard his friend say.

Young took fifty dollars in chips over to Hickok and returned behind the bar. Rich started to deal another hand.

At that moment a young man named Jack McCall entered the bar. He was twenty-five years old, had come out West from Louisville, Kentucky, a half dozen years before. His greatest ambition was to be a famous gunfighter. Few people knew even that much about him. He had drifted into Deadwood, as he had drifted into many other towns, a few weeks before. Doc Pierce claimed to have known him and said of him later, "He was the most repulsive-looking man I have ever met. He was cross-eyed and his nose had been broken with a six-shooter. He told me he was raised in Louisville, Kentucky, but came to the plains when a youth and joined a band of buffalo hunters down on the Republican River . . . He was a queer specimen of the genus homo. I have seen him do some generous deeds while sober, but he was a demon when drinking. He had a dual personality." In a few moments it became apparent which side of his personality was in control that afternoon.

McCall ordered a drink from Harry Young, tossed it back, and began walking toward the table where the four men were playing poker.

It was 4:10 P.M.

Hickok was seated with his back to the approaching McCall; Captain Massey was opposite him against the wall; Carl Mann was on his left and Charlie Rich on his right.

Rich had just dealt Hickok the last hand of a long career at the poker table—a pair of aces, a pair of eights with a queen kicker. Ever afterward aces and eights would be known as the Dead Man's Hand.

259

Hickok was staring glumly at his hand as McCall approached to within a few yards. This time the intuition which he had credited with saving his life on other occasions was oddly inoperative, despite his anxiety of the past days, despite his uneasiness at being seated with his back to the bar.

Before any of the players, intent on the hand just dealt them, became aware of his presence, McCall drew an old .45 Colt revolver and fired just once.

The bullet crashed through the back of Hickok's head, came out under his right cheekbone, and still had enough propulsive force to imbed itself in Captain Massey's left forearm.

The only words McCall uttered, according to the later testimony of Charlie Rich and Harry Young, were, "Take that!"

Then the assassin turned and started to flee. Young began to climb over the bar after him, and McCall tried to snap a shot at him. The gun misfired; McCall threw it aside. A later test showed that, of the six bullets in the revolver, five were defective and would not fire. The only live bullet was the one that fell under the hammer on the first shot and was sent into Hickok's skull.

Hickok died instantly, without a murmur or twitch.

Doc Pierce, who was summoned to the scene immediately as Deadwood's part-time undertaker, recalled that "when they unlocked the door for me to get his body, he was lying on his side, with his knees drawn up just as he slid off his stool . . . His fingers were still crimped from holding his poker hand." The body was removed to the tent shared by Hickok and Colorado Charlie, where Doc Pierce prepared it for burial. He subsequently related these mortuarian details: "When Bill was shot through the head, he bled out quickly, and when he was laid out he looked like a wax figure. I have seen many dead men on the field of battle and in civil life, but Wild Bill was the prettiest corpse I have ever seen. His long mustache was attractive, even in death, and his long tapering fingers looked like marble." Pierce, it is evident from his prose style, would have done splendidly as a latter-day publicist for one of Southern California's more elegant burying grounds.

Jack McCall didn't get very far from the scene of the crime, although Main Street was thrown into such confusion by Hickok's murder that a coolheaded desperado could have easily escaped. Harry Young, in hot pursuit, saw McCall vault into the saddle of a horse down the street. The cinch on the saddle broke and McCall tumbled to the ground. McCall scrambled away as the street filled with shouts and screams.

The whole aftermath of the shooting, in fact, degenerated into low comedy.

Captain Massey thought it was Hickok who had shot him when the bullet from McCall's gun coursed through Hickok's skull and bit into his arm. The river-boat pilot evidently believed Hickok had become irked over his losing streak and had taken it out on the heavy winner. Blood streaming from his arm, he staggered out of the No. 10 yowling, "Wild Bill shot me!"

That started a panic in the south end of town. Men ran up the street shouting that Wild Bill Hickok had gone berserk and was shooting up the town. People bolted their doors and hid under their beds.

It took a few minutes for cooler heads to sort out the facts. Captain Massey was finally convinced that Hickok hadn't shot him. Harry Young, Charlie Rich, and others spread the word that Hickok was dead and McCall was his slayer.

Horsemen rode up Deadwood Gulch, shouting the news to all the camps, Deadwood, Whitewood, Gold Run, Blacktail, Crook City, and Elizabeth City—"Wild Bill Hickok is dead!" The gulch settlements were a turmoil of thousands of excited men and women. The saloons did a roaring business. Some demanded the lynch rope for Hickok's slayer—whoever he was and whatever his motive. Others suggested that the murderer be given a communal vote of thanks and a handsome reward. Most people didn't care much one way or the other; few could work up much moral indignation over the death of a gunfighter; how else could Wild Bill have expected to die?

Amid the clamor and confusion around the south end of Main Street just after the shooting, Jack McCall somehow got himself captured. Just how is still a matter of conjecture. Harry Young said McCall was cornered on the street. The Deadwood *Pioneer* published August 5 reported only that "The murderer Jack McCall was captured after a chase by many citizens and a guard placed over him." Other accounts say McCall was found in a barn across the street from the No. 10 Saloon.

By far the most colorful and least accurate was Calamity Jane's version: "I at once started to look for the assassin and found him at Shurdy's butcher shop and grabbed a meat cleaver and made him throw up his hands, because through the excitement of hearing of Bill's death having left my weapons on the post of my bed. He was then taken to a log cabin and locked up . . ."

The dime novelists made the most of Calamity Jane's story and placed her at Hickok's side as he lingered long enough to satisfy the contemporary literary conventions:

"The great gunfighter knew that he was dying . . . That drop of moisture on his pale cheek was not the rain but a woman's tears . . . Calamity Jane was on her knees beside him. 'Don't go away from me, Bill,' she sobbed. 'I love you . . . Don't you know that? I love you.' And his last message came to her in a whisper she was never going to forget: 'My heart has been yours from the first.'"

The less romantic truth was that Calamity Jane, on hearing the news that Hickok was dead, hurried right over to the No. 10 Saloon and joined the wake. Drinks were plentiful for this grown-up ragamuffin who boasted of her friendship with the dead man. "She knew the worth of her slight contact with greatness and what was due it," as Aikman wrote. "She had intimations, no doubt, that without this mighty patronage her celebrity would lose some of its luster, and so she genuinely grieved that the contact was over." In any event, her mourning was not prolonged. She made a name for herself in Deadwood's night life by invading a bordello one evening and raising the roof with her antics. Nobody dared throw her out, but her conduct was considered shocking even for a Dakota whore house. The madam ordered her locked in a closet until she sobered up because "I won't have her using that kind of language in front of my girls." On another occasion, dressed in men's clothes, she won a large bet by visiting the Chinese red-light district and proving that the girls would not recognize her as a member of their own sex. Once, in one of the Main Street dives, she created so much disturbance that the bartender was forced to remonstrate with her. She picked up a small log near the stove, cracked him over the head, and went on raising a ruckus. . . .

Deadwood, in a state of turmoil, was confronted with the question of what to do with Jack McCall. There was no law in Deadwood, no courts, no officials, not even a proper jail. A mass meeting of the citizenry was convened at the Bella Union Theater a few hours after the shooting to decide on how to handle the problem of jurisprudence. The citizens, after much debate, decided that McCall would be tried by a "miner's court" in accordance with the tradition of such settlements beyond all federal or territorial law. It was not the most reliable of institutions, but it made everybody feel better than a lynching. W. Y. Kuykendall was named to preside as judge of the miner's court, with Colonel May as prosecutor and Judge Miller as defense attorney. Isaac Brown was appointed sheriff pro tem to maintain custody of the prisoner. A jury was to be selected from a panel of thirty-three citizens. The trial was set for the next day, right after the victim's funeral.

While Doc Pierce and Colorado Charlie were laying out Hickok's body and dressing it in his best black broadcloth suit, and the whole town was in an uproar, a new sensation hit the place like a shock wave that night. The Indians were on the warpath and coming to wipe out the settlements in Deadwood Gulch! A Mexican bullwhacker named Francisco Mores galloped into town with a grisly souvenir—an Indian's decapitated head which he swung around by its long black hair. Earlier that day Señor Mores' employer, a freighter named Brick Pomeroy, had come across a stray Indian up in the hills and killed him. The excitable señor cut off the Indian's head and rode into Deadwood to exhibit his prize.

Doc Pierce heard men shouting outside Hickok's tent that "The Indians are coming" and left his task to investigate the excitement.

Somewhat to his disgust, Pierce found that Deadwood had forgotten all about Hickok's murder, had stopped talking about stringing up Jack McCall, and was busy acclaiming Señor Mores as the hero of the day. At No. 10 the Hickok wake was abandoned and men were passing the hat to take up a collection for the Mexican, who was gleefully exhibiting his Indian head and accepting drinks from a throng of admirers. Pierce thought it in bad taste for this Mexican to come barging into the limelight and steal the play from Hickok. He was even more disgusted when the crowd presented Señor Mores with a purse of seventy dollars.

Señor Mores, however, did not live long to enjoy his moment of fame. An hour or so later, down the line, he was spending the money collected for him and still hanging onto his Indian head, which he insisted on shoving into everyone's face. It was getting rather tiresome. A Crook City gambler, irked a little more than most by this exhibitionism, drew his gun and shot Señor Mores dead. Both he and his souvenir were given a hasty burial in the morning. The Indians, it developed, were not coming.

Next day, August 3, Deadwood had a high old time for itself. Thousands filed past Hickok's rough coffin, with his Sharps rifle (seldom used) resting next to him. It was noted that he seemed to be smiling slightly. Whether there was a touch of irony to that smile was not observed.

It was a fine funeral, anyway, the best that Deadwood could provide. The pallbearers were Charlie Rich, Johnny Oyster, Harry Young, Tom Dosier, William Hillman, and Jerry Lewis. He was buried on a slope at Ingleside, with a large stump serving as the grave marker. Carved on the stump was the legend, "A brave man, the victim of an assassin, J. B. Hickok (Wild Bill), age 39 years; murdered by Jack McCall, Aug. 2, 1876." Captain Jack Crawford, who billed himself as the "poet-scout," commemorated the occasion with an effusion which still stands as a mawkish high light in frontier poesy. Its last misty stanza read:

> "You buried him 'neath the old pine tree,
> In that little world of ours,
> His trusty rifle by his side—
> His grave all strewn with flowers;
> His manly form in sweet repose,
> That lovely silken hair—
> I tell you, pard, it was a sight,
> That face so white and fair!"

Since then Hickok, who always loved a crowd and did not mind being the center of attention, has never been lonely. His grave is one of the chief tourist attractions of the Black Hills. Only a few years ago Abilene, which had dismissed Hickok rather rudely as its city marshal, demanded that he be disinterred and buried in Abilene, possibly to keep Phil Coe company. Deadwood strenuously and successfully resisted the Kansans' attempt at body-snatching.

Hickok's body lay in its first resting place for three years, during which time some passing sentimentalist scrawled on his marker, "Custer was lonely without you." In 1879 Deadwood had expanded to the Ingleside slope, and Hickok's remains had to be moved to the new Mount Moriah cemetery, halfway up the slope of the mountain facing Deadwood from the east.

When Hickok's body was exhumed—apparently it was turned into a public occasion—those present (according to the Deadwood *Telegram*) "were astounded to find that by some natural embalming process of the soil, accomplished by water which had percolated through the coffin, the body had been so well embalmed as to preserve even the outlines of his features and the lines of the manifold pleatings of the dress shirt he wore." One of the spectators at this social affair, William Learned, musical director of the Gem Theater, claimed a lock of the dead man's hair.

After the second burial Colorado Charlie Utter had a more elaborate marker erected over the grave. In addition to the usual brief obituary the marker was inscribed, "Pard, we will meet again in the happy hunting grounds to part no more. Goodbye. Colorado Charlie." In the succeeding years souvenir hunters chipped away at the marble headstone until there was nothing left. Around 1910 a life-sized stone statue was placed over the grave and a steel enclosure built around it. None of his effigies proved as durable as his legend, but then, as Robert J. Casey pointed out, "he never had much to do with tourists."

Next to Hickok's grave, in a similar enclosure, Martha Jane Cannary, or Calamity Jane, lies in unaccustomed dignity and peace. She died of pneumonia in a Terry, South Dakota, boardinghouse on August 2, 1903, which was twenty-seven years to the day after Hickok was shot to death in the No. 10 Saloon. Close to death, she had asked that she be buried next to Wild Bill, and Deadwood pioneers saw to it that it was done. In some ways that was the crowning irony of his career—that he would be linked eternally, for all the world to see, with the uncouth and unromantic creature whom he knew only as an occasional drinking companion.

In his sandstone representation Wild Bill Hickok stands looking forever westward, over the Black Hills, toward the high plains. He is, for once, unarmed.

The mystery of Jack McCall and his motive for slaying Hickok has never quite been solved. This is not for lack of theories, suppositions, and confessions; the Hickok Murder Case has been all but smothered in these. McCall himself put forward several tentative sort of explanations, later retracted, and then decided to keep posterity guessing. Was he, as Robert J. Casey has suggested, "a sort of Mr. Mitty who suddenly decided to take a speaking part in one of his own daydreams"? Was he seeking revenge for some real or fancied wrong? Was he a hired assassin? Simply a moronic young man with ambitions to be "top gun of the West"? The reader will have to impanel himself as his own jury and try to bridge large gaps in the story of how the murderer and the victim came together. It cannot even be positively determined, for instance, whether Hickok had ever met McCall.

McCall's first, and extra-legal, trial took place August 3, 1876, the day after the murder, immediately after his victim's funeral. It might be adduced that this informal trial, held almost the same hour as the funeral, was subjected to such emotional pressures that a fair verdict was impossible. On the contrary: most of those who packed the Bella Union to watch the trial were in a jovial holiday mood. All they wanted was a good show. Except for a few of Hickok's embittered friends, they cheered both the defense and the prosecution with a good-natured enthusiasm. Had there been an effective rabble-rouser present, they would probably have seized McCall, with equal good nature, and strung him up.

The jury was drawn by putting the names of the thirty-three men on the panel on slips of paper and picking them out of a hat. Each prospective juror was then questioned on his ability to serve without prejudice. A jury of twelve men, with Charles Whitehead as foreman, was quickly selected. No transcript of the trial was made, so the only record of the proceeding can be pieced together from scattered and fragmentary newspaper accounts.

The prisoner was brought in and seated near Judge Kuykendall. To a reporter in the mob of spectators he "presented a most forbidding appearance. He was twenty-five years old, but dissipation and a low life had painted their stains on his ugly features. His brow was low and retreating, as a sign of his cowardly and brutal propensities, while sandy hair, small mustache and cross eyes completed the unmistakable evidences of his villainous character. He attempted to appear indifferent and assume the role of a desperado who had been accustomed to acting such parts, but despite this effort the chicken liver he possessed made his flesh creep and the blanch and color of his cheeks come and go like a patient badly overcome with intermittent fever."

Three of the men in the No. 10 Saloon when the shooting occurred, Carl Mann, Charlie Rich, and Harry Young, all testified that McCall had come up behind Hickok, fired one shot into the back of his head, said only two words ("Take that!"), and fled from the place.

Not on the witness stand, but much later in his autobiography, Bartender Young gave a curious side light on the murder. He said that Hickok and McCall played cards together all during the night of August 1–2 preceding the shooting. Young said that when he came to work that morning they were still at the table, that McCall had lost $117 and was cleaned out. Hickok, he said, lent the loser "75 cents in shinplasters" to buy his breakfast. Young did not stress the point but implied that the gambling loss was McCall's motive for killing Hickok.

Three men, Patrick Smith, Ira For, and H. H. Pitkin, testified as character witnesses for McCall. Smith, in addition to attesting to McCall's excellent character and high moral standards, told the jury that he had introduced McCall to Hickok in a Cheyenne saloon, that the two men had been friendly and drank together.

Then Jack McCall was called to the stand. Overnight he had managed to cook up a sort of defense for himself. Or possibly he had help. Under the circumstances it was an effective one.

He began bravely enough: "Well, men, I have but a few words to say. Wild Bill threatened to kill me if I crossed his path. I am not sorry for what I have done. I would do the same thing over again."

Then, falteringly, he provided a sort of alibi for the deed. One reporter noted that as he told his story "the eye, face, and in fact everything about the prisoner denoted villainy and iniquity as an innate part of his nature."

McCall claimed he was the brother of "Sam Strawhan," whom Hickok had killed in Hays City seven years ago. The name of the gunman Hickok killed actually was Jack Strawhan, who, like McCall, tried to shoot Hickok in the back.

Furthermore, McCall claimed, he had promised his mother "on her deathbed" to avenge his nonexistent brother's death. Deathbed promises, in those days, were highly regarded; the jurors and other spectators were visibly moved by this portion of McCall's testimony.

And he wrapped up his case with a neat simplicity, "Wild Bill killed my brother, and I killed him."

No cross-examination was permitted, fortunately for Jack McCall.

Opposing counsel then launched into their final arguments, which were stem-winders in the best tradition of frontier eloquence.

"Men, comrades," intoned Judge Miller, the defense counsel, "you have been chosen to decide the guilt and punishment of one of your own companions. Look upon the honest countenance of this poor boy who is being tried for his life because he struck down the assassin of his dearly beloved brother. Note, particularly, that unflinching and innocent eye, which could not possibly belong to a man who could do any wrong."

Judge Miller wisely emphasized the avenged-brother angle and avoided the fact that McCall had shot his victim in the back, which was generally held to be indefensible under any circumstances.

Colonel May, the prosecutor, thundered in reply: "If this is not murder, then there never was murder committed. The deceased in his bloody winding-sheet from his mountain grave demands that a proper punishment be meted out to his villainous assassin."

With this oratory ringing in their ears, the jury retired for an hour and a half before reaching a verdict. From the beginning of their deliberations, it was reported later, they stood eleven to one for acquittal. One of the jurors thought maybe McCall ought to be fined twenty-five dollars for breaching the peace. Finally they marched back to the courtroom with their verdict:

"We, the jury, find Mr. John McCall not guilty."

McCall was set free amid cheers from the spectators, with an almost unheard grumbling from Hickok's friends that the jury had been rigged.

Immediately after the verdict was announced, Colonel May charged that two hundred ounces of gold dust had been slipped into the jury room during its deliberations. No one denied the charge.

Nor did anyone deny that some of the town's leading

underworld characters, with Johnny Varnes and Tim Brady acting on their behalf, had hired McCall to do the job. McCall's recompense was $25 down, $175 on a successful completion of the assignment, and a skinful of cheap whiskey to give him the courage to gun his man down. So Hickok's friends learned. His triumphant enemies did not dispute it.

McCall found himself the local hero, acclaimed in the saloons, congratulated and plied with drinks. He would have liked to stay around and enjoy the notoriety of having killed the most celebrated of the gunfighters. But his well-wishers pointed out that Hickok had friends around town who might be eager to even the score. Then, too, they were concerned about his liquor-loosened tongue. McCall was persuaded to clear out before he blurted out everything he knew.

He was attached to a freighting outfit bound for Cheyenne, and a number of people breathed easier.

Working for a living wasn't much fun after the excitement of having killed Will Bill Hickok. McCall wanted the adulation he felt was due him. He quit the wagon train when it reached Laramie and for several weeks lived in the saloons, re-enacting his deed as long as people kept buying drinks for him.

One night a deputy U.S. marshal was in the audience. He listened to McCall boast how he had "put one over" on the Deadwood jury by claiming Hickok had killed his brother. And he kept saying, over and over, as though still trying to believe it himself:

"I killed the biggest gunman in the world."

The deputy marshal supplied a four-word curtain line for the barroom drama. "You are under arrest."

If he had been able to keep his mouth shut, at least while still comparatively close to the scene of the crime, McCall might have gotten away with Hickok's murder. He might even have survived to tour the eastern theatrical circuit as the star of a Buntline melodrama. As it was, he soon learned the bitter significance of the homily that character is destiny. He was arraigned at Laramie and sent to Yankton, Dakota Territory, for trial in the federal court there.

While McCall was awaiting trial in Yankton, the law finally began to take steps against Johnny Varnes, the supposed instigator of Hickok's murder. The federal government had brought a measure of law enforcement to Deadwood, and on November 11 the Deadwood *Pioneer* reported that a deputy United States marshal and a posse of five men had started searching for Varnes, "now out on a new stampede," for "having procured the death of Wild Bill by paying a sum of money to Jack McCall." The *Pioneer* said the cause of the trouble between Varnes and Hickok was a poker game at the Senate Saloon in which "Bill interfered in a dispute between Varnes and another man. Bill covered Varnes with his pistol and arrogated to himself the position of umpire."

Varnes, however, was never taken into custody. Doubtless he had taken to his heels on learning that a U.S. marshal was coming to Deadwood.

But the law still had McCall in its clutches, and he was placed on trial before Federal Judge Blair November 27 on a charge of first-degree murder. Again there was much public interest in the trial and much sympathy for the defendant. Sentimentalists pointed out that McCall was a "mere boy" and argued that he had advanced the cause of civilization by ridding the world of a professional gunman like Hickok; a trifle misguided perhaps but with good intentions.

The defense, set forth by court-appointed counsel, Oliver Shannon and General W. H. H. Beadle, was simply that McCall was being placed in double jeopardy in violation of the constitutional principle that no man should be tried twice for the same offense. The federal prosecutor, however, maintained that McCall's first trial had no legal standing, that it took place in an extra-legal court in an outlaw town—but that Hickok's death was no less a crime for having been committed in such a place. Judge Blair upheld the prosecution.

The defendant, under brief cross-examination, did not help his case much in the following exchange:

Q. Why didn't you go around in front of Wild Bill and shoot him like a man?

A. I didn't want to commit suicide.

The courtroom rocked with appreciative laughter. Neither the judge nor the jury joined in, however; there was no one to pass around samples of gold dust in McCall's behalf in Yankton.

Prosecution witnesses agreed that Hickok didn't have a chance of defending himself. George M. Shingle, the gold-dust weigher at the No. 10 Saloon, testified under cross-examination that Hickok was "a constant drinker but was sober when the shooting occurred." Captain William Massey told the court that McCall apparently had attempted to kill Hickok on a previous occasion, testifying, "I saw the defendant walk into the same room a day or two before and walk around behind Bill and pull his pistol about two-thirds out. There was a young man with him who put his arm around the defendant and pulled him toward the back door."

The jury deliberated for five hours the night of December 6 and returned a verdict of guilty at midnight. Judge Blair sentenced McCall to hang on March 1, 1877.

In the three months between sentence and execution a number of attempts were made to have the verdict reversed or the sentence commuted. An appellate court only affirmed the verdict, however, and petitions to the President for executive clemency, signed by thousands, were officially ignored.

Late in February 1877, when it appeared that nothing could save him from the gallows, McCall busied himself in his cell writing the truth—so he told his jailers—about his motive for killing Hickok. A few days before the execution date the Yankton *Press and Dakotan* received a note from McCall which said, "I intend to write an article which I wish you would publish in your paper, after my death." But on the night before the hanging McCall destroyed whatever he had written, deciding that the "truth" would die with him. And so perhaps it did, unless the probability that he had been hired to do the job by Deadwood's worst element was indeed the motive. No better one was ever advanced. Some writers have argued that if McCall had been hired to kill Hickok, his employers, hardheaded men, would have selected a real professional and handed him a more effective weapon than the beat-up .45 Colt with defective cartridges used by McCall. Yet, if the most plausible explanation is true (and it was never denied), the men behind McCall had to use a warped and foolish creature like him; no experienced gun slinger would be silly enough to take on the job—it had proved fatal too often in the past. Nor would a real pro be likely to shoot his man in the back. McCall would probably not have been sentenced to death if he had shot it out with Hickok face to face. Western gunmen hardly ever died on the scaffold.

So Jack McCall marched bravely to the gallows the morning of March 1 and would probably have been inordinately pleased by the newspapermen's verdict that he "died game." No doubt he was consoled by the fact that people came from all over Dakota Territory by the thousands to watch him die on the scaffold erected two miles from the prison near the public school and just north of the Catholic cemetery. The Yankton *Press and Dakotan* accorded him some of the fame he sought so avidly:

THE GALLOWS
Jack McCall the Murderer of
Wild Bill Executed
He Meets Death with an
Unshrinking Firmness

The *Press and Dakotan* account related that McCall and his escort left the prison in a wagon at 9:30 A.M. "The mournful train, bearing its living victim to the grave, was preceded and followed by a long line of vehicles of every description, with hundreds on foot and horseback, all leading north, out Broadway. Not a word was spoken during the ride . . . McCall continued to bear up bravely, even after the gallows loomed in full view."

McCall knelt in prayer with a priest at his side, kissed the Crucifix, and rose as the black mask and the noose were fastened on by a deputy marshal. "Draw it tighter, Marshal," he was heard to say. "At precisely 15 minutes after 10 o'clock," wrote the man from the *Press and Dakotan*, "the trap was sprung and with a single choking expression, 'Oh, God,' uttered while the drop fell, the body of John McCall was dangling between heaven and earth."

The real tragedy of those two deaths, Hickok's and his slayer's, was enacted far away, where the only people who really cared about them heard the news in roundabout fashion.

Hickok's widow read of his murder in a Cincinnati newspaper. She had to wait until the following spring to enter the Black Hills with the intention of bringing his body back East for burial. Doc Pierce took her to his grave, waxed eloquent on the theme that "he belongs out here in the West," and persuaded Mrs. Hickok to let Deadwood keep him. The Deadwood Chamber of Commerce, it would seem, owes Doc Pierce a memorial shaft of his own.

In Troy Grove, Illinois, Hickok's mother and sisters learned of his death from a neighbor who brought them the Chicago newspaper. His sister Lydia, twenty years later, told how the news was received. Her sister, she said, hid the newspaper in the kitchen. "Then, composing herself, she went in where Mother was sitting. 'Mother,' she said, 'I am going over to the store a minute and will be right back.' She put on her bonnet and ran to the little store about two hundred yards away to tell one of the brothers. All came back to the house together. When they entered the sitting room, there sat Mother, the newspaper laying at her side, slowly rocking back and forth, while the blood from a hemorrhage of the lungs dyed the front part of her dress. 'I saw you get the paper, Lydia,' she said, 'and when you did not bring it in, I went and got it.' She never fully recovered from the blow, and she died two years later, still mourning his terrible death."

And Jack McCall, however repulsive he may have appeared to those who knew him only as the slayer of Wild Bill Hickok, also had a mother and sisters worrying about him back home. The day after he was executed the U.S. marshal at Yankton received the following letter, dated February 25, 1877, and signed Mary A. McCall:

"I saw in the morning papers a piece about the sentence of the murderer of Wild Bill, Jack McCall. There was a young man of the name of John McCall left here about six years ago, who has not been heard from for the last three years. He has a father, mother, and three sisters living here in Louisville, who are very uneasy about him since they heard about the murder of Wild Bill. If you can send us any information about him, we would be thankful to you. This John McCall is about twenty-five years old, has light hair, inclined to curl, and one eye crossed. I cannot say about his height, as he was not grown when he left here. Please write as soon as convenient, as we are very anxious to hear from you."

Hickok and McCall had left home under similar circumstances to make their mark on the frontier. One found enduring fame, thanks partly to the necessary touch of martyrdom provided by the other. The other wound up dangling from a hangman's noose. With a slightly different shift in circumstances, Hickok might have become a McCall and McCall might have become a Hickok. The gun was their common denominator.

Aside from a vast and swollen body of Bunyanesque fable, Hickok left little behind him when he died. He went out of this world flat broke, in fact, and owing the No. 10 Saloon $50 for the chips he bet on the "Dead Man's Hand." His entire estate consisted of his fancy haberdashery and his weapons. Except for the Sharps rifle buried with him, these possessions were raffled off at twenty-five cents a chance several days after his funeral, apparently to pay for the expenses of that occasion.

One of his guns, a Colt with the serial number 139345, with "Wild Bill" engraved on the butt, came into the possession of Fred Sutton, a friend of Hickok's and a U.S. marshal in the Indian Territory. He in turn had received it from Pat Garrett, the New Mexican sheriff and gunfighter of a renown approaching Hickok's.

Garrett, in a letter to Sutton from Las Cruces, New Mexico, dated January 12, 1902, explained that he had been given the gun by Hickok's sister Lydia, then living in Oberlin, Kansas.

It was the gun, Garrett wrote, which he used to "put Billy the Kid out of business" when Garrett tracked him down on the Pete Maxwell ranch in 1881.

That must have been one of the most lethal revolvers in history.

Bibliography

The author is indebted for assistance in research to Mr. Joseph Fricelli, Jr., of Brooklyn; to the state historical societies of Connecticut, Illinois, Kansas, Nebraska, and South Dakota; to the public libraries of Bangor and Bar Harbor, Maine, New York City, Kansas City, Denver, and St. Louis, and to the Library of Congress in Washington.

BOOKS

Aikman, Duncan, *Calamity Jane and Other Wildcats*, New York, 1927.

Aikman, Duncan, editor, *The Taming of the Frontier*, New York, 1925.

Altrocchi, Julia Cooley, *The Old California Trail*, Caldwell, Idaho, 1945.

Bennett, Estelline, *Old Deadwood Days*, New York, 1928.

Botkin, B. A., *American Folklore*, New York, 1944.

Bradley, Glenn D., *The Story of the Pony Express*, Chicago, 1913.

Buel, J. W., *Life and Marvelous Adventures of Wild Bill*, Chicago, 1880.

Burke, John M., *Buffalo Bill from Prairie to Palace*, Chicago, 1893.

Casey, Robert J., *The Black Hills*, Indianapolis, 1949.

Cody, William F., *Story of the Wild West*, Chicago, 1919.

Connelley, William E., *Wild Bill and His Era*, New York, 1933.

Coursey, O. W., *Wild Bill Hickok*, Mitchell, South Dakota, 1924.

Cunningham, Eugene, *Triggernometry*, New York, 1934.

Custer, Elizabeth, *Following the Guidon*, New York, 1890.

Custer, George A., *My Life on the Plains*, New York, 1874.

Dick, Everett, *The Story of the Frontier*, New York, 1941.

Dodge, Richard J., *Our Wild Indians*, Hartford, 1883.

Eisele, W. E., *The Real Wild Bill Hickok*, Denver, 1931.

Graham, W. A., *The Custer Myth*, Harrisburg, 1953.

Hardin, John Wesley, *The Life of John Wesley Hardin*, Seguin, Texas, 1896.

Harris, Frank, *My Reminiscences as a Cowboy*, New York, 1930.

Holbrook, Stewart H., *Little Annie Oakley and Other Rugged People*, New York, 1948.

Holloway, John, *Wild Life on the Plains*, St. Louis, 1891.

Horan, James D., *Desperate Women*, New York, 1952.

Hough, Emerson, The *Story of the Outlaw*, New York, 1907.

Howard, Robert W., editor, *This Is the West*, New York, 1957.

Jahns, Pat, *The Frontier World of Doc Holliday*, New York, 1957.

Lake, Stuart N., *Wyatt Earp: Frontier Marshal*, Boston, 1931.

McCoy, Joseph G., *Historic Sketches of the Cattle Trade of the West and Southwest*, Kansas City, 1874.

Monaghan, Jay, *Civil War on the Western Border*, Boston, 1955.

Nichols, Alice, *Bleeding Kansas*, New York, 1954.

Nordyke, Lewis, *John Wesley Hardin*, New York, 1957.

O'Connor, Richard, *Bat Masterson*, New York, 1957.

Otero, Miguel, *My Life on the Frontier*, New York, 1935.

Parkhill, Forbes, *The Wildest of the West*, Denver, 1957.

Raine, William MacLeod, *.45-Caliber Law*, Evanston, Illinois, 1941.

Raine, William MacLeod, *Guns of the Frontier*, Boston, 1940.

Sandoz, Mari, *The Cattlemen*, New York, 1958.

Stanley, Henry M., *My Early Travels in America*, New York, 1895.

Streeter, Floyd B., *Prairie Trails and Cow Towns*, Boston, 1936.

Tallent, Annie D., *The Black Hills, or Last Hunting Grounds of the Dakotahs*, St. Louis, 1899.

Vestal, Stanley D., *Warpath and Council Fire*, New York, 1948.

Walton, W. M. *Life and Adventures of Ben Thompson*, Austin, 1884.

Wellman, Paul I., *Death on Horseback*, Philadelphia, 1947.

Wilstach, Frank J., *Wild Bill Hickok*, New York, 1926.

Works Progress Administration, *Illinois Guide*, Chicago, 1947.

Works Progress Administration, *Kansas Guide*, New York, 1939.

Works Progress Administration, *South Dakota Guide*, New York, 1952.

Works Progress Administration, *Wyoming Guide*, New York, 1941.

Young, Harry, *Hard Knocks*, Portland, Oregon, 1915.

Zornow, William F., *Kansas: A History of the Jayhawker State*, Norman, Oklahoma, 1957.

MAGAZINES AND PERIODICALS

Guns Magazine
Outdoor Life
Outdoor Recreation
Human Life
Billboard
American Weekly
Esquire
Holiday
Saturday Evening Post
Journal of the Illinois State Historical Society
Nebraska History Magazine
Collier's
The Trail
Harper's Weekly

NEWSPAPERS

New York *Times*
New York *Herald*
New York *Tribune*
Chicago *Inter-Ocean*
Chicago *Record*
Chicago *Tribune*
St. Louis *Republican*
Kansas City *Star*
Topeka *Commonwealth*
Abilene *Chronicle*
Laramie *Daily Sentinel*
Leadville (S.D.) *News*
Deadwood *Pioneer*
Cheyenne *Daily Leader*
Yankton (S.D.) *Press and Dakotan*